32 Counties

'The phrase "If we don't learn from the past, we are doomed to repeat it", seems more apt about Ireland than anywhere else. To look at Ireland through the prism of class is to see not what might have been but what brightness the future might bring. Kieran Allen's new book is Irish history seen anew, from below, bristling with practical lessons for working-class struggle today.'
—Eamonn McCann, politician, journalist and political activist

'Showing how partition was not to separate two hostile cultures but a strategy to defend the British empire, it traces the grisly story through to the return of the national question today when Irish unity can be posed again on a new socialist basis. Essential reading for anyone who wants to change Irish society.'
—Brid Smith, People Before Profit TD

'An important contribution to a debate that has been reignited. It is an excellent tool for activists who are navigating the arguments in favour of ending partition.'
—Gerry Carroll, MLA Stormont Assembly for West Belfast

32 Counties

The Failure of Partition and the Case for a United Ireland

Kieran Allen

PLUTO  PRESS

First published 2021 by Pluto Press
345 Archway Road, London N6 5AA

www.plutobooks.com

British Library Cataloguing in Publication Data
A catalogue record for this book is available from the British Library

ISBN   978 0 7453 4418 8   Hardback
ISBN   978 0 7453 4417 1   Paperback
ISBN   978 0 7453 4421 8   PDF
ISBN   978 0 7453 4420 1   Kindle
ISBN   978 0 7453 4419 5   EPUB

Typeset by Stanford DTP Services, Northampton, England

Simultaneously printed in the United Kingdom and United States of America

Contents

Preface

In August 2020, UK premier Boris Johnson announced plans to celebrate the centenary of the formation of Northern Ireland. There would be a forum composed of politicians, businessmen and public servants as well as a Historical Advisory Panel composed of academics. Johnson thought that the centenary was a cause for celebration because it joined Northern Ireland with the United Kingdom, 'the most successful political partnership anywhere in the world'.

This book is written to expose this fallacy. It argues that partition was a disaster which helped to keep Ireland enchained in two conservative regimes for decades. The losers were not just a minority who were imprisoned in that state but the wider mass of working people on the whole island – Protestants, Catholics and Dissenters.

The Historical Advisory Panel is chaired by Lord Paul Bew and is mainly composed of historians who have shown a distinct sympathy for the unionist cause. In the name of academic objectivity, it will no doubt produce material to justify an occasion of 'celebration', however muted and nuanced that may be. This book is designed to counter that propaganda and is written from an explicitly left-wing standpoint.

I would like to thank those who have made this possible and two people in particular stand out for their scrupulous reading of an earlier text. They are Sean Mitchell and Willie Cumming. I have taken on board most of their comments and this, I think, has added to the argument made.

1
'A Carnival of Reaction':
The Origins of Partition

In June 2021, Northern Ireland will have existed for one hundred years. It has its own parliament, police force and judiciary and operates like any other state with a civil service who pore over the details of its economy. It is anomalous in some ways, certainly. The Prime Minister is called the First Minister and must seek the agreement of the Deputy First Minister. Tax-raising powers are limited and its finances are dependent on the British Exchequer. Nevertheless, Northern Ireland still exists – and few imagined that it would last one hundred years. Certainly not Edward Carson, the founder of Ulster unionism, whose statue stands in front of Stormont, the Northern Ireland Parliament Buildings, portrayed in a moment of passionate oratory. Were his ghost to unshackle itself from its stone encasement, he could only look aghast as his followers sit alongside former Irish Republican Army (IRA) operatives. But even he would be surprised that his state has lasted so long because he had a profound ambiguity about the precise border and shape of that state.

Edward Carson was primarily a defender of British empire and, consequently, an ardent opponent of Home Rule for Ireland. When the first Home Rule Bill to give limited autonomy to a Dublin parliament was proposed in 1886, he was totally opposed. He switched his allegiance from supporting the Liberals to the Tories but, as his admiring biographer stated, 'Carson knew next to nothing of the northern province of Ulster... Even then "Ulster" was a term which was used loosely.'[1] However, he recognised that the most determined opponents of Home Rule lay there and believed that if they were willing to threaten force, Home Rule for the whole island could be stopped. He was never enthusiastic about a separate Northern parliament and just as it was about to be established, stated that 'I cannot understand why we should ask them to take a parliament which they never demanded and do not want.'[2]

His ambiguity about the very concept of 'Ulster' was evident in two key debates in the House of Commons. In June 1912, a backbench Liberal, Thomas Agar-Roberts, became the first person to propose the partition of Ireland when he moved an amendment to the Home Rule Bill to exclude four counties – Antrim, Armagh, Down and Londonderry – from its scope. Carson voted for this amendment, but a few months later he introduced his own amendment to the Bill, this time proposing that the whole nine-county province of Ulster be excluded from Home Rule. He argued that 'It is far better statesmanship to exclude the whole of Ulster than to select counties which are nearly, so to speak, all the one way.'[3] By 'all one way', he meant either Catholic or Protestant. Carson's voting record is just one indication of the confusion surrounding the exact borders of a partitioned Ireland. In terms of geography 'Ulster' denoted one of the four provinces of Ireland and was composed of nine counties. Yet there was no clarity on what the political term 'Ulster' meant subsequently. Unionist leaders sometimes spoke of the 'North East Ulster', or 'Protestant Ulster' or just plain Ulster.

This ambiguity on the geographical limits of the Northern state is of some significance. Contrary to binary ethnonational explanations of the conflict based on British and Irish identities, or indeed theories of two nations, unionist national 'identity' has never been fixed. The allegiance of unionism to a particular territory was in fact pragmatically driven. It is almost universally agreed that a basic criterion for any definition of nationality is that it points to a defined and delineated territory. Yet unionism shifted from an all-Ireland unionism, to an Ulster unionism, to a six-county unionism. These shifts took place over a very short period of time, in line with the pragmatic interests of unionist elites rather than some deep-seated and immutable nationalism or identity.

The moment of truth came when Walter Long was charged by the British government with solving the Irish question in 1919 by chairing a committee to draft a Government of Ireland Bill. Long was a high Tory, descended from a mix of the English gentry and the Irish ascendency, and an ardent defender of landlord interests in Ireland. He was a former leader of the Irish Unionist Parliamentary Party and, as one of his biographers noted, 'held the Catholic Irish in contempt, thinking of them as clearly inferior to the English, both racially and culturally'.[4] His parliamentary secretary was James Craig, the future Prime Minister of Northern Ireland. As a scion of the British establishment, Long was not motivated by any consideration of a balance between ethnic identities but rather by how best to defend the British empire when faced with rebellion in Ireland.

Long regarded the Sinn Féin rebels, who had launched a struggle for an independent republican Ireland, as 'vile criminals [who] must be exterminated'.[5] In May 1919 he had proposed the hiring of ex-servicemen to bolster the Royal Irish Constabulary – these subsequently became known as the Black and Tans, feared for the reign of terror they launched on the country. Long assumed that the British empire could defeat republican insurgents in a military combat, but he also thought there was need for a defensive political strategy to undermine Irish independence. His parliamentary committee charged with drafting a Government of Ireland Bill, therefore, proposed the creation of an Ulster parliament so that military action was complemented with a political initiative. This was to be a parliament for a nine-county Ulster and would sit alongside a Dublin parliament. This, he regarded, as a temporary arrangement, a prelude to the reunification of Ireland within a more federated British empire. His original proposals included the formation of a Council of Ireland, to which both Irish parliaments would devolve their powers, and which would lead to 'the peaceful evolution of a single parliament for all Ireland'.[6] As an arch unionist, Long did not envisage a six-county state. He never dreamed that it was a natural or inevitable boundary to express a particular identity.

However, Walter Long quickly learnt he was on the wrong track when he visited Ireland shortly after his proposals became known – visit may be a slight exaggeration as most of the time he stayed on his yacht, *Enchantress*, which was docked in Dun Laoghaire. Nevertheless, he got a clear message about the reluctance of Northern unionists and in a memo to Lloyd George, he noted their concern that 'the inclusion of Donegal, Cavan and Monaghan would provide such an excess of strength to the Roman Catholic party that the supremacy of the unionists would be seriously threatened'.[7] In other words, they thought that the loyal, British part of Ireland could not encompass all of Ulster. Or as James Craig MP put it, the six counties were the largest area where there was 'a decisive Protestant majority in which unionist power could be guaranteed, in perpetuity'.[8] This shift in policy brought to the surface tensions within the ranks of Irish unionism. In May 1920, when the Ulster Unionist Council finally voted by a margin of 310 to 80 to accept a six-county state, there was a split in their ranks. Southern-based unionists broke off to form a short-lived Unionist Anti-Partition

League led by prominent businesspeople including Rupert Guinness – Lord Iveagh, Sir John Arnott, Andrew Jameson and Maurice Dockrell.

The current Northern state, therefore, did not arise from a determined plan. It was never the stated goal of any major social or proto-national movement. Nobody suggested before partition that the six counties reflected a 'natural' ethnic identity. Its precise shape arose from a series of discussions between some, but not all, supporters of the British empire. It was forged as a backlash against a struggle to break free of that empire, a 'fall back policy of an imperial state thrown onto the defensive during a revolutionary period'.[9] The result was the creation of not just 'a Protestant parliament for a Protestant people' – but one where Catholics would always be in a minority and viewed as the internal enemy. The addition of counties Tyrone and Fermanagh, which had nationalist majorities, meant that the state was not too small to survive but still had an inbuilt Protestant majority. Hence its peculiarity and hidden in this paradox was a deeper one.

The official rationale for a six-county state was that it rested on a fixed identity. It was to be a home for those who were Protestant, unionist, pro-British and supportive of empire. Yet identities are never one-dimensional or static. The imposition of fixed, permanent identities defined against other fixed identities was vastly strengthened by the creation of the Northern state. Often identities change, become hybrid, or criss-cross with other identities as time progresses. Think of how the city of Glasgow became synonymous with a tradition of working-class militancy – but was also a city riven with sectarian conflict. Support for the soccer clubs like Celtic or Rangers remain to this day markers of 'identity', but they recede in significance when there are battles over issues like the poll tax or wider debates on Scottish independence. Northern Ireland, however, had a different dynamic from the very start. The construction of a Protestant state with an inbuilt large Catholic minority was designed to cement identities into permanent blocks. That in turn depended on drawing communal barriers against a disloyal minority who might undermine it. Put simply, the inclusion of a substantial nationalist minority was not just a matter of creating an economic and material viability for the new state. It was a precondition for maintaining Northern Ireland as a distinct 'loyalist' entity. The unionist elite simply exploited the fact that Catholics and Protestants lived side by side rather than embarking on any attempt at mass ethnic cleansing.

TERROR AND GERRYMANDERING

The new state was born in violence and it could hardly have been otherwise when a third of its population did not want to be part of it. Given their beleaguered status, Northern Catholics were often not openly or actively enthusiastic about the IRA's campaign which was raging south of the new border. Whereas the rest of the country voted overwhelmingly for Sinn Féin in 1918, the older Home Rule party, which favoured limited autonomy within the empire, retained a support base among Northern nationalists, winning four seats in what became Northern Ireland. In 1920, for example, there were fewer than 100 Sinn Féin members in Belfast but there were 7,000 in the United Irish League, the northern version of the Home Rule party led by Joe Devlin. Sinn Féin's main support base lay in the west of the province, particularly in Derry, Tyrone and Fermanagh. Nevertheless, the mere existence of a substantial minority within the proposed boundaries of the Northern state was deemed a threat to unionist power. This became evident in local elections held in January and June 1920, which were conducted under the proportional representation system, just before a Northern parliament was established.

In the six-county area, nationalists won control of ten urban councils, including Armagh, Omagh, Enniskillen, Newry and Strabane and 13 rural councils. In Derry, a city with a mythological status in the history of unionism, nationalists took control. More significant in some ways was the emergence of the Labour Party in Belfast which, with 13 seats, became the main opposition to the Unionist Party. Labour's breakthrough followed a wave of working-class militancy which culminated in a massive strike in 1919 for a 44-hour week involving 60,000 workers. These twin opponents of unionist hegemony needed to be smashed if a stable unionist regime was to be established and this was achieved through systematic violence and state repression.

By 1920 loyalist vigilantes had started calling themselves the Ulster Volunteer Force (UVF), the name that had originally been used by armed militias who pledged to resist Home Rule by force. One of their first major interventions occurred in Derry in response to the electoral victory of nationalists in the local council. On 19 June, the UVF began by firing shots into Catholic areas, killing innocent bystanders. Rioting and IRA retaliation ensued but when a curfew was imposed on the city, the search for arms was concentrated in the Catholic areas. As the historian Jonathan Bardon noted, 'A striking feature of the army's intervention in Derry was its close alignment with the UVF'.[10] In all, 20 people were murdered during the Derry riots, 15 Catholics and five Protestants. In the same month, the Ulster Unionist Council decided to officially revive the UVF and placed advertisements in newspapers calling on loyalists to enlist. Carson then used the occasion of the annual Orange procession on 12 July to deliberately inflame the situation. Adopting his familiar stance of pressing for stronger action from the British empire, he said, 'if the British government are unable to deal with these matters, they ought to ask somebody else to deal with them… we know well that the real battlefields of Ireland in relation to a republic must be Ulster… We in Ulster will tolerate no Sinn Fein'.[11]

One week later, pogroms and ethnic cleansing started in the aftermath of the funeral of Colonel Gerard Smyth, a divisional police commissioner for Munster who had been assassinated by the IRA. Smyth had been one of the main advocates of shooting republicans on sight, telling police officers under his command that 'the more you shoot, the better I like you and I assure you that no policeman will get into trouble for shooting any man'.[12] After his funeral in Banbridge, loyalists attacked Catholics in the town and the neighbouring Dromore.

Shortly afterwards, the Belfast Protestant Association called a meeting in the Harland and Wolff shipyards for all unionist and Protestant workers to which thousands showed up and passed a resolution not to work alongside those who were 'non-loyal'.[13] A mob then assembled to chase out Catholics and 'rotten Prods' who had shown insufficient loyalty to the empire. Among the latter were leaders of the 1919 strike and as one of them, James Baird, stated, 'Every man who was prominently known in the Labour movement… was expelled from his work'.[14] The expulsions spread to the main workplaces in Belfast and by the end of it an estimated 10,000 workers or about 10 per cent of the nationalist population of the city were driven out. The sectarian conflict then spread from workplaces to the streets with injuries and deaths following. In August, the IRA assassinated a police officer, Oswald Swanzy, who had been involved in the murder of Thomas MacCurtain, the Lord Mayor of Cork. Swanzy's killing occurred in Lisburn and in retaliation, loyalists launched a pogrom against the town's small Catholic minority. Over the course of three days, 300 homes were destroyed and Catholics were forced to flee on foot to Belfast. A London *Times* reporter claimed that 'the war on Catholics is a deliberate and organised attempt. . . to drive the Catholic Irish out of North East Ulster'.[15] While this may be an exaggeration, there can be little doubt that the birth of the Northern state coincided with attempts to terrorise the minority who did not want to belong to it. The period from 1920 to 1922 is one of escalating violence, reaching its crescendo in May 1922 when 66 civilians were killed – 44 Catholics and 22 Protestants.

Despite the fact that the violence was often led by the illegal UVF, this force was soon integrated into the official apparatus of the British state. James Craig, who was then a junior minister in the British cabinet, proposed the creation of a new volunteer constabulary which would be raised from the loyal population. Craig, who would soon become the first Prime Minister of the Northern state, wanted a local force that would be controlled by unionists. The volunteer constabulary was supposed to assist the police force but was organised on military lines and operated exclusively within the six-county area. Wilfrid Spender, the former UVF quartermaster in 1913–14, was appointed by Craig to form and run the Ulster Special Constabulary (USC). UVF units were incorporated en masse into the new force and it was composed of full-time A Specials, the much larger part-time B Specials and a C Special reserve. By the end of 1922 it comprised 48,000 members and was fully paid for by the British state. Approximately one in five Protestant males were to serve in this force which gained a reputation for extreme sectarianism. While the full-time A Specials were disbanded in 1926, the much larger part-time B Specials continued right until 1970.

Coinciding with a strong security apparatus, the unionist state introduced legislative measures to ensure that nationalists had a second-class status. In April 1922, twenty-one nationalist-controlled councils were suspended. The proportional representation system of voting was also abolished so that, as James Craig put it, there would be a 'simple system' that would elect 'men who are for the Union on one hand or who are against it and want to go to a Dublin parliament, on the other'.[16] This was designed to eliminate the threat from Labour. Oaths of allegiance were demanded of teachers and state employees. Electoral boundaries were changed to produce artificial unionist majorities at the local level. The aim was to set up a system which facilitated discrimination in housing and jobs, administered mainly through local authorities.

Through these mechanisms, two key victories were achieved for unionism. First, the exercise of violence and legal authority intimidated the minority population and forced them to accept their role as second-class citizens. Second, unionism was consolidated into a single homogenous bloc. As Eamonn McCann put it, 'The significance of the Holy War which erupted in Belfast in July 1920 was that it welded the classes within the Protestant community together.'[17] It did not stop in that year because there were recurring waves of violence directed at the Catholic population in subsequent years. This helped to discipline the Protestant population and the measure of that success was that the Unionist Party remained in power from the state's formation in 1921 until the abolition of Stormont in 1972 – a feat unparalleled in the Western world. In that time, only one opposition bill was passed – the Wild Birds (Protection) Act in 1931. These birds, it seems, were neither Catholic nor Protestant.

BRITISH IMPERIALISM

In 1962, a Dutch political geographer, M. W. Heslinga produced a book entitled *The Irish Border as a Cultural Divide*. He argued that the 'Irish land border represents, however arbitrary, an important spiritual divide… most marked by religion'.[18] Today it is not uncommon to analyse the Troubles in Northern Ireland as a conflict between two cultures. Instead of a 'spiritual divide', terms like 'ethno-nationalism' are used and it is assumed that partition reflects the conflict between cultures. The border grew out of a long-standing conflict between two 'ethnicities' according to this schema, who were then driven into mutual hatred of each other because both wanted a different type of state. Even if its precise line on a map was unclear, the border is fundamentally a reflection of differences within Ireland. This cultural understanding is sometimes supplemented by a discussion on the uneven nature of capitalist development that derives from a left perspective: namely, that the 'North East' had industrialised and was part of a triangle that linked Belfast to Manchester and Glasgow whereas the rest of Ireland needed protectionist measures to develop. Whether a culturalist or materialist outlook is deployed, it is then supposed that there was an inevitability about partition. The script for the border, it appears, was written long before it became a reality.

The problem with both these approaches is Britain's imperial role slips into the background. At most, it becomes a paternalistic overseer responsible for a messy compromise between two opposing groups. Instead of having an active interest, it is embroiled in an Irish conflict and has few options. To this day, British Secretaries of State for Northern Ireland claim that they only want a 'mutual understanding between two communities' as if their role was that of an independent arbitrator. Yet, in a very basic sense the partition of Ireland was foisted on the country by a British government. Irish people, no matter what their religion, identity or geography, had little say in that policy. In a very real sense, the border was the product of British imperialism.

Imperialism, however, is not a thing or a slogan. It is a concept that indicates how strong states dominate others and subordinate their economies to the interests of the metropolis. This is a very general description and the forms of that domination change over time. Crucially, however, it must be managed by a ruling class who develop coherent strategies despite their own internal divisions and debates. They need to develop ways of neutralising internal opponents and intimidating external rivals. Yet this is by no means an easy task as few rulers enjoy a permanent, stable situation of domination in an uneven and competitive world. At the turn of the century, the British ruling class faced two central problems and these helped to condition their response to the 'Irish question'.

The first was the entry, after the Reform Acts of 1867 and 1884, of workers into the political system. Just under a third of men over 21 became eligible to vote but it was enough to transform politics. Before this, the battles between the Conservatives and Liberals were essentially parlour games fought between a landed aristocracy and big business leaders. After the spread of popular suffrage, the style of politics had to change, and elites had to take some account of the mass of their male electorate. Politicians learnt to mask their support for privilege, to speak their real intentions only within the corridors of power and, crucially, to co-opt elements of the lower orders to their political projects. In the main, the Liberals emphasised co-option, seeking to forge an alliance with Labour representatives. The Conservatives appealed more to social imperialism to inculcate a spirit of empire within the population. In the words of Cecil Rhodes, 'The empire is a bread and butter question', providing bigger crumbs to working people of Britain.[19] And even if the crumbs were confined to a small minority, there was also a 'psychological wage' bolstered by identifying with queen and country.

Second, overlapping with the problem of how to deal with the entry of working-class voters was the growing strains within the British empire. The British army had to fight a terrible war against the Boers in South Africa to retain control over diamond and gold mines. It also faced the rising economic power of Germany. And then, despite their studied moderation, the Tories regarded the Irish Home Rule Party as a threat because it had mass support and was endangering the unity of the empire. All of these issues provoked a debate within the British ruling class on how to maintain their hegemony. Some promoted a more federal arrangement to give autonomy to emerging nations within the empire. Others wanted to surround the empire's economy with protectionist barriers. Splits and division grew more acute, and in the crucial period between 1911 and 1914 the British ruling class were divided as they had not been for centuries. The eventual strategy for dividing Ireland was directly intermeshed with these ruling class divisions.

These tensions started really to come to a head with the Parliament Act of 1911. In 1909, the Liberal Party agreed to introduce a 'People's Budget' which proposed taxes on land to fund social protection programmes. This measure was designed to appease Labour allies and project the party as friendly to working people. However, it infuriated the landed ascendancy and they used their power base in the House of Lords to veto it. In response, the Liberals introduced the Parliament Act to remove the veto over laws passed in the House of Commons. It turned the conflicts within the ruling class to an outright conflagration.

At the time the Liberal Party was supported in office by the Irish Home Rule Party and they were promised support for a parliament in Dublin with limited autonomy. Stung by the Parliament Act and riven with divisions within his own supporters over the issue of tariffs, the Conservative leader Andrew Bonar Law decided to focus on opposing Home Rule as 'the glue' that would cement his party together.[20] To do so, he forged an alliance with Edward Carson, and his agenda was not simply Ireland but rather a full-frontal defence of empire, upper-class 'leadership' and tradition. Loyalty to the British nation was defined as allegiance to a monarch or, in the earlier words of Disraeli, 'the King at the centre, the people at the circumference'.[21] This he saw as the key themes to mobilise a mass base for the Conservatives in a new age.

Carson was the ideal ally for such a project. He was son of a landed aristocrat on his mother's side, a protégé of the sixth Marquis of Londonderry and a fanatical defender of the ascendancy's role in the empire. He had been appointed as public prosecutor by a Tory government and won the nickname 'Coercion Carson' for his role in charging tenants who resisted landlords under a special Crimes Act. He was described as a 'castle bloodhound' for prosecuting a writer who organised a public meeting against the notorious Hugh de Burgh, Lord Clanricarde. This absentee landlord was a sworn enemy of the Land League, evicting tenants at will with particular cruelty. Carson also represented Clanricarde at the Morley Commission, established to discuss the plight of evicted tenants, trenchantly arguing against any public assistance for the victims. He also conducted the Tory attack on the Trade Union Disputes Act 1906 which gave the unions some immunities so that they could not be sued for damages incurred during a strike. Famously, he won the legal case against Oscar Wilde, sending him to jail for homosexuality. More significantly, for his later project, Carson was an enthusiastic support of Dr Jim Jameson, an associate of Cecil Rhodes, who staged a raid on the Boer republic of Transvaal to expand the British empire. As Carson's biographer explained, both men were inclined to 'flout the law for the good of the empire'.[22]

This was the real core of his project. Carson was an outlier in the ranks of the British ruling class, willing to take extreme measures to advance the cause of the landed aristocracy in governing the empire. But as the crisis of the British ruling class deepened, this ultra-conservative imperialist moved into the limelight, offering a solution to their dilemmas. In an age where mass politics was starting, Carson showed the Tories how a section of the working class could be won to a renewed social imperialist project. By enlisting tens of thousands of unionists in mass mobilisations, Carson and the Tories demonstrated that defence of empire could generate a movement that stopped the backsliding of the Liberals. Force, insurrection and mutiny were the stuff that dictated the course of history rather than parliamentary majorities.

The crisis within the British ruling class came to a head in 1912 when another Home Rule Bill was introduced to the British House of Commons. It was a very modest measure which gave Dublin limited powers within the empire. Carson, however, began to preach open sedition, promoting an Ulster Covenant, signed by over 218,000 people which pledged to resist Home Rule by 'all means' and 'to refuse to recognise the authority of such a parliament'.[23] These were no idle phrases. A provisional Ulster government was established, enlistment began in an Ulster Volunteer Force and a business committee, chaired by a leading shipbuilder, was charged with procuring arms. Thirty thousand rifles and three million rounds of ammunition were subsequently landed.

Such was the scale of the divisions inside the British ruling class that the Conservative Party tore apart the façade of parliamentary democracy and supported naked physical force to destroy their opponents. When the Tory leader Bonar Law reviewed the mass ranks of the Ulster Volunteers, he told them explicitly that 'you hold the pass for the Empire'.[24] In words not heard since the English Civil war, he denounced his government as:

> a revolutionary committee which has seized power by fraud upon despotic power. In our opposition to them, we shall not be guided by considerations which would influence us in ordinary political struggle. We shall use any means to deprive them of the power they usurped.[25]

As if that was not clear enough, a future Lord Chancellor, F. E. Smith, Earl of Birkenhead, talked gleefully of ministers 'swinging from the lamp posts of London'.[26] This rhetoric encouraged British army officers stationed in Ireland to mutiny in 1914 when asked to move against unionists, demonstrating again that you could 'flout the law for the good of empire'. While the Liberal government was willing to send the army in to shoot down strikers in Liverpool and Llanelly in 1911, they backed off before this mutiny. The Home Rule Bill was eventually postponed due, apparently, to the outbreak of the First World War.

The Ulster crisis of 1912–14 was not simply a conflict between two communities. Once we situate it within the split in the British ruling class, we can see it as part of a project to renew and harden support for the British empire. Sectarian tensions certainly existed in Belfast between Catholic and Protestant workers as Catholics from rural areas migrated to the city looking for work. In their defence of sectional interests, Protestant workers drew on a tradition of settler versus native, Protestant versus Papists, civilised versus barbarian. But a key ingredient in taking this forward and solidifying it into permanent sectarian identities was the intervention of a Conservative Party whose primary aim was to unite the British ruling class around a fulsome defence of empire.

In December 1918, the first election involving all men over 21, and a limited vote for women, was held on an all-Ireland basis. With the passing of the Representation of the People Act, the total Irish electorate rose from 701,475 in 1910 to 1,936,673 in 1918. Sinn Féin stood on a platform of national independence, the creation of a republic and opposition to a Home Rule party which had acquiesced in the temporary exclusion of Ulster. Of the 105 seats, Sinn Féin won 73, wiping out the Home Rule party who only gained six. Unionists won 26 seats, two in Dublin – for Trinity College and Rathmines – and 24 in Ulster. In any democratic society, this was a clear mandate for independence, yet the rulers of the British empire had no intention of respecting Irish democracy. Their failure to do so led to the launching of the Irish war for independence by the Irish Republican Army (1919), starting with an ambush in Soloheadbeg in Tipperary. The response of the British empire was repression and partition.

1919 was a fateful year for the British empire. In Egypt, a revolution was launched against British protectorate rule, with women to the fore in organising demonstrations. Eight hundred people were murdered to suppress it. In India, hundreds of people were murdered by British soldiers in the Amritsar massacre as they put down a non-violent protest. Carson was a strident supporter of General Reginald Dyer, who had ordered his troops to fire live rounds into the crowd. He portrayed Dyer as a defender of imperial power against a revolutionary conspiracy that linked Ireland and India. In Britain itself there was major unrest with mutinies in the army, a police strike and a workers' fight for a 44-hour week. Given this background, the British ruling class thought it vital to crush the Irish rebellion. Under the leadership of General Macready, who had previously threatened to shoot striking Welsh miners, they increased their security apparatus in Ireland recruiting the Black and Tans and Auxiliaries. Targeted assassinations and collective punishment of towns and villages were the method; the aim was to use military superiority to drive the IRA to the negotiating table and force them to compromise. The strategy was partially successful mainly because the IRA leader, Michael Collins, had no interest in fomenting a social revolution against the British empire, and saw the conflict in military terms. Given that the IRA was 'down to its last bullet' he saw no option but to sign up to the Anglo-Irish Treaty. The full fruits of the British strategy came into view, when Collins, supplied with British guns and finance, mobilised a national army to crush his former republican comrades in a bloody civil war.[27]

The other element of the British strategy was partition. After the 1918 election, the British government, now dominated by the Conservatives, moved rapidly to divide Ireland into two states. It provided the Northern state with massive financial resources enabling it to create a security apparatus and civil service. Without that support, there was little prospect that such a state could survive. In doing so, the British ruling class created a template for dealing with other countries that tried to liberate themselves from its grip. The price of independence would be partition, with all the violence and mayhem that would ensue. In order to gain international support, Britain presented itself as protectors of the rights of minorities, claiming there was an intrinsic cultural difference between Protestant and Catholic. Such differences, they emphasised, required separation and partition. Yet the same logic was never applied to a large number of Catholics who were forced to belong to a state that was designed to establish unionist rule in perpetuity.

DISCRIMINATION AND ORANGEISM

The unionist leaders who came to power after the foundation of the Northern state in 1921 were drawn from both the landed ascendancy and the captains of industry. The big landowners provided three of Northern Ireland's premiers for a total of 28 years: Sir Basil Brooke, Terence O'Neill and James Chichester-Clark. James Craig, the first premier, was a wealthy stockbroker and son of a whiskey millionaire. His cabinets from 1921 to 1937 included three former presidents of the Belfast Chamber of Commerce, a partner in a large firm of solicitors, an industrialist, a company director and another titled owner of a large landed estate. This type of government was unusual in Europe after the introduction of mass suffrage because the 'captains of industry' tended to withdraw from public life and leave it to professional political managers to govern in their interests. Barristers and solicitors made the ideal candidates as professional politicians as they were skilled in the art of rhetoric, while big business got on with making profits. In the Northern state it was different. The most privileged elements of society were so confident that their positions were secure, that they took on the role of political leadership. But how did they hold the allegiance of workers for so long?

One way was through systematic discrimination in housing and jobs. Control of local authorities, often through gerrymandering to create an artificial unionist majority, was crucial as these allocated thousands of jobs and housing. Sometimes, however, the local authorities restricted their housebuilding programme lest allocation go to too many Catholics. Even when public housing was in a poor state of repair, unionist councils refused to build new ones if it meant that the delicate electoral balance between unionists and nationalists was upset. The Orange lodge became a space where Protestant workers rubbed shoulders with 'their betters' and got access to jobs and housing. As the big enterprises in the private sector were also in unionist hands, the same techniques of discrimination applied. Of the 10,000 workers in Harland and Wolff in 1970, for example, Catholics only made up 400. Even when factories like Mackies or Sirocco Engineering Works were located in Catholic ghettoes, they only employed a handful of Catholics. Support for discrimination was articulated by Basil Brooke, the then Minister for Agriculture, when he stated that:

> I recommended these people who are Loyalist not to employ Roman Catholics, 99 percent of whom are disloyal... You people who are employers have the ball at your feet. If you don't act properly now, before we know where we are we shall find ourselves in a minority instead of the majority. I want you to realise that, having done your bit, you have got the Prime Minister behind you.[28]

The other way to cement unionist unity was through the enforcement of a specific ideological concept of Protestantism, many aspects of which have come to define a specific 'culture'. Like any religion which functions as an ideology, Protestantism is contradictory. On one hand, there are elements of a radical democratic tradition when believers rejected bishops, papal guidance and asserted their individual right to read the bible in their own language without guidance from a priest claiming special access to God. At its high point, this radical tradition was expressed in the Putney debates in England in 1647 with their call for greater equality among the community of believers. As a Leveller leader put it, 'the poorest he that is in England hath a life to lead, as the greatest he'.[29] The sentiment was limited in terms of gender but it was a challenge to a feudal concept of status. Elements of radical Protestant tradition surfaced in Ireland in the late eighteenth century when the Presbyterians in Belfast played a major role in creating the United Irishmen. The leaders of this movement tended to fuse the dissenting aspects of their faith with an Enlightenment tradition that challenged the 'divine right of kings' and the superstitions that fed from it.

But if the original anti-papist rhetoric contained elements of progressive thinking when it was directed at the aristocracy, the unionist version of Protestantism simply targeted ordinary Catholics as both disloyal and feckless. The 'good Protestant' was someone who was saved and who gained stability in life through thriftiness and hard work. The 'fenian' or 'taig' on the other hand was enslaved to superstition, unable to enjoy the civil and political liberties that freeborn Ulster men enjoyed. If Catholics were unemployed or their countries suffered from lack of industrial development, the fault lay in their religion. The organisation which did most to promote this ideology was the Orange Order which was, officially, a religious organisation that targeted the Church of Rome as the embodiment of evil. Not only did it exclude Catholics from membership but, even to this day, it forbids its members attending Catholic services. Its religious ethos was mixed with an unctuous admiration for monarchy as the institution that defended the Protestant faith and held the British nation together. By creating a space for respectable workers to mix with their betters in local lodges, the Orange Order provided a key mechanism to tie Protestant workers to the Unionist Party. It only had to encourage its members to look across the border into the Southern state to see an enemy that was steeped in a Catholic ethos. This allowed it to suggest that the Protestants were permanently under threat of invasion or liable to be tricked by its devious machinations.

THE MIRROR IMAGE

There was no such threat because the Southern state had no irredentist ambitions. While politicians might sing republican ballads with great gusto, the last thing the Southern elite wanted was the incorporation of a troublesome non-Catholic population. George O'Brien, the author of *The Four Green Fields* and one of the leading economists of his day, probably expressed their feelings most accurately when he stated that:

It would be most regrettable if the sectarian dividing lines between the parties in the north were to spread to the south, and it is hard to see how the infection could be prevented from spreading if the border barrier were destroyed. At the present, sectarianism is safely confined in its Ulster quarantine.[30]

The 'infection' was not just sectarian conflict. The North was also the associated evils of urbanism, foreign influences and a Godless opposition to the ethos of Catholicism which was being inscribed into the Southern state. Partition was used as a symbol of national wrong and an emotional focus to revive anti-colonial memories, but the purpose was to construct a 26-county identity; indeed, one that would become obsessed with security, particularly around its border.

The civil war of 1922–23 brought the most conservative elements within the nationalist movement to power. Having achieved victory over their republican opponents, the Free State embarked on a counter-revolution to crush any radical sentiments that had emerged in the War of Independence. The new state owed its very existence to an uprising of the mass of people against British rule, but its elite wanted to stop all talk of revolution, to replace 'anarchy' with a social order that respected hierarchy. The figure who most personified this ambition was Kevin O'Higgins, the Minister of Justice, who defined continuing talk of revolution as 'a weird composite of idealism, neurosis, and megalomania' that verged on 'a national hysteria'.[31] He despised 'the attitude of protest, the attitude of negation, the attitude of sheer wantonness and waywardness and destructiveness… which has been to a large extent the traditional attitude of the Irish people'.[32] Determined to impose order on this people, O'Higgins and his party introduced measures such as the Enforcement of Law (Occasional Powers) Act of 1924 to give more powers to bailiffs to seize the property of tenants who resisted landlordism. His government cracked down on a strike by post office workers and denied the right of civil servants to join a trade union. The aim of the new state was to advance commercial interests – not the ambitions of the poor.

It was not easy, however, to simply assert naked class privileges, particularly to a population who had sacrificed so much during their fight for freedom. An ideological cover was needed and the form it took in the 26 counties was a spiritual antidepressant – Catholic fundamentalism. If the Irish revolution changed little in material existence, the people could at least have the comfort of living in the most Catholic of countries. The use of Catholicism as both a badge of pride and a mechanism to discipline the population began in the midst of the civil war when Cumann na nGaedheal formed an alliance with the Catholic bishops to condemn opponents of the Anglo-Irish Treaty. In one of their pastorals issued during that conflict, the bishops gave an indication of the role that religion would play in the new state:

> No one is justified in rebelling against the legitimate government, whatever it is, set up by the nation and acting within its rights… 'Let every soul' says St Paul 'be subject to the higher powers' – that is to the legitimate authority of the State. From St Paul downwards the Church has inculcated obedience to authority as a divine duty as well as a social necessity.[33]

The sentiment was echoed by a key backroom figure, Kevin O'Shiel, a legal advisor to the Free State government, who wrote that Cumann na nGaedheal should:

> link up therefore with some great class interests such as Church or agriculture, that it should become in fact a Christian people's party to defend religion against the Atheist and Freemason and property against the Bolsheviks.[34]

To establish a disciplinary power over the population, the Southern state enforced a Catholic identity at every turn. Irish society was defined as primarily agrarian, de-anglicised and Catholic. The new government banned divorce and imposed a strict censorship on films. It established a Committee on Evil Literature and created a system whereby many books by key Irish writers were banned. From a very early stage, unmarried mothers were targeted for shaming and incarceration with special inquiries reserved for those who were 'recidivist'. The road for the expansion of the Magdalene laundries, a space for incarceration and slave labour for single mothers, was open within the first few years of the new state.

Yet contrary to Orange propaganda, the creation of a Catholic state in the South was accompanied by a rejection of nationalist rebellion in the North. After the death of Michael Collins, who, for his own tactical reasons, had tried to unite republicans around armed resistance in the North, the Southern state moved rapidly to a policy of abandonment. The Free State government urged Northern nationalist-controlled local authorities not to pledge allegiance to the Dublin government and encouraged MPs to take their seats in the Northern parliament. They agreed to stop any border incidents by the IRA and hand over any offenders who were caught to the Northern authorities. The only proviso was that they should not be flogged!

When Fianna Fáil came to power in 1932, the rhetoric about the 'fourth green field' was stepped up but the policy of creating a distinct 26-county Catholic identity continued. If anything, it was strengthened as Fianna Fáil presented themselves as more nationalist and, therefore, more Catholic than their rivals. In a celebrated case, the Fianna Fáil leader Éamon de Valera supported the decision of the Mayo County Council not to appoint a Protestant librarian. He argued that 'as over 98 percent of the population is Catholic, they are justified in insisting on a Catholic librarian.'[35] Once they settled into a long hold on government office, Fianna Fáil were even more vigorous in creating the legislative framework for a Catholic state. They banned the sale and importation of contraceptives. They imposed a marriage bar for civil service and teaching jobs, forcing women to leave on marriage. They passed a Dance Hall Act which made it a requirement to obtain a licence from a district justice before holding an event deemed to be 'an occasion of sin'. Behind all these legislative moves, a shadowy theocracy came into existence as de Valera formed an intimate relationship with the Catholic Archbishop of Dublin, John Charles McQuaid, to oversee Irish society. One fruit of this relationship was the Constitution of 1937, which recognised the 'special position' of the Catholic Church. While that clause has since been removed, aspects of that legacy remain to this day as the Irish Constitution starts with the sentence 'In the Name of the Most Holy Trinity, from Whom is all authority and to Whom, as our final end, all actions both of men and States must be referred.'[36]

Yet the more that Fianna Fáil strengthened the Catholic ethos of the South, the less involved they were with Northern nationalists. This infuriated one of their TDs, Eamonn Donnelly, who had previously been elected as an abstentionist MP in Stormont in 1925. He made several efforts to draw the party closer to Northern nationalists but each time was rebuffed. In 1936, he backed up a proposal, originally made privately by two leading Northern nationalist MPs, that elected representatives should leave Stormont and take their seats in the Dáil Éireann. Donnelly believed that this tactic would accelerate the pace of anti-partition agitation and make Irish unity the stuff of practical politics. The plan was rejected. In 1937, he proposed that Fianna Fáil would contest all parliamentary seats in the North and reorganise itself as an all-Ireland party. Once again this was rejected. This was something of an anomaly because Fianna Fáil originated as a split from Sinn Féin, which had been organised on a 32-county basis.

Despite its rhetoric, Fianna Fáil's aim instead was to build up the 26-county state and it saw this occurring though an expansion of Southern capitalism, initially through a strategy of protectionism. Seán Lemass put this succinctly during an election campaign in 1933 when he stated that 'the triumphant nationalism of the people of the South' would eventually secure 'the unity of our historic country'.[37] By triumphant nationalism he meant both the gradual weaning of the South away from the entanglement with the British empire in which it had been trapped by the Anglo-Irish Treaty and the development of a successful 26-county economy. Two years later in May 1935, de Valera spelled this out when he confessed that 'we have no plan… which can inevitably bring about the union of this country' and argued only that an economically prosperous 26 counties would prove irresistible to Northern Protestants.[38] There was, however, a contradiction at the heart of this ambition. The primary mechanism for economic expansion until 1958 was protectionist tariffs but this was precisely what Belfast capitalists did not want. As Desmond Ryan, an early biographer of de Valera pointed out, the small-time industrialists behind Fianna Fáil feared competition from Ulster's more powerful industrialists. Both, it seems, had a vested interest in partition.

Fianna Fáil's role in not just opposing but bolstering partition became evident in the way it cracked down on the IRA. In 1939, it introduced an Emergency Powers Bill to allow for internment, Military Tribunals and executions of IRA members. This was later used to execute at least six IRA volunteers in Ireland between 1940 and 1944. In 1957, after Fianna Fáil returned to power, they reintroduced internment without trial after the killing of a Royal Ulster Constabulary (RUC) man during the IRA's border campaign. The use of internment on both sides of the border made it impossible for the IRA, most of whose leadership was imprisoned, to maintain the momentum of their campaign. Rhetorically, Fianna Fáil leaders still attacked a national wrong, but in a very practical sense they cooperated on security matters. The attitude of the Southern establishment towards partition best resembles that between the contemporary leaders of many Arab nations and Israel. These regularly denounce Zionism and its treatment of Palestinians but at the same time they engage in security cooperation to help crush any real resistance. In a similar fashion, far from any real desire to reclaim the 'fourth green field', nationalist rhetoric was used by Fianna Fáil only to unite people within their part of partitioned Ireland. The last thing it wanted was the actual realisation of their rhetorical ambitions.

A CARNIVAL OF REACTION

In March 1914, after the socialist leader James Connolly learnt of the agreement of the Home Rule Party to the partition of Ireland on a temporary six-year basis, he wrote:

the betrayal of the national democracy of industrial Ulster would mean a carnival of reaction in both North and South, would set back the wheels of progress, would destroy the oncoming unity of the Irish Labour movement and paralyse all advanced movements whilst it endured.[39]

It was an accurate prediction. Partition produced two Irish states that became mirror images of each other in their conservatism, one of the few countries in Western Europe where there was no left–right divide. Instead, voters in the South were locked into supporting parties which emerged from the settlement of 1922. The North became effectively a one-party state, dominated by the Unionist Party, while Fianna Fáil held government office in the South from 1932 to 1973 with two brief interludes. Both parties drew their votes almost equally from all social classes.

In most other Western European countries, the workers' movement produced social democratic parties, giving some expression to the aspirations of workers. They were limited by the fact that they worked within a wider consensus that upheld profit-making and American 'leadership' during the Cold War. Nevertheless, after the Second World War, in the 'golden age of capitalism', they won some reforms and carved out a distinct political identity. Not so in Ireland because the official labour movement quickly adapted to partition, splitting into two parties. The Northern Ireland Labour Party moved to a pro-union stance and refused to challenge loyalism. At a special conference in 1949, it officially supported partition and in 1964 some of its prominent councillors voted to keep playground swings closed on Sunday in a concession to Sabbatarian unionists. Occasionally, it appeared to be about to make an electoral breakthrough, only to be pushed back by the beating of the Orange drum. The South produced a Labour Party that was scarred by its overweening loyalty to the state and to the Church, splitting in 1944 over who was the most anti-communist. After unity was restored, it positioned itself as a permanent minor party, available at different intervals to prop up Fianna Fáil or Fine Gael in government. Both parties were ineffective, marginal and beholden to the dominant conservative forces.

Working people were the ones that lost out. In the South, Catholic social teaching, with its emphasis on charity and voluntary welfare provision, became the core of state policy. In 1933, the Minister for Local Government and Public Health informed an audience in Geneva that his government's policies were based on the same principles as the papal encyclical *Quadragismo Anno*. Foremost of these was the concept of subsidiarity, whereby the state should only delegate to itself functions which could not be performed by the family or by voluntary effort. As the papal encyclical put it, 'social charity… ought to be the soul of this order, an order which public authority ought to be ever ready to protect and defend'.[40] This ran directly counter to the idea that citizens had social and political rights. Instead, every family was to be led by a male breadwinner who looked after his wife and children. If that was not possible, he needed to join the ranks of the deserving poor who appealed to charity. This philosophy led to a situation where many state benefits excluded 'non-working' wives. It also led to directly the debacle over the Mother and Child Scheme in 1950 when the Catholic bishops joined the medical profession in condemning a bill which would have provided free health care for women and their children up to the age of 16. Its architect, Noel Browne, was told that his free health measures would 'constitute a ready-made instrument for future totalitarian aggression'.[41] The defeat of this bill led to modern Ireland's bizarre two-tier health system whereby those who can pay for private insurance jump ahead of the queue for medical treatment.

In the North, workers made some gains because of the efforts of a wider British labour movement. In contrast to the defeat of free health care in the South, Northern workers saw a national health service come into existence. At a time when British capitalism was quite strong, they also benefitted from the creation of a welfare state. The Unionist Party were ideologically opposed to these measures but accepted them, partially because they wished to maintain their hegemony over Protestant workers and partially to distinguish themselves from a backward South. However, the sectarian divisions among workers and the weakness of capitalism in the North created its own problems. The unionist policy of restricting council housing meant that a high proportion were in a state of poor repair. In 1969, for example, there were still 100,000 homes, 22 per cent of the total, officially classified as unfit for human habitation.[42] The divisions among workers made them less combative in facing employers and as a result the income of Northern workers was 25 per cent less than the British average in the mid-1960s.[43]

Overall therefore, the workers' movement was weakened by partition as Connolly had predicted. The 'carnival of reaction' meant that it was ideologically disarmed and did not produce any independent political representation. Instead, it was in thrall to the hostile twins of Unionism and Fianna Fáil. Social rights and even basic wages suffered as a result.

2

Republicans and Loyalists

If you tell someone to change the world in the morning, they may simply stay in bed. If you urge them to take small steps, they may not just get up but change the whole political system. That at least is what occurred in Northern Ireland in 1968. It was a year of international revolt and it was also when the contradictions in the Northern state erupted.

The roots of the social explosion stretch back to 1964 when a tiny group of professional Catholics set up a Campaign for Social Justice to distribute facts about discrimination and gerrymandering. While the approach was moderate, it contained the germs of a revolt. Before this, the main vehicle for Catholic anger was passive support for an IRA campaign or voting for the ineffectual nationalist party. By seeking the basic reforms they were entitled to as British citizens, however reluctantly they accepted the designation, a possibility was created for mass mobilisation. This only became a reality when the demands for civil rights were connected to smaller left-wing networks. Activist networks exist in most countries where there is even a minimal democratic space to organise and, generally, they are marginal but on other, rarer, occasions, they provide a focus for mass anger. Such was the case in Northern Ireland when these networks took up the cause of civil rights.

Different networks overlapped in shaping the strategy. The one which proved to be most cautious in the longer run were the Wolfe Tone Societies, a grouping of republicans who had aligned with members of the Irish Communist Party.[1] After the failure of the 1956–62 border campaign, the republicans had turned to social agitation and were encouraged in this direction by a small number of intellectuals who had originally been associated with the Connolly Association, a network of Irish emigrants with links to the British Communist Party. Communist influence also won the republicans to a new strategy of focusing on a call for civil rights in the North and this implied a set of goals that involved a rigid application of the 'stages theory'. The movement, it was suggested, should focus exclusively on

civil rights within the Northern state and then, at a later stage, the achievement of these demands would create the space for pursuing a united Ireland
by purely political means. Talk of socialism was to be postponed still further
until after a united Ireland had been achieved. Anything that might collapse
these stages – such as questioning the existence of partition – was to be
avoided. In practice, it meant that unity inside the newly formed Northern
Ireland Civil Rights Association was to be enforced by a studied moderation
that would not scare off any 'progressive' allies.

A different network of activists emerged from left-wing students and
the more radical sections of the Northern Ireland Labour Party. Formally,
the NILP was opposed to discrimination but its leadership periodically
succumbed to pressure from unionist politicians, particularly when there
was any talk of a republican conspiracy. As the British Labour Party shifted
left in the 1960s, a number of young activists joined the NILP only to be
disillusioned with its backsliding. Simultaneously, the student revolt of
1968 led to the formation of People's Democracy, a radical left organisation. Alongside the Derry Labour Party, these promoted a series of militant
tactics which pushed the civil rights movements beyond the limits set by
its original leaders. Their aim was to challenge the state and to expose the
manoeuvres of 'moderate' unionists such as the Prime Minister, Terence
O'Neill.

The differences between the two group of activists came to the fore in
two key protests. Left-wing activists in the Derry Labour Party pushed for
a civil rights march in Derry on 5 October 1968 to go ahead in defiance of
a state ban and despite the reluctance of others. This march has gone down
in history as the moment which turned the call for civil rights into a mass
movement. Later, in 1969, when the leaders of the Northern Ireland Civil
Rights Association were looking at the possibility of a truce with O'Neill,
People's Democracy staged the Burntollet march. This was inspired by the
Selma to Montgomery march led by Martin Luther King in America. On
both occasions, the Northern state's response was violent repression – which
in turn led to a renewed questioning about its very existence.

It would be a mistake, however, to think that a small number of activists
simply created the events that triggered 'The Troubles'.[2] Far deeper structural
changes were at play which brought to the surface the contradictions within
the Northern state. Instead of attributing responsibility to left-wing activists
for the events that followed – much like the sacrifice of the leaders of 1916 is

supposed to explain the subsequent fight for Irish freedom – it is necessary to look at the underlying structural conditions which gave a new impetus to the political agitation.

By the late 1960s, the original basis for the partition settlement was undermined. When the Northern state was first created, its British architects assumed that it would be self-supporting and the province was supposed to make an 'Imperial Contribution' to the British government each year.[3] However, soon after its foundation unionist-controlled industry began to decline and the British government was forced to subsidise social services and government administration. The process accelerated after the Second World War with employment in linen falling by 50 per cent between 1949 and 1967, while the numbers in shipbuilding dropped from 25,000 to 10,000. The British government then sought to revive the North's industrial base by inviting in multinationals to take advantages of the abundant supply of cheap labour. Synthetic fibre manufacturers such as Dupont, Chemstrand and British Enkalon replaced the linen mills. The North began to project itself as an outward-looking modern society but eventually this led to pressure to shift its political style of rule. The multinational companies had little reason to discriminate against Catholic workers as they had not been traditionally aligned with the unionist project. The manager of a Dupont plant sent over from New Jersey, for example, saw no reason to join the local Orange lodge. If they wanted to recruit workers, they just employed the hiring methods used in any other capitalist country rather than using Orange patronage networks.

The South was also undergoing a similar change after it relaxed the Control of Manufacturing Act in 1958 which had stipulated that Irish shareholders must make up 51 per cent of a company. This was a signal that this part of Ireland was also 'open for business' from foreign direct investment. The first group of multinational companies who came into Southern Ireland were British companies who tended to concentrate on food and confectionary production. Partially in recognition of this and partially to prepare for further integration into the global economy, the Irish government concluded an Anglo-Irish free trade agreement which cut the tariffs between both countries. It signalled that Fianna Fáil's strategy of using protectionism to build up native capital had run its course. Hostility to Britain at the level of the economy was over.

These developments meant that it was in Britain's interest to promote the modernisation of Unionism. In practice, this meant persuading unionist leaders to make symbolic gestures to appease the nationalist minority. London's aim was to remove an historic sore that was an obstacle to their relations with the South and to create the possibility that Catholics could be embraced as British citizens. Here, however, the British strategy ran into a difficulty. Unionism was founded in the belief that violence and law-breaking were justified to push the British state into a fulsome defence of empire and Protestant identity. It was not going to easily concede to new-fangled ideas coming from London because even the moderates within the unionist camp held a deeply sectarian view of Catholics. The unionist Prime Minister, Terence O'Neill, who was seen as the key moderniser, was willing to shake hands with nuns and meet the Southern Taoiseach, Sean Lemass. But after he left office, he explained his real attitude in a language that could only come from the upper-class squire:

> It is frightfully hard to explain to Protestants that if you give Roman Catholics a good job and a good house they will live like Protestants because they see their neighbours with cars and television sets. They will refuse to have eighteen children but if a Roman Catholic is jobless and lives in a ghastly hovel, he will rear eighteen children on National assistance.[4]

If this was the voice of moderate Unionism, one can only imagine the anger that swept through the unionist hardliners. British imperialism had created a Frankenstein's monster to suit its original interests, but as those interests changed, it needed to dismantle some of its worst features. However, Northern Ireland had been maintained through constant propaganda about a disloyal minority and the threat of invasion from a Catholic-dominated South. While the British elite might want a more modernised form of rule, the Orange machine had developed interests of its own. It had created a system whereby there was active discrimination against Catholics and this system would not be given up so easily. Catholics were more likely to be unemployed, to be employed in unskilled labour and less likely to get social housing. The original basis for these differences was the relatively late entry of Catholics into the Belfast working class and the fact that Protestant workers were more established in the city, sometimes in exclusive craft unions. In most other parts of the world, these differences and divisions would have lessened over time as Catholics became more established within the labour movement. However, the unionist elite exploited these differences and deployed an active discrimination policy against Catholics once the Northern state was established. There was a perception that Protestant workers were better off even though working-class division meant that both Catholic and Protestants lost out. As Sean Mitchell pointed out, 'Protestants tended to have a better position than Catholics in Belfast, but workers in areas like Manchester or Glasgow had a better position than both.'[5] Nevertheless, from an Orange perspective the wider working-class interest was irrelevant – the key issue was sustaining a system of discrimination, against the wishes of any British modernisers. The contradiction between the wider British policy and its unionist allies in the North eventually gave rise to the two forces that were to shape the future – republicanism and loyalism.

REPUBLICANISM

Prior to 1968, republicanism in Northern Ireland was a marginal and demoralised force. On the fiftieth anniversary of the 1916 rising, the Belfast IRA could only send a minibus to the annual republican commemoration at Wolfe Tone's grave. Danny Morrison, who would later become its major propagandist, wrote at the time, 'As far as we were concerned, there was absolutely no chance of the IRA appearing again. They were something in the history books.'[6] Yet by 1971, the Belfast Brigade had over one thousand members and in the minds of many, civil rights within the Northern state had been replaced with a call to end partition. Two key elements brought about this transformation.

One was the traditional unionist response of suppressing any disloyal rebellion with violence. Not all Protestants supported this but the use of violence to intimidate the disloyal ran deep in Orange 'culture'. Here is Richard Seymour describing his memories of growing up in a small Protestant town in the 1980s in a *New York Times* article:

The annual Twelfth of July bonfires and parades, celebrating the history of Ulster Loyalism, saw effigies of wicked Papists burned for public edification and the delight of inebriated Loyalists. This was 'our culture'. These festivities helped create a lynch mob atmosphere, leading to the murder of Catholics. Every year, the stories were the same: Bonfire night was a night for petty terror and bricking Catholic windows. Parades day was a day for blood.[7]

Given this background, it is not surprising that the civil rights movement was met with violence both from state forces and unofficial vigilante networks. One of the first deaths of the Troubles, for example, was Samuel Devanney who was beaten to death at his home by RUC officers who had gone on a punishment rampage in Derry's Bogside. In August 1969, an attack was launched against Catholics living in Belfast's Bombay Street and similar incursions were made on the Unity Flats on the Falls Road. The Scarman Tribunal reported that over 10,000 people or 5.3 per cent of Catholic households in Belfast were left homeless in the 1969 riots.[8]

The second factor was the role of the British army. Originally it was sent in to quell riots and were welcomed in Derry's Bogside. It was not, however, trained to take the side of the oppressed against a police force and the defenders of a local variant of the British state. British army generals preferred to work through an existing state apparatus even as their political masters sought to professionalise and modernise it. Their main role was to prop up the Northern state as the exhausted and beleaguered RUC were losing control. Even though they were initially seen as giving the besieged Catholic population of Derry a brief breathing space, the British army's strategy soon became apparent. It was to *first* shore up the Northern state by a policy of repression against Catholic areas and then to wean Unionism gradually towards reform. The path to Catholic confrontation with the British army was thus paved by a series of events like the Falls Road curfew in 1970 where four civilians were shot dead; internment in 1971 when hundreds of Catholics, republican or otherwise, were locked up without any evidence of committing a crime; and Bloody Sunday, 30 January 1972, when 14 civilians were murdered by the Parachute Regiment. Many drew the conclusion that the fight for democracy in Northern Ireland had become a fight against the state itself and the British army that was propping it up.

An interesting study based on interviews with 50 IRA volunteers shows that there were three pathways into IRA membership in this early period. The first were those who joined before 1969 who largely came from families steeped in the republican tradition. Those who joined later were composed of two groups. One consisted of those who were already political but because of 'transformative events' had come to believe armed activism was the only way forward. Another younger group joined 'after experiencing state repression or violent sectarian attack by loyalists rather than the holy grail of the Republic of 1916'.[9]

In the decades since the Troubles began, a mythological narrative has grown that the conflict was caused by 'men of violence on both sides' who resorted to 'terrorism'. Only the intervention of skillful politicians like Tony Blair, Bill Clinton and Bertie Ahern brought them to their senses and offered a peaceful, political way of resolving their differences. From a different angle, Sinn Féin's Gerry Adams is seen as someone who came to a late realisation that terrorism had to be replaced by a peace process and, on these grounds, enters the pantheon of peacemakers. Even if one disagreed with their politics, gratitude needs to be expressed to these men who weaned away people from the path of violence.

There are problems with this view. For one thing, the image of 'statesmen' leading former terrorists to a peace process confuses who exactly were terrorists. It is estimated that the Provisional IRA killed 1,696 people during the Troubles but, while these killings were horrific, they pale in significance when compared to the murderous activity of the statesmen. Tony Blair, for example, was involved in a terrible war in Iraq, launched with lies about 'weapons of mass destruction' which led to the death of over 1 million people. He gave orders for bombings, military assaults and, possibly, torture, but few have described him as a 'reformed terrorist'.

The notion that there were 'two sides' who were both 'evil terrorists' is equally problematic because it ignores the origins and political motivations of those involved. One can look with horror and outrage at the human cost of a war fought in a small corner of Europe. The casualty figures may not seem high when compared to the bloodshed in the former Yugoslavia but they are the equivalent, if measured per head of population, to 125,000 deaths and nearly 2 million injuries in Britain, or half the British death toll during the Second World War.[10] Given this carnage, it is easy to demonise those involved but this will not help explain what happened. According to Martin McGuinness, at least 10,000 people passed through the ranks of the main protagonist of the conflict, the IRA, during the Troubles.[11] It makes little sense to dismiss these people as morally bankrupt or mindless operatives controlled by paramilitary godfathers. While their actions brought terrible suffering, they risked imprisonment and death for deeply held political motives. The loyalist paramilitaries sometimes organised more openly and at its height, the Ulster Defence Association (UDA) claimed 40,000 members.[12] A much smaller number went on to join its armed campaign but, again, it is necessary to assess their political motives and objectives.

As we have seen the IRA grew when a movement for civil rights was met with state violence and loyalist attacks. Its stated aim was a democratic goal, the ending of partition: democracy, in this case, being exercised on the whole island. The origins and purpose of loyalist organisations, by contrast, was to resist civil rights by violence. The Ulster Defence Association, the largest loyalist group, was formed in 1971 in response to Catholic opposition to internment. A leaflet at the time claimed that 'the enemies of our Faith and Freedom are determined to destroy the State of Northern Ireland and enslave the people of God'.[13] The *UDA Bulletin* contained a letter from a reader which posed the question, 'Why have they not started to hit back in the only way those nationalist bastards understand? That is ruthless, indiscriminate killing.'[14] Soon the organisation answered this call with random, indiscriminate attacks on Catholics. One UDA activist, Alec Calderwood, recounted an incident where after drinking in a pub, he set out to walk home and encountered a crowd who had two young men up against a wall:

Someone I knew shouted to me that they were Fenians and had I got a gun on me. He knew I was in the UDA. One of the two they had caught made a run for it, but they hung on to the other one. I took him along the street a little way to a derelict garage and there was a loose slab of concrete there. I was a big strong fellow and I picked it up and smashed his skull in with it. I beat him to death, and I felt good about it. It wasn't the drink.[15]

This was not just a random, brutalised account of one individual. The action grew out of a wider tradition that Fenians did not belong to the 'people of God' and had to be collectively punished.

IRA activists also engaged in sectarian murders, most notably in Kingsmills, La Mon and Enniskillen. As the requirement for 'balance' dominates most of the mass media, helping shape our mindset, this might suggest that both sides were equally involved in sectarian killing. However, such a balance is usually struck from a vantage point of official society, which ignores or hides its own history of violence. When we examine the specific nature of each side's strategy, a different picture emerges. There was a specific period, 1974 to about 1976, where the IRA consciously set out to kill Protestants in retaliation to loyalist attacks. In September 1975, IRA members machine-gunned an Orange hall in Newtownhamilton, killing five Protestants. In January 1976, IRA members used the cover name of the South Armagh Republican Action Force to shoot dead ten Protestant building workers in Kingsmill. Two weeks later, the IRA issued a statement that contained an implicit justification by framing it as a form of retaliation: 'The Irish Republican Army has never initiated sectarian killings... [but] if loyalist elements responsible for over 300 sectarian assassinations in the past four years stop such killing now, then the question of retaliation from whatever source does not arise...'[16]

That period also fuelled the rise of the Adams faction who largely put an end to explicit sectarian murders like Kingsmill, but not to the killing of Protestant civilians through indiscriminate bombs. Essentially, these killings of the IRA arose from a car-bombing campaign that hit city centre targets rather than businesses in Catholic areas. Car bombs have been described by Mike Davis as the 'poor man's air force' because they can ravage a city with little cost to the perpetrators.[17] However, like the smartest of aerial bombs, they are 'indiscriminate' and 'collateral damage' is inevitable. After 1976, most IRA violence was focused on state forces, those assisting state forces and on a bombing campaign designed to create economic sabotage.

Loyalist paramilitary violence was focused on collective punishment of Catholics, often as punishment or revenge for IRA actions. In 1992, after four Catholic building workers were murdered in Castlerock, a UDA spokesman told a Belfast journalist, 'If you are talking in terms of success rates, yes, this week has been a success – and it is still only Thursday.'[18] The most accurate summary of the conflicting patterns of violence was undertaken by Robert White who concluded that:

> Between 1969 and 1993, the Irish Republican Army killed more than 340 Protestant civilians in Northern Ireland. However, most of the deaths occurred in the early years of the conflict, and many of them resulted from the IRA's focus on military activity and on destabilizing Northern Ireland... of 307 Protestant civilians killed by the IRA between 1969 and 1989, 181 (59 per cent) were killed in the years 1972–76.... Over time, the IRA changed its approach, but not its focus on breaking the link between

Northern Ireland and the UK, and the number of Protestant civilians killed by the organization declined.[19]

Differences, however, do not amount to a justification. We can still ask if the violence achieved the stated purposes of those involved. In other words, was the amount of human suffering worth it and here the answer must be negative. At first, the emergence of the IRA from a mass movement offered hope that Catholic areas could be defended and resistance to the Northern state was possible. The armed struggle, however, came to subsume and undermine the mass movement and the more it did so, the less it was able to achieve. This occurred because a militarist attitude characterised the early leaders of the IRA. The founders of the Provisional IRA associated left-wing politics with the running down of armed struggle and asserted that 'Red agents' had infiltrated the IRA and 'brainwashed young men and girls into departing from the traditional republican emphasis on armed struggle'.[20] In order to stop this occurring again, there was a return to an earlier tradition whereby the IRA Army Council was put in charge of the wider republican movement, including its political wing, to ward off any compromise emanating from Sinn Féin. The main strategy of the IRA leaders was targeting of security forces and a bombing campaign, which, they believed, would create economic sabotage and draw away security forces from Catholic areas. This was pursued regardless of its political impact.

It was counterproductive at many different levels. It led to an outlook that played down mass mobilisation in favour of the 'cutting edge' of armed struggle.[21] After internment, for example, tens of thousands took part in a rent and rates strike and 8,000 workers in Derry joined a one-day strike. But the republican strategy was a bombing campaign directed at shops, offices and city centre pubs. The bombing campaign also played into the hands of a Southern establishment. In the aftermath of Bloody Sunday in 1972 there were mass strikes and occupations of British businesses in the South. Yet within months, the Southern establishment was able to quell this mood, establish Special Criminal Courts and step up security cooperation on the border. They used the car bombings in Dublin organised by loyalist paramilitaries and British intelligence to frighten people and to present the IRA as the cause of threats to their security. Another factor which played into the hand of the Southern establishment was the tactics of the IRA itself. The southern population had – and still has – an historic memory of a 'war of independence' but by the 1970s there was a massive difference between working-class communities like Ballymurphy in Belfast and Ballymun in Dublin. In Ballymurphy, people saw the British army kick in their doors, arrest young men, beat them up and intern them. Support for an armed struggle grew spontaneously in response. In Ballymun, there was no British army, no loyalist attacks – so there was no spontaneous support for armed action. Quite the opposite – it helped to alienate people from the struggle.

Support for the armed struggle, therefore, came from a minority of the minority community in the North – and could not break out of this to win solidarity in the South. While it was not the cause of the division between Catholic and Protestant workers, the IRA campaign confirmed in many Protestant minds that they were a community under siege. The result was that sections of the Protestant population were drawn ever closer to support, tacitly or implicitly, for the more hardline unionists. Given all this, it was never possible for the IRA to win. Whereas conditions for a nationalist movement spearheaded by a guerrilla army were favourable in countries like Vietnam or Algeria, none of this applied in Northern Ireland. The success of many guerrilla armies has been their ability to build a territorial base among the peasantry by addressing the land question or resisting a parasitic state. Once that base has been consolidated, they are often able to surround and conquer cities. The IRA was one of the most effective guerrilla movements in the late twentieth century, but it lacked conditions that could secure victory. The end result from all the suffering, therefore, is that IRA leaders now sit in government in a Stormont regime they once pledged to oppose.

LOYALISTS

Between 2003 and 2005, a major shift occurred within the politics of the Protestant population. On 29 November 2003, the Ulster Unionist Party, which had governed the Northern state from its foundation until the suspension of Stormont in 1973, lost an election to the Democratic Unionist Party (DUP). Then, as if to compound its demise, the Orange Order cut its links with the Ulster Unionist Party. Afterwards, the DUP reduced its rival to a marginal force in successive elections. The shift can broadly be characterised as a shift to the loyalist end of the political spectrum.

The categories unionism and loyalism are not absolute but they point to an important contradiction. Traditional unionism makes support for the

British state conditional on its defence of a Protestant identity. Mobilisation and defiance of its laws might be necessary to make that state live up to its imperial obligations. Hence the veneration of Edward Carson, who supported armed insurrection to make the empire act like an empire. In practice, conditional loyalty means bolstering the position of Protestants within the Northern state. Yet here is where the distinction matters. The more you asserted loyalty to the British state, the more you veered to a unionist outlook. The more you emphasised the needs of Protestant Ulster and were willing to defy that state, the more you veered to loyalism. The category and its earlier 'plebeian unionist' incarnations tends to be based inside poorer sections of the Protestant population, reflecting elements of class polarisation in a sharply refracted manner. However, they are often organised under leadership of some section of the Protestant petit bourgeoisie, be they small business people, church pastors or community leaders.

These tensions within unionism–loyalism overlapped with divisions on social class. For decades, the 'big house' or the 'fur coat brigade' dominated the ranks of Unionism. The leaders of the Orange Order, the Unionist Party, the Stormont Cabinet were drawn from the landed aristocracy, industrialists or upper professionals. The all-class coalition between the upper class and workers was held together both by discrimination and deference. As an example of the latter, note an invitation by a Fintona Orange Lodge in Tyrone in 1967:

> In view of the vacancy for Grand Master, the lodge recommend the Marquis of Hamilton, MP... it would be an honour for County Tyrone to have such a worthy brother in this high office. He would bring grace and dignity to this office (and this would mean) much good will for the Orange Institution of Ireland.[22]

This deference was never absolute as Protestant workers had a history of looking to both labour opponents but also, sometimes, to a tradition of Independent Orangeism that combined class resentment with opposition to any form of 'appeasement' of Catholics. The wealthier elements identified more closely with the United Kingdom as they did not feel the same need for support from the local state. In the more secure, professional areas such as in the suburbs stretching out of Belfast, this version of Unionism was dominant. Sometimes, their political representatives, such as James

Molyneaux or Enoch Powell stressed integration into the British state rather than devolution of powers to Stormont. Others, such as David Trimble, imagined that a more liberal version of Britishness could attract upper-class Catholics into the ranks of Unionism. The poorer elements of Unionism viewed the matter differently. They wanted the devolution of powers to Stormont and dreamt about better access for jobs and housing. They did not trust the British state or the 'Lundies' in their own ranks. Their outlook was conditioned by insecurity about their own living standards and, through that, about the state itself. Hence the shift to loyalism.

Ian Paisley's Democratic Unionist Party won the leadership of many Protestants by relating to that sentiment. The origins of the party lay in the outer fringes of fundamentalist evangelicalism as Ian Paisley began his career by claiming that the leaders of the main Protestant churches were not standing up to 'Romanism' and 'Papism'. He suggested that the 'born again' and those who were 'living in light' of pure Protestantism were closer to God than Catholics who were enslaved to superstition and the priesthood. His theological claims about the 'saved' and the Calvinist notion of a predestined 'elect' offered a thinly disguised discourse of ultra-sectarianism. One of the first organisations which he founded, the National Union of Protestants, asserted that 'Roman Catholics are buying up Protestant farms, houses, land and property in their efforts to establish Papacy in Ulster. The NUP has helped Protestant employers to obtain Protestant employees.'[23] From an early stage, Paisley developed a style of fomenting physical attacks on Catholics and then departing the scene. Well before the Troubles began, he addressed a rally as follows:

> You people of the Shankill Road, what's the matter with you? Number 425 Shankill Road, do you know who lives there? Pope's men, that's who. Forte's ice-cream shop, Italian papists on the Shankill Road. How about 56 Arden Street. For 97 years a Protestant lived in that house and now there's a Papisher in it. Crimea Street, number 38. Twenty-five years that house has been up, 24 years a Protestant lived there but there's a Papisher there now.[24]

When a violent 'Taigs Out' march followed after his speech, Paisley was nowhere to be seen. It was pattern that was to be closely followed in future decades.

The shift from Ulster Unionism to the DUP began when British imperialism tried to nudge the unionist leaders into an accommodation with moderate nationalists. When the conflict grew, their strategy was to shore up the Northern state by offering power-sharing and a Council of Ireland to encourage cooperation with the South. But every move in this direction was viewed as an attack on the very tradition that founded the Northern state. Moreover, as the focus of the civil rights movement was on equal access to jobs and houses, this was seen by many Protestant workers as fewer jobs and houses for them. And insofar as there was little talk of expanding the numbers of houses or decent paid jobs, there was a certain cruel logic to this sentiment. Against this background, an evangelical message that won a hearing in rural areas was combined with an appeal to the working class in the cities.

This has given rise to a mistaken view that the DUP articulates working-class interests, even if in a distorted sectarian way. Thus, Clifford Smith suggests that it was 'right wing in the sense of being strong in defence of the Constitution but to the left on social issues'.[25] Dixon put it differently when he acknowledged that while 'the party is conservative on social issues (contraception, gays and women's liberation) it is to the left on economic issues'.[26] Ironically, a similar argument has been made about Fianna Fáil in the South – conservative on social issues but to the left on economic issues. The distinction rests on the assumption that one can support social oppression and that this has no economic impact. It assumes, for example, that one can oppose a woman's right to choose but this will not adversely affect women, in their real economic existence. This makes little sense. The DUP is a thoroughly right-wing party and this is evident at many different levels.

First, its lower middle-class cadre cultivates an image of respectability. It has managed to do this even while whipping up sectarianism to mobilise its base. It successfully marginalised loyalist paramilitaries by presenting itself as a law and order party that did not associate with ruffians. This has been achieved by rhetorically dangling the possibility of strong resistance to British government efforts – while lurching back to respectability later. In 1981, the party called for a 'Third Force' to back up the security forces and when Paisley reviewed a parade of thousands of masked men, he said 'my men are ready to be recruited under the crown to destroy the vermin of the IRA. But if the crown refuses to recruit them we will destroy the IRA.'[27]

Yet when the British Secretary of State for Northern Ireland declared that a private army would not be tolerated, Paisley backed down. Similarly, in 1986, the DUP leaders announced the formation of an Ulster Resistance Movement to take direct action. A year later, however, the party cut its links with the movement when it was involved in smuggling arms. The party's modus operandi has been, in the long tradition of Carson, to threaten illegal action – and then rush back to the shelter of the mainstream to protect its middle-class base.

Second, the party's record does not support the view that it has a left-wing stance on economic issues. It may vote at Westminster against items like a bedroom tax, but this is only to distinguish itself from *British* Tories. It plays on being an outsider on the fringes of the British state and fighting strongly for a bigger share for Northern Ireland. As the province is more heavily reliant on the public sector, the DUP demands billions from the British exchequer to fund services. However, where it has direct control over finances such as at local council level, it pursues a vigorous policy of privatisation. This sometimes takes the form of outsourcing facilities to private trusts or simply selling off public assets. The NIPSA union has detailed how DUP-dominated councils in Ards, Belfast, North Down have divested themselves of public facilities.[28] Even while advancing these Thatcherite policies, the DUP will still pose as champions of areas which are decimated by these programmes. This is not an uncommon feature of right-wing parties in other countries. They do not simply defend the privileged but rather combine this with claiming to win resources for their own regions. In the case of both the DUP and Fianna Fáil in the South, their representatives vote for right-wing economic measures, but then claim to be standing up for their constituency and even pose as advocates for the victims of austerity. If there is any doubt about the social class that the DUP protects, one has only to look at its role in the corruption scandals that have mired its presence in Stormont. The events around Project Eagle will serve as just one example.

The scandal arose when the NAMA, the 'bad bank' agency of the Southern state, wanted to call in debts owned by Northern creditors and threatened to sell off their property. The top property speculators called Sammy Wilson of the DUP and within 24 hours Wilson put through a phone call to NAMA's chairman in Dublin. A few weeks later, the outline of a solution for the business elite came into view with moves to sell off the whole of the NAMA-controlled property empire in the North to just one US investor. Section 172 of the NAMA Act, passed by the Dáil in 2009, forbade the agency from selling property back to developers who were in default of their loans. However, if all of NAMA's properties in the North could be sold off to one big US investor, that investor could then sell the properties back to the developers at cut-price rates. This is precisely what happened when Cerebrus got the Northern portfolio for a fraction of its original value and then signed a letter to the DUP leader Peter Robinson stating that 'Cerberus will release personal and corporate guarantees as a key part of consensual workout plans with corporate borrowers.'[29] The Northern business leaders were protected and throughout the complex negotiations 'fixer fees' were paid to an offshore bank account. It was an apt illustration of how the DUP has little difficulty working with Southern 'papists' if they can help their friends in business.

Third, the DUP has had to cover some of its fundamentalist views in order to win urban working-class support. Thus, under Peter Robinson's influence, it has dropped its Sabbatarianism – a ban on all work and most play on Sundays – in favour of a 'local option'. Instead of using their council seats to close swings or pubs on a Sunday, the DUP now allows local communities to decide on the issue. Nevertheless, Christian fundamentalists play a big role in the party and their views coincide neatly with right-wing positions. One recent study found that 40 per cent of DUP councillors and a third of its Members of the Legislative Assembly (MLA) were members of the Free Presbyterian church even though this denomination made up only 0.6 per cent of the total population.[30] The fundamentalist element of the party promotes policies which are directly at variance with the majority of the population – and bring significant economic hardship. This is most evident in the case of abortion, which 65 per cent of the North's population believe should not be a crime.[31] Nevertheless, the DUP fought tooth and nail against any legislation, with every one of its MLAs, except one, opposed to extending the 1967 Abortion Act to Northern Ireland. Despite the fact that it was passed by a British parliament, the DUP aligned with Catholic fundamentalists in Both Lives Matter to oppose it. The direct result was that an average of over one thousand women a year had to travel to Britain to obtain this service. One report presented to the Northern Ireland assembly detailed the cost:

The cost of accessing abortion ranges from £70 from internet providers to £600–£2000 for those who travel to England (this includes clinic fees and flights/ferry costs). Such costs create a significant burden to women with low incomes and can also lead to delays in obtaining an abortion, thereby increasing costs.[32]

While the direct economic costs of the DUP's policy on abortion are quantifiable, the same cannot be said for other aspects of their fundamentalist policies. Nevertheless, they exist. The party has a long history of verbally abusing gay people, with Iris Robinson, the former DUP MP for Strangford, stating that 'I cannot think of anything more sickening than a child being abused. It is comparable to the act of homosexuality. I think they are all comparable. I feel totally repulsed by both.'[33] So vehement were the DUP in its opposition to gay rights that even though a majority of MLAs in Stormont voted to legalise homosexuality, they vetoed it through a petition of concern in 2015. Once again, gay marriage was only legalised in Northern Ireland when the Stormont assembly was not operating. However, the damage in terms of scapegoating and abuse of gay people will continue for some time afterwards. Like most fundamentalists, the DUP is also a leading exponent of climate change denial. The former Environment Minister at Stormont, Sammy Wilson, banned UK government advertisements on television and radio that were encouraging people to cut their carbon emissions. Wilson described the ads as insidious green propaganda and believes the ideas of man-made climate change is a 'gigantic con' and an 'hysterical semi-religion'.[34] Not surprisingly, the DUP was an avid supporter of Donald Trump and three of its prominent MPs, Sammy Wilson, Ian Paisley Jr and Paul Girvan, posed outside the Houses of Parliament with a banner reading: 'Trump 2020, Keep America great.'[35]

These right-wing views rest uneasily on a Protestant working class whose lived experiences do not conform to evangelical dogmas. The DUP's road to leadership of its 'community' has, therefore, rested on a rhetoric that combines an apocalyptic vision of a united Ireland with one of betrayal by other unionist leaders. The IRA was supposed to have engaged in a 'genocidal' campaign against Protestants; the Southern state was pursuing a plan to wipe out their religion; the IRA ceasefire was a devilish shift in tactics to gain control over policing. With these doomsday scenarios, the main issue facing unionism was betrayal. After the signing of the Belfast

Agreement in 1998, Paisley claimed that 'those who should be in the front line are in cahoots with the enemy' and that the leader of Ulster Unionism was 'the worst and most loathsome person in society, a Judas Iscariot'.[36] Nevertheless, after 30 years of the Troubles, the majority of Protestants rejected this rhetorical bluster and by a slim majority voted to accept the Belfast Agreement.

This rebuff to the DUP led to a rapid change of tactics. Despite objecting to the peace process and the Belfast Agreement, the DUP agreed to take part in its institutions. Its stated aim, however, was to 'destroy' the agreement from the inside.[37] Later, this position was amended to seeking a 're-negotiation' of the Belfast Agreement.[38] By promoting rhetoric about traitors making concessions to Catholics and republicans, the DUP managed to recover ground. The two key themes it focused on were the IRA decommissioning and the Royal Ulster Constabulary. In both arenas the focus shifted to symbols. Paisley wanted visible decommissioning of weaponry to show republicans that 'they need to wear their sackcloth and ashes, not in a backroom but openly'.[39] Despite Paisley's call for symbolic repentance, the reality was that the IRA was coming to an accommodation with the state, rather than seeking to militarily overthrow it. Similarly, the DUP's main attack on police reform was the fact that the RUC had been renamed the Police Service of Northern Ireland and that it no longer wore an emblem of the British monarchy. Behind the symbols, however, there was a much more salient fact – republicans had agreed to support recruitment to a police force formed to protect the Northern state.

The focus on symbols was to be a harbinger for the future because in 2008 the DUP did an about-turn and decided to enter a power-sharing agreement with Sinn Féin. Naturally, the evangelical wing of the party was upset and Paisley was pressurised to step down as moderator of the Free Presbyterians. His wife, Eileen, however, was at hand with a biblical reference to defend her husband:

Like the Israelites of old treated Moses so they treat today's God-anointed leader. They refuse to believe that God is already working in the most unexpected places and in the hearts of the most unexpected people. Again, like the Israelites, they prefer to remain in the wilderness of the past than move into the promised land of a better and happier future.[40]

The new 'promised land' was one where 'God's anointed leader' sat in the same government cabinet as Martin McGuinness, a self-proclaimed leader of the IRA. In the past, the DUP had refused to sit quietly in local authorities when Sinn Féin councillors spoke but the relationship between McGuinness and Paisley became so warm that they were known as the 'Chuckle Brothers'. After all the bluster, defiance and threats, the hardest voice of loyalism was consorting with the former terrorists they had denounced so fiercely. Two factors had produced the change. The first was the determined pressure of Westminster. The British government had threatened a further involvement of Dublin in a Council of Ireland if power sharing did not occur and despite all its protestations, loyalism was still dependent on the will of British imperialism. If Westminster was determined to modernise the sectarian structures of the Northern state there was little that the loyalist forces could do at that stage. For decades loyalism resisted but there was no final option for independence as had occurred when the white population unilaterally declared independence in Rhodesia in 1965. After 30 years of conflict, war weariness eventually set in. The second was that the institutional structure of the Belfast Agreement provided ample scope for the DUP – and for Sinn Féin – to pursue their communal conflicts. They had only to focus on symbols and 'legacy issues' to remind their electorate that they were the strongest defenders of 'their side'. Then after the public spats and arguments, they could do deals quietly behind the scenes with their sworn enemies.

The current status of Northern Ireland is thus, based, on the failure of two ideologies. The republicans claimed that an armed struggle could force Britain to a negotiating table and lead to their withdrawal. It did not happen. The loyalists claimed they could defy the overlords at Westminster and push measures that would crush the republican enemy. They also failed. Today, the North lives in an uneasy, sectarian peace. Betrayal has come back to haunt its accusers like a boomerang.

3

British Imperialism

Ireland has a new export industry as the Belfast Agreement has become a model for mediating conflicts over identity. From the Basque country to Cyprus, discussion of the Irish case has become a reference point for new solutions. If Protestants and Catholics in Northern Ireland can agree to share power, then similar mechanisms can be created for other divided societies. Or at least that is the theory.

The key 'architects' of the agreement have gone onto greater things. The US politician George Mitchell became a special envoy to the Middle East and now gives lectures on the art of mediation. Former UK premier Tony Blair has rebranded himself as a peacemaker and, according to one newspaper report, can earn up to €1 million an hour when acting as a Mr Fix-It.[1] His former chief of staff Jonathan Powell took up a position as 'special envoy to the Libyan Transition' and then became a CEO of Inter Mediate, an NGO dedicated to conflict resolution around the world. Even Gerry Adams, the former advocate of armed struggle, has jokingly released a cookbook about the 'pees process'.[2]

Criticism of the 1998 Belfast Agreement has been muted and it has assumed an almost sacrosanct place in Irish political discourse. One reason is a belief that peace in Northern Ireland will always be fragile, almost like walking on eggshells, and any mishap or abrupt change could trigger a return to violence. Given this nightmare scenario, many believe that the 'peace process' is the only viable option and that gratitude is to be expressed to its architects. Thus, the late Ian Paisley and Martin McGuinness are now praised as men of peace. The irony of enshrining the memory of a former chief of staff of the IRA in a peace foundation seems lost on many.[3] The transformation of a promoter of sectarian hatred into a 'statesman' is equally strange.

However, it is possible to separate 'peace' from the 'process'. When the historical record is examined more carefully, it will appear that the architects of peace were not just politicians. The demand for an end to all violence came from mobilisations from civil society and, particularly, organised labour. In

1992, a rally was organised by the Belfast Trades Council after the murder of five people in a bookmaker's shop on the Ormeau Road. In 1993, 7,000 people gathered outside Belfast City Hall for a rally called by the Irish Congress of Trade Unions (ICTU) to express opposition to the Shankill Road bombing and a massacre in Greysteel, while in Derry another 5,000 people gathered.[4] In 1994, workers from Harland and Wolff walked out of their jobs after a 50-year-old Catholic welder was murdered by the UVF. In 2002, thousands attended protest rallies organised by the ICTU against loyalist paramilitary death threats to postal workers and school staff.[5] The demand for peace came from below and acted as a pressure point on paramilitaries. Ownership of that peace cannot, therefore, be appropriated by any one group.

The 'process' is a different thing. The Belfast Agreement laid down a set of institutional arrangements through which the North was to be governed. These are based on theories of consociation which were originally developed by the political scientist Arend Lijphart and then modified to include all-Ireland cross-border institutions linking the two sovereign governments of Britain and Ireland.[6] Essentially, it involves a power-sharing arrangement in Stormont where 'each of the main communities share in executive power';[7] a system whereby elected representatives designate themselves as nationalist, unionist or other; a form of veto whereby measures require 'cross-community support'. On top of these internal arrangements, which are designed to give due recognition to 'equally legitimate political aspirations',[8] there are a series of interlocking institutions which acknowledge the British and Irish dimensions. These include a North–South Ministerial Council, a British and Irish Council and a British–Irish governmental council.

Underlying the Belfast Agreement are three main assumptions that deserve far closer scrutiny. The first is that Britain is not engaged in an imperialist project but retains sovereignty over Northern Ireland only because it is responding to the wishes of the majority. If this were true, then it is possible that Britain might shift focus and respond to other aspirations. Republicans, for example, suggest that Britain should go one step further and advocate for a united Ireland. A recent document from Sinn Féin stated that 'the British government should instead become persuaders for agreement on political structures in Ireland'.[9] The notion of Britain playing a more beneficial role in terms of Irish unity is quite novel for Irish republicans but it is premised on a belief that Britain has no direct imperialist interest.

The second key assumption is that there are two irreconcilable cultures and identities in the North which have equal validity and must be represented at governmental level. So deep was the conflict over culture and identity, that the original theorist of consociational democracy in the North suggested that a repartition should be given serious consideration. Even if that were unlikely, Lijphart argued that 'it should be possible to create areas with relatively homogenous population without the necessity of dividing these areas into or among different sovereign states'.[10] These were theoretical speculations from an academic in the mid-1970s and after the horrors of ethnic cleansing in the former Yugoslavia, few now support repartition. However, Lijphart's notion of a deep clash of identities lies at the heart of the Belfast Agreement. Political structures have been organised around the recognition of this clash and it is suggested that only over time might hatred be replaced with understanding.

The third assumption was that the Belfast Agreement would be followed by a peace dividend. This arose from a recognition of the link between material deprivation and violence. Contrary to popular mythology, the Troubles did not affect everyone equally but were overwhelmingly skewed towards the poorest areas. Of the 94 postal codes in the North, half of the fatalities were concentrated in just twelve of them. If a map was drawn between areas of highest deprivation and fatal incidents, the two would be almost interchangeable.[11] As the Belfast Agreement brought peace to the two communities, it was claimed this would bring a flow of inward investment. When combined with substantial EU funds, this would then create favourable economic conditions lifting areas of the North out of poverty and thus reduce violence.

Each of these assumptions, however, can be questioned. In this chapter, we shall examine the first assumption and deal with the other two in the next chapters. The overall argument is that far from offering a stable long-term settlement, the inherent failures of the Belfast Agreement are reopening the question of partition itself. Let us see how.

DOES BRITAIN HAVE AN IMPERIAL INTEREST?

In November 1990, the Northern Ireland Secretary of State, Peter Brooke, delivered a speech where he stated that:

The British government has no selfish strategic or economic interest in Northern Ireland: our role is to help, enable and encourage. Britain's purpose, as I have sought to describe it, is not to occupy or exploit but to ensure democratic debate and free democratic choice.[12]

The speech was an important signal that helped lay the basis for informal peace talks as it suggested that some sections of the British ruling class were willing to consider withdrawal. But just as there were sections of the US ruling class who were willing to privately consider withdrawing from Vietnam in the early 1960s, it did not mean the US ruling class as a whole had no interest in staying. Nevertheless, too many people have accepted Brooke at face value.

Apologists for imperialism often claim, like Peter Brooke, that it is a benign power which seeks only to mediate differences between locals by establishing the rule of law.[13] Thomas Babington Macaulay, a member of the Supreme Council of India in the 1830s, for example, thought that the purpose of British rule was to bring the blessings of good government to the subcontinent. The empire would educate diverse ethnic groups in the benefits of Western civilisation to produce a 'class of persons, Indian in blood and colour, but English in taste'.[14] In more recent times, Britain and the US claimed that they went to war with Iraq to bring democracy to the Middle East. And when asked why they remained after toppling Saddam Hussein, the answer was to manage the conflict between Shias and Sunnis. Belgian authorities introduced identity cards to formally separate Hutus from Tutsis in Rwanda and then presented themselves as a referee between both. Almost everywhere imperialists invariably find differences within conquered populations and then classify and make these divisions more rigid. They justify their rule as mediators between communal rivals – but also exploit and use those divisions to maintain their rule. The notion, therefore, that Britain's purpose in Northern Ireland is to bring 'democratic debate and free democratic choice' might equally be a specious piece of paternalism.

Brooke's argument, however, may appear to gain some support because there is a lack of clarity about imperialism. Sinn Féin, for example, in one of its early documents countered Brooke's claim by suggesting that 'strategic interests' were the main reason why Britain remained in Ireland. It suggested that the prospect of a neutral Ireland would be a 'serious threat to British and NATO's strategic interests'.[15] This was mainly because it might become a 'European Cuba' and deprive Britain of bases in the North Atlantic. However, this was a weak argument because as the Cold War ended the need for such bases to counter Warsaw Pact military manoeuvres seemed to disappear. A somewhat stronger argument rested on a claim that British capitalism had an economic interest in Ireland. 'British involvement in Ireland', the party claimed, 'serves a wider role in securing the interests of Britain's multinational capitalist allies from the potential or perceived threat posed by an independent Irish state.'[16] This of course is undoubtedly true, but it begs a question: have not the Southern political elite been more than enthusiastic about looking after foreign direct investment? In other words, why would you need a British presence in Northern Ireland to look after multinationals when the Southern government is doing such a good job?

To understand the modern imperialist system and Britain's role within it, we need to digress and look at some classic accounts of the concept. In his book *Imperialism: The Highest Stage of Capitalism*, Lenin argued that imperialism arose from the growing concentration of capital and the emergence of monopolies. This changed the nature of competition so that instead of smaller companies competing on a free market, bigger corporations aligned with their states to divide the world up between themselves. The process by which this occurred was highly uneven and this led to growing conflicts. Thus, while British companies were an early starter in the development of industrial capitalism, it faced major rivals in Germany at the turn of the twentieth century. The point of Lenin's argument was that German and British corporations required the protection and support of their states to advance their interests. Inter-state competition blended in with and reinforced capital accumulation. Or to put it differently, the logic of economic expansion and spatial expansion coincided, leading to the deadly consequence of the First World War.[17]

Viewed from this perspective, a distinction can be made between precapitalist colonialism and imperialism. The former was driven by the needs of state power and involved the physical conquest of a territory because in a feudal or semi-feudal society plunder and the imposition of rent or labour services were the main mechanisms for expanding wealth. The final defeat of the Ulster clan leaders O'Neill and O'Donnell in 1603 and the subsequent plantation of Ulster was a clear example of colonial expansion. Modern imperialism, however, arose from a change in the dynamic of capitalist competition. Instead of market-based competition on price or technical innovations, oligopolistic corporations linked up with their state bureaucracy to forge a national interest. The strength of different states rested on the health and vibrancy of their economies and this was principally shaped by the bigger corporations. Similarly, these corporations needed the protection and support of their states to advance their interests. In the words of David Harvey, it is best to 'reserve the term imperialism… for a property of inter-state relations and flows of power within a global system of capital accumulation'.[18]

Some of the specific features of imperialism that writers like Lenin and Rudolf Hilferding identified are no longer relevant. Thus, both identified 'finance capital' as the main driver of the process. While this may appear as a prediction about financialisation, they meant something different to the modern term. 'Finance capital' signified the role that banks played in organising industrial cartels to press for the seizure of raw materials and the creation of markets in the colonies. While finance plays an even bigger role within global capitalism today, the banks do not direct industry in this manner. Moreover, there has been a period of decolonisation whereby the old imperial states of Britain and France withdrew from colonies like Algeria or Kenya. A variety of factors were involved, including the success of national liberation movements and the growing hegemony of the US over the old empires. However, it was also the case that late capitalism did not have the same reliance on colonial raw materials in an era of artificial fibres or factory farming in the metropolitan countries. There are exceptions to this general pattern, of course, and conflict over oil helps to explain the regular interventions of imperial powers in the Middle East. It is, therefore, pointless using classic texts on imperialism to check if specific features such as the role of finance capital or the super-exploitation of indigenous raw materials apply. If that method were used, then the US war in Vietnam would not fit a 'tick the box' method of assessing an imperialist relationship.

The core of the theory of imperialism, however, remains valid for today, namely, that we live in an uneven world where the big corporations have a home base and need a state that protects their interests. They are not disembodied globalised entities that only engage in economic competition. Otherwise how can we understand how the power of the US state is deployed to enforce currency manipulations such as occurred with the Plaza Accord in 1985 when the Japanese yen and the German mark were revalued against the US dollar? Or the way hundreds of corporate lobbyists join US trade delegations at WTO talks? It would be difficult to understand the growing rivalry between China and US without acknowledging the declining share of the global economy going to US corporations. As Trump constantly reminds us, the slogan *Make America Great Again* is about restoring advantages to US corporations and it is backed up by military might. Thomas Friedman put the issue quite succinctly:

> The hidden hand of the market will never work without the hidden fist. McDonalds cannot flourish without McDonnell Douglas, the designer of the US air force F-15. And the hidden fist that keeps the world safe for Silicon Valley's technologies to flourish is called the US army, air force, navy and Marine Corps.[19]

Once we look at imperialism from this vantage point, we can more readily assess the nature of the British variety today.

BRITAIN'S ROLE WITHIN GLOBAL CAPITALISM

Britain is a substantial player within global capitalism and is the sixth largest economy, but it has been in decline for some time. In the nineteenth century, Britain was the workshop of the world, and, at its high point in the 1870s, capital invested per worker in UK manufacturing was approximately 10 per cent higher than in the USA and 30 per cent higher than in Germany.[20] The power of the British state was central to the growth of this economic success, creating markets for the sale of its commodities and protecting its corporations. British state power, in turn, can be traced back to a long historic process of state formation and adaption. It began with the Tudor monarchy uniting the peripheral regions of Scotland, Ireland and Wales under its leadership. In the case of Wales, this occurred through an earlier conquest and was completed when Henry VIII made it part of the realm of England. In the case of Scotland, this occurred though dynastic marriage and the creation of a joint monarchy. In Ireland, the Tudor reform to bring the country into the English legal system appeared successful at first. But subsequent resistance from Gaelic chieftains led to the plantation of Ulster and a more thorough conquest of that province.

If Britain's absolute monarchy built a strong state, its overthrow by parliamentary forces in the Civil War of the 1640s created the conditions for the accumulation of capital by the 'middling sort' – an intermediate social class between the nobility and the peasantry. Arbitrary control by the king was ended and a system of common law was put in place. Royal monopolies on trading companies were abolished and a forward-looking commercial policy was undertaken. The Navigation Act of 1651 laid the basis of England's commercial prosperity in the next century. It made English shipping the main carrying trade of Europe by banning rivals from trade with its colonies. The state developed new forms of military power, including a navy and a strong army, based on an officer class, promoted on merit not birth. Cromwell put it like this, 'I had rather have a plain russet-coated captain that knows what he fights for and loves what he knows, than that which you call "a gentleman" and is nothing else'.[21] Overall, the English revolution of the 1640s produced a state that gave Britain a head start on its continental rivals, displacing commercial rivals like Holland. It carried though the full conquest of Ireland, partially by buying off the more radical elements of that revolution, the Levellers, with land bequests. The emergence of a strong state, empire, military conquest and the expansion of the British economy went hand in hand.

However, Britain's dominance was by no means uncontested and by the end of the nineteenth century it faced growing rivals. By 1900, US investment was 90 per cent more capital intensive per worker and Germany had caught up with Britain.[22] In response, it became more reliant on the markets of its empire. As Hobsbawm put it, 'the international position of the British economy became increasingly dependent on the British inclination to invest or lend their accumulated surpluses abroad' and this entailed 'a steady flight from modern competitive markets into the underdeveloped'.[23] Moreover, this was linked to the importance of 'invisible earnings' – interest and dividends received from abroad. Through it emerged the dominant position of the City of London which was intimately involved in insurance, brokerage commission and distribution of dividends.

After the Second World War the US assumed the role as the world's leading imperialist power. The symbolic moment of transition came in 1956 when a disastrous attempt by Britain and France to punish Egypt for nationalising the Suez Canal was ended with US intervention. Thereafter Britain came to play a subordinate role to the US. It continued to have its own distinctive interests and occasionally came into conflict with the US, but broadly its main imperial interests were pursued as part of an Anglo-American alliance. To see why an imperialist policy remained vital for Britain and why it operated as part of this alliance, we need to note a few features of British capitalism.

The first is that the British capitalist class have largely turned away from manufacturing and towards an economy heavily dependent on 'financial services'. Economists measure the level of non-financial investment through Gross Fixed Capital Formation. In Britain, this has declined from 26 per cent of GDP in 1974 to 17 per cent in 2019, and has been less than its rivals for the past two decades.[24] By contrast, British companies pay out a higher level of dividends to their shareholders than most other countries as short-term greed trumps long-term gains. Not only is the level of investment low, but it is mainly flowing towards property and finance. For every pound British banks lent to manufacturers in 2014, they lent almost £36 to home-buyers.[25] As a result it has become a service economy, with 80 per cent of its exports coming from services. Financial services now represent 6.9 per cent of Britain's economy compared to just 11 per cent for manufacturing. The near parity between the two sectors is in sharp contrast to Germany, where finance is only a fifth the size of its manufacturing sector, which represents 23 per cent of its economy – more than twice the proportion of Britain.[26]

The low level of investment and the shift to services helps to explain the prevalence of low pay and a precarious jobs market. The productivity of the British workforce is relatively low – because of the lack of investment in machinery – and so, low wages have become the key driver of the economy. Michael Roberts describes the situation accurately:

> British employers, rather than invest in new technology that could replace labour, have opted for 'cheap unskilled labour', both British and immigrant, with full knowledge that with little employment protection and weak trade union backing, they can hire and fire as they please.[27]

The scale of the disaster facing British workers today is enormous because although Britain has had full employment in the recent past, real wages for the average household have fallen further and for longer than at any time since the Great Depression of the 1930s. A TUC analysis indicates that a 17-year period of wage stagnation up to 2018 was the worst for two centuries.[28] An interim report from the Institute for Public Policy Research Commission on Economic Justice noted that:

The UK's high employment rate has been accompanied by an increasingly insecure and casualised labour market. Fifteen percent of the workforce are now self-employed, with an increasing proportion in enforced self-employment driven by business seeking to avoid employer responsibilities. 6% are on short term contracts and 3% are on zero-hour contracts. More workers are on lower pay than ten years ago. Insecure and low paid employment is increasing physical and mental ill-health.[29]

Despite this position of relative weakness and decline, the British ruling class has climbed back towards the top of the leading world powers.

British capital is, firstly, more internationalised than many of its rivals. The stock of British investments abroad amounted to £11 trillion in 2017 which represented five times the value of its GDP and was twice the size of the foreign investment of France, which is an economy of similar size.[30] Almost half of this investment goes to the US, which helps to explain the strategy of attaching the country to the fate of the US economy. Similarly, the US and, significantly, British overseas dependencies, are the main investors in Britain. The internationalisation of British capital has helped to offset its decline in trade in manufactured goods. In 2017, for example, earnings on direct investments abroad brought in £95.4 billion.[31]

Secondly, British financial services are one of the dominant players in the world. British banks, for example, have the largest total of claims (loans to) and liabilities (deposits from) to other countries. London has also the biggest share of the global foreign exchange market and even though it is weaker than the US in trade in goods and services, it has twice the volume of currency dealings. This reflects both the country's historical lead in international commerce and its current role as the broker for global capitalism. The City of London also accounts for nearly 50 per cent of the world's interest derivatives.[32] This is where major financial speculators trade in different types of interest-bearing transactions that can change every six months. Overall, the reliance on financial services has helped modern Britain deal with a persistent balance of payments deficit. The British economy has run a deficit in trading on goods for nearly forty years, but this is partially compensated for by the key role it plays in financing global capitalism. Financial services, business management and business consultancy were its key services exports in 2018.[33]

Thirdly, linked to the central role of finance, Britain has become a major centre for deregulation and tax dodging. It has used its overseas territories and the Crown Dependencies as a network of tax haven jurisdictions linked to the City. It has also consciously created a major UK offshore centre through the development of the so-called euro-dollar market.[34] Instead of the City of London functioning as the centre of a formal empire, it has become the centre of a vast network of offshore jurisdictions.[35] Taken together, these decisions have made Britain into the primary driver of tax haven capitalism since the Second World War. Of the eleven remaining UK Overseas Territories for example, seven are tax havens, including Bermuda, the Cayman Islands and the British Virgin Islands. In addition, there are the Crown Dependencies of Jersey, Guernsey and the Isle of Man. The Irish Financial Services Centre has also become a successful outpost of the City of London.[36]

This offshore web provides British finance with strategic advantages. Tax havens hoover up vast wealth and foreign investment from around the world, before channelling it to British capitalism. They function as less regulated storage centres for global financial assets and as 'a money-laundering filter that lets the City get involved in dirty business while providing enough distance to maintain plausible deniability'.[37] Collectively these advantages helped the UK to maintain its role at the heart of the global economy even as its empire declined. These developments have also made UK firms some of the biggest tax dodgers on the planet. Of the 100 largest companies currently listed on the Financial Times Stock Exchange (FTSE) for example, 98 have tax haven operations. Of these, the worst offenders are found in energy and banking, with Barclays, HSBC, Lloyds and RBS using 1,649 shell companies between them and Shell and BP using more than 1,000 between them.[38]

Fourthly, Britain is one of the leading arms dealers in the world. While the US tops the list for arms sales, Britain comes second or, sometimes, third behind Russia. The British-based BAE Systems is the third biggest arms manufacturer in the world and the activities of the arms industry is underwritten by strong support from the British state through a UK Export Finance credit scheme. In 2018, for example, 47 per cent of its guaranteed liabilities were for arms sales.[39] Most of Britain's arms exports are sent to the Middle East and mainly to countries with human rights abuses. Their biggest customers include, for example, Saudi Arabia and Qatar.

These four features of British capitalism were crucial to halting its decline in the ranking of the world largest economies. However, they were intimately connected to an imperialist strategy that seeks to capture an extra share of the world's resources. British corporations operate far beyond its borders and they need a state that can overreach itself to protect those investments. At a very basic level, Britain wants to ensure that its companies are not national-ised or taken over by a left-wing government. Generally, British companies need a strong state that will pressurise weaker governments to open up their economies. Crucial to this is a requirement that foreign investors will not suffer 'discrimination' in terms of local content agreements or technology transfer agreements. With the passage of the Trade Related Investments Measure at the WTO in 1994, Britain, the US and others pushed through such an 'opening' on weaker governments.

Britain's role as the world's broker for finance also requires the presence of a strong state willing to promote the interests of the City of London. The use of credit, the sale of derivatives, the myriad of transactions carried out between financial institutions brings a privileged cut to the British economy that others might like to take. The predominance of the City of London has been unofficially supported by the US, but it is not without rivals in Frankfurt or Paris. All sorts of seemingly technical discussions revolve around who exactly is going to get the bigger cut. There are disputes over interest rates on interbank lending. There are disputes over regulation versus the freedom of over-the-counter transactions. There are continual conflicts over which currency is used in transactions. There are longer-term disputes over which is used as the reserve currency because this carries economic advantages. In most of these conflicts there are common interests between the US and Britain, as the latter effectively operates as a broker for financial interests based in both countries.

The power of the British state is regularly invoked to promote these interests. That was evident at the negotiating tables of the European Union – when Britain was a member. It appears at international forums from the WTO to the Bank of International Settlements. Most of the time the British state speaks with 'authority' and uses that to gets its way, but it also periodically demonstrates its military power to show that it is a top-ranking state. Since the start of the twenty-first century, Britain has been involved in military interventions in Sierra Leone, Afghanistan, Iraq, Somalia, Nigeria, Mali, Libya and Syria. On many of these occasions, it cloaks its motivation in the language of humanitarian relief, suggesting that Britain is a guardian of decency, tolerance and human rights. Its support for the brutal regime of Saudi Arabia, however, should disabuse anyone of this notion. Military intervention is clearly designed to demonstrate the power and 'leadership' of the British state – most often in conjunction with the US. It does not always directly benefit from robbery of natural resources and there are sometimes little direct linkages between the countries Britain intervenes in and the location of British investments. Nevertheless, the authority of the British state rests on regular demonstration of its military prowess. That authority in turn is deployed to support its own corporations.

BRITAIN'S IMPERIALIST INTEREST IN NORTHERN IRELAND

In many ways, Britain's involvement in Northern Ireland appears as an anachronism from the days of its formal empire. In 1921 it partitioned Ireland against the wishes of a significant majority of elected representatives to stymie a national liberation struggle that had all the appearance of a revolutionary upheaval. The Tory party and their ally Lloyd George believed this was necessary to halt the fragmentation of the wider empire. By carving off a section of Ireland, they wanted to show that there was a working class who valued the ideals of empire, monarchy and British order. Yet that empire has now collapsed and in every other country which they partitioned they have left. Gibraltar is the only equivalent in this sense.

In the last few decades British imperialism has sought to clean up the mess they created in Northern Ireland. They were forced into this position when the sectarian nature of the state was exposed to all the world through the agitation for civil rights. Having become embroiled in a fulsome defence of the unionist state, the British eventually developed a strategy of managing sectarianism within the Northern state – rather than undoing partition. Their first attempt to do this was in Sunningdale in 1973 when they put in place most of the elements that later formed the core of the Belfast Agreement, namely power sharing and an Irish dimension. In addition, they opened an informal communication channel to the IRA and established a formal truce with them on two occasions, in 1972 and 1975. This strategy failed in the short term and the British subsequently turned to 'Ulsterisation' that was modelled on the US policy of Vietnamisation. It meant pushing the police and the Ulster Defence Regiment to the fore to reduce British army casualties and thus lessen any sentiment for troop withdrawal from the wider British population. Simultaneously, the British government sought to criminalise their republican opponents by denying them political status when imprisoned. However, even while adopting this strategy, a secret military intelligence document written by a senior officer of the Defence Intelligence Staff, Brigadier J. M. Glover, noted that 'The Provisional IRA has the dedication and sinews of war to raise violence intermittently at least to the level of 1978, certainly for the foreseeable future.'[40] He could only recommend a continuation of direct rule from London to avoid a further escalation of the situation. Britain was quite literally caught in a bind.

As a major imperialist power, Britain could not be seen to be defeated by a guerrilla army. If they withdrew from the North, this would have had wider implications for their global activities as a junior partner in the Anglo-American alliance. Quite simply, the same type of consequences that the US suffered after its defeat in Vietnam would have been visited on Britain many times over because it was a weaker power. They were stuck in a long war, from which they could not extricate themselves because they could not be seen to be forced out by a guerrilla army. The republican leader in the 1970s, Ruairí Ó Brádaigh, was fundamentally mistaken when he detected 'vibrations' that the British were considering a withdrawal.[41] His nationalism gave him a blinkered view that failed to look at Britain's wider imperial role outside of Ireland. For 20 years, therefore, Britain fought to contain and infiltrate the IRA. It was stuck in a quagmire where it could not defeat them, but neither could the IRA force it to withdraw.

The British ruling elite had to await the involvement of their more senior imperial ally the USA in the 1990s before returning to their original strategy – the management of sectarianism within Northern Ireland. This aspect of how the Belfast Agreement came to be established has been underplayed and instead a mythology has developed that a series of influential Irish nationalist politicians got the ear of Bill Clinton to take an interest in the conflict. Within the ranks of Irish republicanism, a similar interpretation has been promoted as a vindication of a pan-nationalist strategy. An internal IRA document, known as 'TUAS', noted that 'all nationalist parties are rowing in roughly the same direction' and that 'Clinton is perhaps the first U.S. President in decades to be substantially influenced by such a (Irish American) lobby'.[42] The formation of an alliance which straddled Sinn Féin, the Irish government, the SDLP and Irish America is supposed to have reached into the White House and persuaded a US, freed from the demands of the Cold War, to play a progressive role. It would be far better, however, to view the Belfast Agreement as resulting from the hard cop-soft cop routine of two close imperial allies.

The Belfast Agreement and the wider peace process emerged out of a series of choreographed moves whereby the US started offering enticements to Irish republicans to enable them to visit and fundraise. This helped to legitimise figures like Gerry Adams and allowed republican leaders to reassure their followers that 'Sinn Fein now, though our President, Gerry Adams has direct access to the corridors of power in the White House'.[43] At the centre of those pushing for US intervention was a group called Americans for a New Irish Agenda, described as 'Irish American corporate people', who wanted to take 'the issue out of the bars and into the boardroom'.[44] However, as US engagement with Sinn Féin grew, so too did attempts to influence their direction. In the words of one writer, the 'incentivising leverages turned to more pressurising leverages'.[45] Effectively the US – in consort with the other allies in the pan-nationalist alliance – acted as a powerful external broker pushing the IRA on the road to 'de-radicalisation'. Meanwhile, their British partner presented itself as the custodian of unionist interests even as it sought to push them towards power-sharing. Thus, while the White House was acting on the IRA, Tony Blair in Westminster pushed the unionists to concede on the release of prisoners and reform of the RUC as necessary steps for an historic compromise. By working in consort, the Anglo-America alliance arrived at its strategic goal – the management and modernisation of sectarianism within the Northern state.[46]

The achievement of the agreement brought key advantages for the wider project of Anglo-American imperialism. It occurred in the context of 'a post-Cold War new order internationalism'[47] when the victorious Western powers proclaimed their right to intervene in other countries to promote human rights and democracy. In the words of Tony Blair, the 'international community' should engage in humanitarian interventions for 'mutual self-interest and moral purpose in defending the values we cherish'.[48] One of the pretexts for doing so was the management of ethnic conflicts and Clinton and Blair used the Belfast Agreement as a model. It helped show that by acting together Britain and the US could take on a leadership role in shaping the post-Cold War world where the older excuse of protecting countries from communism was gone and a new rationale was needed. By reconfiguring themselves in the dual role of policeman and mediator, Anglo-American imperialism could justify a new series of military interventions. In this strategy, peace-making became the flip side of military intervention. Clinton was quite explicit about this when he said, 'I have a very strong feeling that in the aftermath of the Cold War, we need a governing rationale for our engagement in the world, not just in Northern Ireland.'[49]

However, while the Belfast Agreement provided reputational support to Britain and US, there were more tangible benefits for the imperialist powers. Foremost among these was the creation of an enclave that would give multinational corporations special advantages. The political elites knew that sectarian conflict was bad for business as bombings and riots discouraged investors. However, if there was peace and the historic divisions still persisted, they could assist in creating a low-pay economy. While this may not have been an explicit or conscious aim of its architects, the effect of such tribal agreements is to weaken trade unionism and left-wing solidarity. The legacy of past economic failure might also lead the state to offer generous grants and low taxes. Since the signing of the Belfast Agreement there has been a high level of foreign investment into the province. One study found that Northern Ireland, with its population of 1.8 million people, attracted 16 per cent of all US foreign direct investment going to 31 European locations reviewed.[50] Low wages have been a key factor. One study on the drivers of US investment found that the average wage in the North for three common occupations – administration, customer service representatives and office service assistant – was $22,027. This represented 72 per cent of the US figure and was well below both the Republic of Ireland and the rest of Britain.[51] For higher skilled jobs, such as scientist, software programmer or engineer, the average salary in Northern Ireland stood at $34,038 and was just 67 per cent of the US figure.[52]

It is not just low wages because Northern Ireland also offers a 'highly attractive package of financial incentives' to companies. There are special grants for training, for marketing, for research and development. There are different agencies which offer support, with Invest NI giving out financial assistance of £500 million between 2014 and 2018.[53] This, however, is an underestimate of the amount of corporate welfare that was made available because other agencies such as Intertrade Ireland encourage collaboration on research. In order to support business, the leading universities in the North, Queen's University and Ulster University, conduct research which directly benefits it. However, the major breakthrough for business interests came in the Fresh Start Agreement whereby it was proposed to cut the corporation tax rate to 12.5 per cent, significantly below the rate for the rest of Britain and equal to the headline rate in the South. This could set off a competitive chain reaction in the two parts of Ireland. If the North offers low tax plus lower wages, then the South responds with even more special tax concessions. Overall therefore, through low wages, high grants and more tax concessions, an enclave has been created in the North that benefits US multinationals and business interests generally.

These are significant advantages that British imperialism also gains from involvement in Northern Ireland. But it begs the question: is it worth the cost of an annual subvention of £9 billion? Part of the answer to that question lies in understanding how the political can triumph over the economic in certain circumstances. If accountancy were the criterion for determining British interventions, it is doubtful that they would ever have fought a war over the Falkland Islands. In the past, when Britain occupied countries like Afghanistan, they hardly did so to secure immediate economic advantages. An imperialist power is more than aware of how its wider global interests mean that it must bear certain costs in particular regions to assert its overall 'leadership'. The success of British capitalism rests on its ability to promote itself as a strong state on the world stage and it is seen as a United Kingdom that incorporates a periphery of Wales, Scotland and Northern Ireland.

The problem for the British ruling elite is that they now preside over a population whose experience of low wages and precarious employment clashes with an historic legacy of 'greatness'. The tensions involved in this relationship has led the Conservative Party to make a bold move and promote a Brexit break from the EU. Many of their current leaders started out on this path, hoping to whip up anti-foreigner sentiment and develop a nostalgia for Britain's past greatness. Politicians like Boris Johnson surprised themselves when this rhetoric caught fire with many workers who saw it as an opportunity to express their anger. Once the referendum was concluded, however, the Tories took it as an opportunity to advance their own economic agenda by reviving British capitalism as a bargain basement, deregulated economy. Freed from EU rules, they thought they could conclude trade deals with the rest of the world that would give Britain a competitive advantage. It is a gamble which many of the leading elements of the Confederation of British Industry – the bosses' organisation – are deeply sceptical of. Nevertheless, under Boris Johnson, the Tories see it as an opportunity to rebuild their support base by breaking through Labour's 'red wall' particularly in the north of England. They hope to renew their hegemony in an uncertain era by the refurbishing of an English nationalism. However, while this rhetoric may be satisfying to a radicalised right in the Tory party, it presents major dangers for the future, as the *Economist* magazine outlines:

> It has divided the British Isles and exposed constitutional problems that wise statesmen have done their best to conceal. Britain has always been a peculiar multinational kingdom because one of its component parts, England, accounts for 84% of its population and more than 85% of its income. Brexit has thrown this contradiction into sharp relief and revealed growing weariness with the union. In 2018 a poll showed that three-quarters of Tory voters would accept Scottish independence and the collapse of the Northern Ireland peace process as a price for Brexit.[54]

The unintended consequence of Brexit, therefore, is that it has exposed the fault lines in the UK itself. Scotland and Northern Ireland voted overwhelmingly to stay in the EU but their views have been ignored in Westminster. The tensions that have arisen from this dynamic have been further exacerbated by the Covid-19 pandemic where the Tory dalliance with a 'herd immunity' approach has provoked opposition in the regions. Despite its own failures, there has been a high level of support for how the Scottish parliament has handled the crisis and a scepticism about Boris Johnson's approach. There is a real prospect that the Scottish National Party will gain over half the votes in the election in May 2021 and push for a new referendum on independence, provoking a new constitutional crisis.[55]

All of this bodes ill for the British ruling class. A shrunken United Kingdom without Scotland or Northern Ireland would appear as a far more minor player on the world stage. In contrast to Germany which successfully united East and West, Britain would be seen as a defeated power and would not have the same control over military resources or financial clout. The 'authority' of its leaders would be weakened, and they would be less able to impose their will on others. Where working people are already experiencing low wages and deprivation, the hegemony of the rulers would be weakened. All of this means that British imperialism will deploy its considerable resources to retain both Scotland and Northern Ireland. Increasingly, it will see Scottish nationalism or Irish unification as twin dangers that can reinforce each other and threaten the break-up of its state. This is why the political class in England, from the Tory to the Labour parties, are united to defeat a Scottish referendum for independence. Just like the Spanish state and Catalonia, they will resist any call for a new referendum, even if its parliament votes to have one.

This is also why they are resisting calls for a border poll on the constitutional status of Northern Ireland. The Belfast Agreement created the possibility of such a referendum to show the republicans there was an alternative to armed struggle, a peaceful way to Irish unification. Yet more than twenty years after that agreement has been signed, British rulers reject calls for this elementary democratic procedure. A referendum on Irish unity takes decision-making out of their hands, if only for a temporary period. It gives the mass of people an opportunity to pass judgement on the link with London and there is a distinct possibility that they will vote to cut it. Despite all their protestations about having 'no selfish strategic or economic interest' in Northern Ireland, they have a direct interest in stopping it leaving the United Kingdom. Yes, they see the province is a messy place that soaks up economic and security resources. And even though it provides a special enclave for US and British multinationals, these do not compensate and, moreover, could be replicated elsewhere. The direct interest of British imperialism in the North is to be found in its need to project itself as a global power, able to extract advantages for its corporations on a world stage. This demands that they show that they will not be forced by disloyal natives or armed guerrillas into withdrawal. Everything must be seen to proceed on its terms.

Which is not to say British imperialism will always win. The pressure for a border poll will continue to grow and if the Irish Republic government is forced to endorse that call, Britain could be forced to concede. Should a referendum happen, however, the British state will not stand aside as a benign observer. The Conservative Party, certainly, and probably others will do everything in their power to ensure that a vote to remain in the UK is successful. They will whip up the ugliest fears about economic devastation and loss of 'civil and political liberties', that supposedly come with British citizenship, in a united Ireland. All of this brings a risk of deeper instability and, therefore, the British ruling class will resist for as long as possible a border poll.

Their preference is to continue with a managed and modernised sectarianism in a Northern Ireland statelet joined to the UK. Only in the event of a profound defeat in a referendum that they do not want would they be forced to consider other options to safeguard their position as a global power. They might reluctantly retreat to accepting a federal or confederal Ireland but they know a wider process that led to the breakup of the UK would represent a calamitous outcome for their role as a 'world leader'. If Northern Ireland could be treated in isolation or the new threats to the unity of the UK, it is theoretically possible that Britain could actively endorse options, such as a federated Ireland. In such an event, no doubt, they would seek to maintain significant influence or even a measure of joint authority. Even then it would want guarantees that the South signs up as a fully-fledged member of the Anglo-American alliance by dropping all pretence at neutrality. No doubt, the Southern ruling class would have little difficulty with that. However, the North cannot be viewed in isolation from the current issues which face British imperialism. It will, therefore, seek to stay there for as long as it can and will continue to oppose Irish unity by presenting itself as a benign mediator between rival communities.

4

Managed Sectarianism

Northern Ireland is a very divided society. In Belfast, 91 per cent of Housing Executive estates are described as 'highly polarized', meaning that they are almost exclusively inhabited by one or other denomination. Outside Belfast, between half and a third of estates are in a similar situation.[1] In some areas Union Jacks or Irish tricolours are flown and the kerbs painted to delineate the unionist or nationalist affiliation of communities that live side by side. Spatial separation is reinforced by segregated education with over 90 per cent of pupils educated in schools dominated by one denomination. State schools are de facto Protestant schools while 'maintained' schools are run by the Catholic Church. Given this level of segregation, it is not surprising that only about one tenth of marriages are mixed. There is even some truth in the joke about the atheist who is asked 'but are you a Catholic or a Protestant atheist?' because since 2001, the Northern Ireland census adds a background question to those who declare 'no religion', asking which religious community they were brought up in.

However, while the divisions run throughout Northern society, they affect the working class more. This is most evident in Belfast where peace walls separate communities that would otherwise have a common class interest. One study found that 86 per cent of those living within 400 metres of the walls came from the poorest fifth of the population.[2] Instead of a shared working-class demand for more public housing, political discourse is framed as one group intruding on the territory of the other. As the Catholic population of Belfast is growing, unionist politicians stoke up fears in older Protestant areas suggesting that they will literally lose ground if housing is allocated according to need. Housing density is, therefore, higher in nationalist Belfast than in loyalist areas, but through a combination of DUP moves to stop new builds in areas like North Belfast, and loyalist paramilitary intimidation against Catholics, this state of play is maintained. By contrast, wealthier people are more likely to live in mixed areas and the Catholic upper professional class face few obstacles to integration. In some of the most affluent areas of the North, Wallace Park for example, the proportion of Catholics has grown steadily over the years with little outcry from older residents who do not compete for scarce public resources.

These divisions between working people have little to do with theology and, contrary to writers such as Padraig O'Malley, they do not result from political outlooks shaped by religious beliefs.[3] Rather religious denomination is a marker for deeper political divisions. In no other part of the world does the seemingly divergent forms of morality – 'evasive' for Catholics or 'strict' for Protestants – give rise to such conflict. German Catholics and Protestants, to take one example, do not segregate or fight over how houses are allocated because they have different theological views. Explaining division by differences in religious belief simply ignores its root cause, how the Northern state was constructed. Partition, as we have seen, could only have worked in a six-county state with a beleaguered Catholic minority, rather than an even smaller four-county state. The existence of that minority was then used by 'big house' unionism to cement an all-class alliance around it. The enemy within, it was claimed, was the reason why unionists should stick together and not be tempted towards any left-wing politics. The Troubles, which lasted a full 30 years, exacerbated those divisions and led to greater segregation as people moved for safety into their own 'ghettoes' or, in the case of 15,000 people, fled Belfast altogether. But the Troubles arose directly from the contradictions inherent in the Northern state – not from any divisions over religious belief.

After the signing of the Belfast Agreement, the Northern state was reconfigured so that its political structures would accommodate two traditions. As the theorists of consociationalism argued, this was the best way to deal with ethnic disputes. The conflict over partition was effectively parked and battle lines were redrawn around what constituted 'parity of esteem'. The First Minister and Deputy First Minister are drawn from the unionist and nationalist traditions but unlike the Taif consociational agreement in the Lebanon there is not a 'lock-in' mechanism which specifies how many seats are awarded to each community in a power-sharing arrangement.[4] Instead, electoral fortunes dictate that whichever party wins the most votes in the Northern Ireland Assembly election selects the First Minister. On the surface, this appears as a liberal version of consociationalism which gives due recognition to the relative weights of both identities. According to one theorist of consociationalism, 'this is more likely to transform identities in the long run'.[5] In reality, the Belfast Agreement has become a mechanism to maintain, strengthen and manage sectarian division in a statelet over which Britain retains sovereignty. Let's see how that works.

COMMUNALISM

There is a fundamental ambiguity in the term 'parity of esteem'. Theoretically, it derives from a liberal notion of respecting diversity, meaning that if one does not like the identity of the other, one recognizes their right to be who they wish to be. What exactly constitutes 'parity', however, is open to question when past sectarian divisions have not been eradicated or replaced. Once the rhetoric about 'respect for difference' has been ventilated, the conflict begins over what exactly is 'parity'. Thus, while liberals assume that the respect eventually leads to tolerance, the Belfast Agreement shows that this occurs at only an elite level. Below that it strengthens communalism of the respective blocs and sets off a process known as 'ethnic outbidding' or more simply, people vote for the strongest party that will bargain for their communal bloc.[6]

This is exactly what happened after the signing of the Belfast Agreement in 1998. In the election of that year, the Ulster Unionist Party took 28 seats as against their rivals in the Democratic Unionist Party who won 20. At the time, the leader of the UUP, David Trimble, was attempting to rebrand the party as advocates of 'civic unionism'.[7] Alongside his advisor, the ex-Marxist professor, Paul Bew, he was a signatory to the principles of a right-wing think tank, the Henry Jackson Society. This advocated an imperialist agenda whereby the Western powers would intervene around the world in the name of liberal values. The think tank supported 'the necessary furtherance of European military modernisation and integration under British leadership, preferably within NATO'.[8] As part of this liberal imperialism, Trimble and Bew tried to show that 'Britishness' involved accommodation and inclusion. The subtext was that there was a place inside the unionist party for upper-class Catholics whose identity could be safeguarded within a British state. However, while this indicated a longer-term strategic vision, Trimble was mangled in the intra-communal competition set off by the Belfast Agreement. While Protestants voted by a slim majority to accept the agreement, the process it triggered encouraged many to find a stronger 'ethic outbidder' to promote their bloc. The result was that in the next election in 2003, the

DUP – who opposed the Belfast Agreement – overtook the UUP and went on to become the dominant party of unionism. Against Trimble's more sophisticated attempt to modernise unionism, the competitive dynamic of the Belfast Agreement led to support for a party whose principal agenda was 'getting one over on the other side'. The DUP has since fought a constant war over symbols to suggest that the unionist bloc now had a strong negotiator who could deal with the other side.

A similar dynamic was at play on the nationalist side. In the 1998 election, the SDLP won 24 seats to Sinn Féin's 18, but in the subsequent election of 2003 this was exactly reversed with Sinn Féin winning 24 and the SDLP 18. Once again, this set off a longer-term trajectory whereby the SDLP went into decline and Sinn Féin became the dominant nationalist force. Before the Belfast Agreement, the SDLP was the preferred choice of the Catholic hierarchy and the better-off, professional Catholics. It was much weaker in manual working-class areas like West Belfast, which the Archbishop of Armagh, Cathal Daly, once described as 'anti-Establishment, anti-authority, anti-everything'.[9] Sinn Féin by contrast was seen as a radical voice that supported the armed struggle and wanted a 32-county socialist Ireland. However, after the Belfast Agreement, the Catholic middle class concluded that the SDLP had served its function in winning a settlement which acknowledged their identity within Northern Ireland. They wanted a stronger communal party to represent their interests and increasingly they turned to Sinn Féin.

The process was by no means automatic and to win their allegiance, Sinn Féin repositioned itself as favouring more 'pragmatic' politics. The transformation can be illustrated by the change in rhetoric. Back in the late 1970s, in a document written for the IRA known as the 'gray document', Gerry Adams argued:

Furthermore with James Connolly, we believe that the present system of society is based on the robbery of the working class and that capitalist property cannot exist without the plundering of labour. We desire to see capitalism abolished and a democratic system of common or public ownership. This democratic system, which is called socialism, will we believe come as a result of the continuous increase in working class power.[10]

It could hardly sound more radical. However, by 2005 Adams was advocating an:

> economic policy [which] would take all practical steps to encourage indigenous enterprise and investment. It would welcome foreign capital while ensuring that foreign economic and financial interests did not become too powerful an influence on national economic policy.[11]

By agreeing to work through the institutions of the Northern state and moderating its leftish rhetoric, Sinn Féin became the vehicle of choice for middle-class Catholics and so moved outside its traditional heartlands. The structures of the Belfast Agreement facilitated this change as it put a premium on 'ethnic outbidders' who could strike better bargains for their side.

Originally, the British and Irish governments had hoped that the 'moderate' SDLP and UUP would form the new partnership to run the Northern state but the change within the respective blocs did not fundamentally alter their strategy. Their aim was to transform a fight over partition and the existence of the state into one of competing identities within that state and, so far, they have been highly successful. The key to this has been the structures laid down in the Belfast Agreement. Reacting to claims by a former leader of the SDLP, Mark Durkan, who suggested that sectarian attitudes and structures would prove 'politically biodegradable', Eamonn McCann argued that one of the reasons this did not happen is to be found in the text of the Agreement itself:

> Under 'Safeguards', the Agreement lays down that, 'At their first meeting, members of the Assembly will register a designation of identity – nationalist, unionist or others.' That's as good as it gets for others. Mentioned along with nationalists and unionists, and then ignored. Arrangements 'to ensure key decisions are taken on a cross-community basis' require either 'parallel consent' (a majority of nationalists and a majority of unionists voting together), or a 'weighted majority' (60 percent of the overall vote, including at least 40 percent of unionists and 40 percent of nationalists). 'Others' have disappeared and are simply not mentioned again. This explains how a DUP MLA was able to tell Anna Lo of the Alliance Party after she'd made a speech on equal marriage: 'You can say what you like. In a few minutes when we come to a vote, you won't count.'[12]

The communal parties, principally Sinn Féin and the DUP, sustain their dominance of their bloc through three main mechanisms.

First, the concerns and issues raised by 'Others' are marginalised because they do not fit into the framework of communal division. This category is growing; in a recent survey, 20 per cent of adults in Northern Ireland identified as having 'no religion'.[13] Holding no religious view does not mean that one has no views on the constitutional status, but it indicates, at a minimal level, a refusal to identify with sectarian designation. More importantly, many of the concerns of 'Others' are articulated in broader social movements which cut across the sectarian divide. Thousands of people join May Day parades each year to promote working-class interests. Yet even though the Northern Ireland Assembly has power to alter legislation to make strike action by workers more effective, neither of the communal parties has sought to do so. Similarly, the LBGT movement has grown dramatically. In 1991, the first Belfast Pride was attended by just 50 participants but today attracts thousands. Despite this, the DUP – which at one stage mounted a Save Ulster from Sodomy Campaign – used its communal veto to block gay marriage.

The movement for abortion rights has also grown but the communal parties have been behind the changing public mood. The DUP, as an outright right-wing party, opposed any move to create abortion services in the North, while Sinn Féin favours abortion only in limited circumstances. The marginalisation of the issue meant that the Northern Ireland Assembly refused to extend the 1967 Abortion Act that permitted abortions to Northern Ireland and instead allowed a crackdown on 'illegal' activities such as supplying an abortion pill. Between 2011 and 2015, the Police Service of Northern Ireland (PSNI) are estimated to have seized 3,000 abortion pills.[14] In 2017, they carried out raids on houses in Belfast looking for abortion pills and invited people for interviews. Yet none of the communal politicians spoke out against this blatant attack on women's rights. In a shocking case, a mother was threatened with prosecution for procuring an abortion pill for her 15-year-old daughter. She faced two charges of unlawfully procuring and supplying drugs with intent to procure a miscarriage, contrary to the 1861 Offences Against the Person Act.[15] If found guilty, she faced five years in prison. Fortunately for her and many others, the suspension of the Northern Ireland Assembly allowed Labour politicians in Britain to extend abortion rights to Northern Ireland and legislate for gay marriage. Both Sinn Féin and the DUP opposed this 'interference' and at Belfast City Council joined together to reject a motion welcoming the Westminster move.[16] Later when the abortion legislation required Assembly assent for implementation, both parties sought more restrictive measures than those in the rest of Britain. In the case of the DUP, this was particularly ironic because, as a party which loudly proclaims its adherence to the union, it was opposing 'interference'. In the case of Sinn Féin, the issue was framed as opposition to a British parliament legislating on an Irish issue. But in both cases, the communal parties were out of step with a new generation that wanted a woman's right to choose.

One group which does not fit the binary divide of nationalist versus unionist are migrant workers and opinion polls indicate that many regularly experience casual racism. A 2017 Northern Ireland Life and Times Survey found that 36 per cent of respondents would not accept an Eastern European as a close friend while 47 per cent would not accept a Muslim.[17] Yet the new normal in the Northern state does little to combat such attitudes. In 2016–17, there were more racist than sectarian attacks yet 83 per cent of these did not result in a prosecution or even a warning.[18] The political discourse is centred on the older conflict of Irish/British identities and the issue of racism is almost seen as an annoyance which cuts across this. This was graphically illustrated during Black Lives Matter protests in Derry and Belfast. While many people of colour wanted to talk about their lived experience, the PSNI went around issuing fines and prosecutions for breach of Covid-19 regulations. Yet a week later, loyalists gathered in Belfast to protect war memorial statues. Some wore British army uniforms and draped the Union Jack on the city hall and even though there was no social distancing – unlike the Black Lives Matter protest – no fines were issued. The state apparatus is far more comfortable regulating the old identity politics and not only marginalises but represses those who challenge racism.

The reconfiguration of the Northern state around two competing identities leads to a tremendous parochialism of politics. Issues which cut across the sectarian divide are locked out of political decision-making or sometimes they are reframed to fit into the pre-existing sectarian categories. Thus, Polish migrants or East Timorese meat-plant workers get slotted into the identity as 'Catholic' and, therefore, are categorised as an intrusion into Protestant territory. Bigger global issues such as the conflict in the Middle East are reflected through a local sectarian prism with unionists backing

Israel and Sinn Féin supporting Palestinian rights. Yet when a US President visits the province both parties unite to welcome them – with little discussion on US foreign policy. By normalising and strengthening the sectarian divide, the Belfast Agreement helps to play down issues which cut across it.

The second mechanism through which the communal parties sustain their dominance over their respective blocs is by very public rows over symbols and legacies of the Troubles. At the very start of the 'peace process' this began, as we have seen, over how decommissioning would be conducted or over which badge appeared on a PSNI officer's cap. The conflicts have become shriller since and yet the loudness of arguments helps disguise a silent agreement between Sinn Féin and the DUP on economic issues. Fighting over symbols renews communal loyalties without disrupting their partnership in government. The balancing act between public fights and private cooperation might appear difficult to achieve but Sinn Féin and the DUP have developed a talent in knowing when to agree to disagree. Which is not to say that they come to this game as equal players.

The main instigator of such conflicts are loyalist politicians and paramilitaries. These tend to initiate conflicts to solidify their base but the reaction to their moves also strengthens Sinn Féin. The main reason why loyalists tend to start the battles over symbols is that historically the Northern state was constructed as a Protestant state for a Protestant people. As the material base for discrimination in favour of Protestants has been largely eroded, so the culture wars become a substitute for deep resentment over the changes. Thus, the Orangemen's 'right to march' through Catholic areas is defined as an intrinsic part of Protestant identity and, according to proponents, cries out for respect. The leader of the Portadown Orange District Lodge put it like this, 'When we are being denied the right to march, we are being denied our Protestant culture.'[19] However, Eamonn McCann gives a different view:

> The Orange marches are triumphalist and sectarian and designed in the name of Protestantism to put Catholics in their place. But one of the reasons they are currently so important to Orange leaders is precisely that Protestant power is now largely illusory – and an entirely fraudulent concept as far as Protestant working-class people are concerned. The North is no longer a 'Protestant State for a Protestant people', and ordinary Protestants ought to be pleased about this as many of my own friends are.[20]

A classic example of how the battle over symbols is used to discipline the Protestant working class occurred over the issue of flying the Union Jack at Belfast City Hall. In 2011, Sinn Féin became the biggest party on Belfast City Council and proposed that the Union Jack would no longer be flown. As they did not have an absolute majority, it fell to the Alliance Party to present a compromise resolution which proposed that the flag should only be flown on eighteen designated days each year. This, in fact, is the policy in Stormont and in most councils throughout Britain. Despite this, the DUP and loyalist paramilitaries spotted an opportunity to attack 'the betrayal' of Alliance. The Alliance politician Naomi Long had recently defeated the DUP leader Peter Robinson in the traditional unionist seat of East Belfast because his party was mired in a property scandal at the time. In the aftermath of the Alliance resolution, the DUP printed 40,000 leaflets charging Alliance with making Belfast a 'cold house for Unionists'.[21] Simultaneously, loyalist paramilitaries began staging protests that quickly turned to riots. The office of the Alliance Party was destroyed in an arson attack; pickets were placed on the homes of Alliance representatives, and Naomi Long received death threats. These activities were directed at a party which officially supports a continuation of the Union, but the aim was to drive the Protestant population back into supporting their strong communal party, the DUP.

If the flags protest illustrated in a dramatic way how symbols of identity are used to discipline votes in the communal blocs, more banal and less violent means are also used to play the identity game. In 2016, Belfast City Council decided to invite football teams from Northern Ireland and the Republic of Ireland to a reception but at the next meeting the DUP and UUP opposed players from the Republic attending.[22] In 2019, the absurd tit-for-tat game was started by Sinn Féin. A proposal that a local artist be allowed to draw a portrait of the Belfast City Council was rejected by Sinn Féin on the basis that he had been 'involved in some controversial cartoons – namely about our party as well'.[23] Then there is the key issue of which piece of sculpture is the most appropriate for a public space. On one occasion, Sinn Féin proposed Winifred Carney, a trade unionist, a suffragist and a republican while a unionist councillor suggested a memorial to the Belfast Blitz. A more important issue than pure symbols for some residents are the local council boundaries. Should an area like Dunmurray or Poleglass be allocated to the Lisburn council where the DUP has a majority or to Belfast where Sinn Féin is the biggest party? By structuring politics around the identities of the two main communities, the Belfast Agreement did not create sectarian divisions, but it helps to maintain and strengthen them by putting a focus on the parallel representation of two blocs.

The failure of the Belfast Agreement to promote genuine reconciliation is evident in the inability of the two main parties to address the legacy of the Troubles. Instead this has become another issue used by the communal parties to shore up their base. In 2017, 26 per cent of the Northern population said that they or a family member continued to be affected by a conflict-related incident and it is estimated that 213,000 people are experiencing significant mental health problems.[24] A series of institutional arrangements were created to address this legacy, but little satisfaction has been provided because the key method has been to open the possibility for prosecution in the hope that this would give succour. However, since 2012 there have been just four prosecutions – two republicans and two loyalists.[25] Instead of creating an atmosphere which enabled genuine truth-giving, the issue has become another arena for dispute between communal parties. This suits the British state as it lets them play the role of 'piggy in the middle' and, crucially, stops members of the security forces having to testify about aspects of their 'dirty war'. For different reasons, the republican leadership have no interest in revealing IRA operations particularly as they might tarnish their electoral image. The long history of loyalist death squads and their collusion with state forces also remains hidden. Instead, legacy issues provide ample material for old-style traditional conflicts between the two communities.

There is a further mechanism by which the Belfast Agreement strengthens the communal blocs. The binary opposition of unionist versus nationalist is not just sustained by regular, public battles over symbols but also gains support from a grant culture that underpins community relations. The community, voluntary and social enterprise sector is big in Northern Ireland, comprising 6,122 organisations employing 53,620 people and, in total, 7 per cent of the workforce is employed in this 'third sector'.[26] Traditionally, community development was more highly organised in Catholic communities where the church used its parish network to supply some services normally provided by the state. During the Troubles, this network was often used to build a base for the SDLP but since the 1990s Sinn Féin moved into the space of community development and social enterprise. The sector then got a major boost after the signing of the Belfast Agreement with a massive influx of international and state funding. Money from EU funds, government and private donors were all used to expand the sector. Simultaneously, the policy of New Labour was to promote 'active citizenship' and 'empowerment' as an alternative to the delivery of proper public services. The policy language spoke of building up 'social capital' and 'partnership' but it was the flip side of a neoliberal policy to reduce public services.

However, if this was the wider British context for support for community development, it took on a distinct character in Northern Ireland as some of the funding of the community sector was linked to the consolidation of the two power blocs. One of the key mechanisms by which this occurred was though the Community Relations Unit of the Office of First Minister and Deputy First Minister. This office is controlled by the two main parties, the DUP and Sinn Féin, and they were able to carve up resources for both their sides. In one research report it was found that:

> some interviewees point to what they see as a damaging colonisation of the sector by party-political interests... Recent media coverage that suggests funding mechanisms have been used to channel funding to favoured groups has brought to the fore some long-standing concerns of those involved in the voluntary and community sector... For many in the sector, the systems can be manipulated for political purposes, creating closed networks of favoured interests that benefit from the distribution of resources.[27]

In 2011, the Stormont Executive set up a Social Investment Fund and by 2017, it had spent €80 million. The fund had a somewhat unusual structure which led to subsequent criticism. Steering groups were made up of community, political and voluntary representatives which allocated funds for their areas but sometimes there was no formal application process for groups seeking funds or minutes taken of meetings where decisions were made. A report from the Northern Ireland auditor noted that:

> the processes used to prioritise projects lacked transparency and were inconsistent. Such variation in assessment processes gives rise to concerns over the robustness and transparency of project selection and prioritisation. Documentation does not exist to show clearly how ranking was carried out in each group. The Department did not require steering

groups to submit scoring matrices with area plans, and therefore it does not hold a clear audit trail in relation to the award of public funding.[28]

This structure allowed all sorts of 'community' organisations to successfully apply for grants, especially if they had some influence on the 'inside track'. Between 2014 and 2016, for example, UDA-affiliated organisations applied for and were granted £5 million in funding for projects in Belfast, Lisburn and Bangor. One of these projects was for Charter NI, whose CEO was Dee Stitt, a UDA boss. A DUP assembly member, Alex Easton, had written a glowing reference in support of Stitt's application to join a Social Investment Fund Steering Group. Another DUP politician acknowledged that the party gets 'a lot more co-operation at local level from the UDA because it doesn't have political ambitions. So, they are prepared to work with the mainstream Unionist parties.'[29] In other words, by funding a UDA-sponsored project the DUP won allies 'on the ground' and strengthened their domination over the Protestant community.

Overall then, the Belfast Agreement has not lessened sectarianism but institutionalised it. It has enabled the two big parties, Sinn Féin and the DUP, to dominate their respective communities by organising a political system on consociational lines. The effect has been to either marginalise discussion on issues which cut across the sectarian divide or else reframe them through the lens of sectarian competition. Crucially, the agreement enables the communal parties to stage public rows while privately cooperating in governance. One of the ways this occurs is through a shared economic agenda that seeks to make Northern Ireland an enclave for low taxes, cheap labour and reduced public services. In brief, behind the vigorous conflicts on communal lines, there is a shared embrace of neoliberalism.

NEOLIBERALISM AND CORRUPTION

The architects of the Belfast Agreement in the British, Irish and US governments had an agreed strategy for the Northern economy. They thought it had not made the transition from having an industrial base to a desirable postmodern economy. After the Second World War, Northern Ireland had experienced a successful period of expansion, particularly in shipbuilding and textiles, but when this slowed due to the lack of investment from the family-owned Orange firms, the British state invited in multinationals.

To attract them, they gave higher level of subsidies and grants than were available in the rest of the UK. While this worked during the 1960s, it faltered in the 1970s and the Northern Ireland economy fell back considerably.

This resulted in the creation of a strong state sector which led to a caricature that it was more like East Germany before the Berlin Wall came down.[30] The neoliberal statesmen were horrified with an 'overreliance' on the public sector for jobs, illustrated by the fact that by the mid-1990s a full 37 per cent of total employees were in the public sector.[31] The state sector had expanded through recruitment into the security services but also because it was compensating for a decline in private industry. This growth of the public sector meant that the subvention from the British state rose from the equivalent of half a billion in the mid-1960s to €3.3 billion in the mid-1990s. The absolute figure, however, is not so important as its impact on the size of the economy. In the mid-1960s there was a 7 per cent deficit between revenue and spending in the North, but by the 1990s this had risen to 17 per cent, a very high figure which was plugged by the British state. One of the subtexts of the Belfast Agreement was to bring the representatives of the two communities into government so that they could address these problems.

In the mindset of all three governments, there was a straightforward path ahead which entailed the shrinking of the state and expanding of the market. There was to be a 'rebalancing' of the economy away from the public sector and measures taken to support private industry. In the words of a subsequent 'economic vision document':

> The NI Economy has been overly dependent on the public sector for too long. We need to re-balance our economy by growing the private sector... the path we have chosen to economic competitiveness is to increase employment and wealth by building a larger and more export-driven private sector.[32]

These were familiar neoliberal platitudes promoted by private economic consultants all over the world. While the rhetoric in the North placed the usual emphasis on an 'export driven private sector', there was also a focus on creating a 'social enterprise economy' to help shrink the state.

The political structures established by the Belfast Agreement provided a key mechanism for this shift from public to the private sector. The Stormont Executive is based on a silo structure whereby each party runs its own allocated department without much accountability. Sinn Féin, DUP and the other parties in the Executive appoint special advisors, or SPADS, who do private deals with each other. Few people in Northern Ireland were aware of the precise role or influence that these SPADS had on state policy until the breaking of the Renewable Heating scandal. During the subsequent public inquiry into the huge waste of public money, Timothy Johnson, a DUP SPAD, gave an insight into the internal culture of the Stormont state apparatus. Explaining why there was a lack of transparency and public accountability, Johnson said, 'We didn't always want the public to see the elements of the [Stormont] sausage machine because it wasn't always pretty. It may not always be possible to be as pure as what is done in other places.'[33] The dealing between Sinn Féin and the DUP was also revealed by a senior civil servant, David Sterling, who told the same inquiry that the DUP and Sinn Féin were 'sensitive to criticism' and that it had become 'common' not to keep records because such records are subject to Freedom of Information.[34] The secrecy and fragmented nature of the Stormont Executive gives ample scope for plausible deniability because each party can allocate responsibility to the other for decisions that are not popular. Moreover, there is hardly any viable opposition in the wider Assembly. For a brief period in the past, the SDLP and the UUP occupied opposition benches but as they too joined the Executive after January 2020, opposition and scrutiny over government decisions fell to a tiny number of MLAs. The official opposition now comprises just one People Before Profit MLA, two Green MLAs and one from the Traditional Unionist Voice.

This type of secret government is ideal for the wheeling and dealing between business leaders and state officials. In most Western democracies, businesses engage in lobbying state officials and submitting ideas for consultation but they do so through formal procedures. Typically, business will, for example, use accountancy and consultancy firms to promote their ideas on privatisation and deregulation. At a later stage, they may benefit from winning contracts from the outsourced public agencies. Officially, they adhere to a hands-off culture whereby meetings between business and the political elite must be recorded to safeguard undue influence. The formal mechanisms are like a pinch of sand in the wheels of commerce – they are mildly annoying but they do not stop rotation.

Business lobbyists, however, would prefer more secretive frictionless structures that hide their activities from prying eyes. They like structures like those which operate at the EU level whereby a myriad of decisions are taken in special 'trilogue' meetings which are surrounded by corporate lobbyists.[35] However, of all these templates the Northern Ireland arrangement is probably most favourable for business. They can approach a communal party with a proposal that is slanted towards their community. They are guaranteed more secrecy in dealings with ministers as few records are kept. The tiny size of the opposition means that troublesome meddlers do not have the resources to investigate their manoeuverings. In brief, they have a clear field to push through a neoliberal restructuring.

This started with Private Finance Initiative (PFI) which Sinn Féin ministers embraced with some enthusiasm. PFI is a system whereby a state makes a contract with a company to design, build and operate a project over 20 or 25 years. It differs from a more standard relationship whereby a public authority tenders out for a private company because PFI involves a longer-term relationship where the state pays a regular fee for the maintenance of the project. Examples of the North's PFI projects include schools, court houses, hospital car parks – all which entail the payment of fees to a private operator over a long period of time. While the PFI system has been described as another form of privatisation, the form it took in the North was particularly repugnant because it essentially became a means by which private companies ripped off the public purse for billions.

The total cost of all Northern Ireland's PFI contracts when paid off will be £6.8 billion, almost four times the initial £1.73 billion in construction costs paid by the private investors. The North's taxpayers will continue to pay out these huge sums each year for decades to come. In 2018, for example, these amounted to annual pay-outs of £264 million and one example may serve to illustrate the scandal. St Genevieve's High School in West Belfast was a much-needed facility which opened in 2002. The initial cost of the building was £11.5 million but because the state entered a PFI arrangement it will continue to pay a private company fees until 2027. By then, it will have paid out £73.6 million, more than six times the original cost. As Deputy First Minister, Martin McGuinness was a particularly enthusiastic advocate of PFI schemes. At the opening of St Genevieve's, he stated that:

> The award of... PFI contracts highlights the opportunities for partnership with the private sector in the pursuit of good value for money and the effective use of resources to meet the needs of schools. It is now clear that

PFI does offer real potential for value for money solutions to the pressing capital investment needs of our schools generally.[36]

Which begs a question: how could a party which espoused a left rhetoric back a plan which most unions and socialists oppose? The answer takes us to the heart of how the structures of the Belfast Agreement assist in 're-balancing' the Northern economy. The Sinn Féin Education Minister John O'Dowd explained that Sinn Féin was not actually in favour of PFIs but because the British government was not allocating sufficient funds, they had to be used. By framing the issue in anti-British terms, O'Dowd and McGuinness could justify extracting money for projects in their community while, through private deals, the DUP would be enabled to get projects for theirs. In both cases, however, there was a massive rip-off of the public purse.

The other element of 're-balancing' meant giving big corporations the gift of tax breaks and handouts. After 2010, Sinn Féin and the DUP came to an agreement to cut corporation taxes on profits to just 12.5 per cent which is the same rate as in the South. To do so, they had to first ask the British government for permission to devolve decision-making authority to the Northern Assembly. The Fresh Start agreement of 2015 contained a joint agreement by DUP and Sinn Féin which stated that:

As a means of rebalancing the economy and addressing the social and economic challenges facing Northern Ireland, the Executive is committed to an affordable and more competitive Corporation Tax rate...

On this basis: The NI Executive commits to a commencement date of April 2018, and a Northern Ireland rate of 12.5%.[37]

However, while the intention was there, reality proved to be more complicated. To benefit from the reduced tax rate, a business had to show that most of its earnings were generated in the North and this entailed new accountancy costs. Moreover, Westminster's devolution of tax reform powers came with a caveat that there would be a cut in the block grant. As a result, the Stormont Executive has so far not implemented its tax cut.

However, if the plans for tax cuts have stalled there have been other ways to help big business, particularly those in the all-important 'export driven' sector. One of the most important companies in Northern Ireland is Moy Park Chickens which employs nearly 10,000 workers. The Renewable

Heating Initiative (RHI) scandal has helped to unearth the extremely close relationship that the owners had with the DUP. This was a scheme which sought to incentivise the burning of 'renewable' pellets but, bizarrely, the more pellets were burnt, the more free cash was given out. The scandal, which helped bring down the government led by Arlene Foster, is sometimes seen as unionist politicians getting a lucrative stream of payments for their supporters. There is certainly an element of truth to this – although Sinn Féin's Michele O'Neill was also advising supporters to avail themselves of the scheme. However, this framing of the issue misses an even more important context, namely that half of all the boilers that used the renewable pellets were linked to Moy Park.

The Renewable Heating Initiative gave money to cover the heating costs of farmers who supplied chickens to Moy Park. This then enabled the company to slash that proportion of what it paid to farmers to heat poultry sheds. In the words of the investigative journalist, Sam McBride, 'in essence, RHI was a backdoor subsidy to Moy Park'.[38] Moy Park had already benefitted from big grants from the Northern state as it was given €5 million in 2010 to upgrade its Ballymena plant and was offered another £9.5 million for further expansion. It worked extremely closely with a DUP SPAD to unlock further subsidies for a biogas facility that was funded though charges on household energy bills.

The same pattern of extremely generous subsidies is also evident in the case of Bombardier, the aircraft manufacturer. Airplane manufacturers all over the world receive state grants for creating jobs but the level of support to Bombardier reaches beyond generous. To build its C series in Belfast, Bombardier received £52 million from the UK government, but on top of that, Invest Northern Ireland gives its own subsidies. Between 2002 and 2015 Invest Northern Ireland also offered £75 million of financial assistance to Bombardier, including £21 million for the C Series.[39] In 2018, it got another £15 million for three new research projects employing one hundred workers.[40]

Another way the Stormont Executive has promoted a 're-balancing away' from direct public sector employment has been through the social enterprise model. This is now worth £625 million to the Northern economy and its employment base has grown from 12,200 in 2013 to 24,860 in 2018 while growth in turnover has increased from £592.7 million to £980 million.[41] Many of these projects have a positive impact as a high proportion are located in areas of high social deprivation. However, they have also been used to reduce direct public services and increase forms of patronage which help bolster the rival communal parties. Thus, under the Fresh Start agreement, the DUP and Sinn Féin announced that £48 million would be allocated to the Department of Health in order to reduce waiting lists but, like the policy in the South, the money was not used to pay for procedures in the NHS but rather through private healthcare providers. As the funding for social enterprises can come through Stormont or local authorities, it has created a new arena for patronage. We have already seen how the DUP helped fund a UDA-inspired project in East Belfast but in nationalist West Belfast similar mechanisms are in place to help bolster the dominance of Sinn Féin. Here is how one group of writers describe it:

> Community organisations, GAA football clubs and capital projects closely associated with Sinn Fein representatives and activists either directly, through family connections or through business sponsorship, have been earmarked for millions in public funding via the notorious and nakedly sectarian SIF initiative in order to shore up flagging electoral support in targeted constituencies. Sinn Fein apparatchiks have also become adept in the formation of third sector organisations that conceal party representative interests in agencies that draw down government funding and taxpayers' monies.[42]

While many social enterprise projects are a welcome addition to poor areas, they also tend to employ people on more precarious contracts. A TUC study, for example, found that 42 per cent of contracts in the third sector are zero-hour contracts.[43] There is also no democratic control over these enterprises, as they sit outside the state, where at least there is a modicum of democratic accountability. In other words, it would be better if people were employed directly by the public sector on decent contracts.

Twenty years after the signing of the Belfast Agreement, it is worth asking how successful the strategy of 're-balancing' has been. Success in any economy, however, is a relative term, mediated by social classes which have different interests. The Sinn Féin–DUP project has brought about a modest shrinkage in public sector employment but the re-balancing has not been as thorough as they might have wished. Public sector employment has declined to around 27 per cent of the workforce but the private sector has not grown as quickly as they might have hoped because investment is still spectacularly slow. One way of seeing that is to look at the respective share of investment in output in Northern Ireland compared to Scotland and the Republic, as Fitzgerald and Morgenroth did in their study of the Northern economy. In Scotland and the UK as a whole, investment amounted to 17 per cent of output and in the Republic it was 20 per cent, but in the North it was a mere 10 per cent. In their study of the Northern Ireland economy, the two economists made the pointed comment that it was normal throughout the EU to devote 20 per cent to investment to 'maintain a reasonable level of growth'.[44] On that measure Northern Ireland is a capitalist failure.

The main reason for the low level of investment is that foreign capital has come to the North for low wages and this in turn acts as a disincentive to capital investment. After all, if the price of labour is so low why invest heavily in machinery to replace it? The big growth in foreign direct investment has been in call centres where a host of firms service banks and insurance companies by employing graduates on very low levels of pay. Work is stressful and heavily monitored, with employees subject to high overperformance targets. Beyond the call centres, there are a small number of large firms, such as Moy Park or Bombardier which, as we have seen, are heavily subsidised.

The failure of private industry means, that contrary to expectations, the subvention from Britain has risen as a share of the economy. Thus, while the subvention amounted to 15 per cent of GDP between 1980 and 1999, it has risen to an average of 20 per cent since the Belfast Agreement and has now reached over £9 billion a year. From that point of view, the economic strategy of the British ruling class has failed. But, ironically, the increased role that the subvention plays in the economy is not something that concerns the DUP, Sinn Féin or the other Executive parties. One of the interesting aspects of the RHI scandal was the way in which the DUP were as enthusiastic as Sinn Féin in extracting as much as possible from London. As Sam McBride put it, 'The DUP unionism was infused with Ulster nationalism. The party prided itself on extracting what it could from London – or anywhere else – for its constituents, and was not afraid to boast about it.'[45] For both parties, the key goal was to get as much as possible from London to dispense patronage to their communities. Beyond that they will buy into neoliberal measures as a trade-off. However, while they can give subsidies to attract investors, they cannot force capitalists to actually invest. They, therefore, preside over a failed economy.

Failure, however, is a relative term and it depends on what class you are from. Even though the North is a failed economy in terms of normal measures of capitalist development, it still provides a privileged lifestyle for a few. According to the *Belfast Telegraph*, there are now 12,500 millionaires living there, bringing the regional share of millionaires to 2 per cent of the UK as a whole.[46] Throughout the North an emerging nationalist capitalist class and an upper professional class are joining their unionist colleagues in this elite. One of their main routes into wealth has been construction and property speculation as the repeated property booms in the South have had a ripple effect on the North and the construction industry increasingly operates on an all-Ireland basis. Alongside the small number of successful business people, there has been a much larger growth in the Catholic upper professional class. In the past, this layer was often recruited from the likes of principal teachers or doctors who were serving their own community. But as the opportunities for patronage have grown, this layer has expanded into the high-paid positions in the civil service, in the upper echelons of the social enterprise economy and into the wider managerial strata. From their vantage point, the change wrought by the Belfast Agreement has been a success.

For most workers it is a different story. The peace dividend that was promised with the Belfast Agreement has not appeared. There has been an increase in jobs but these are predominantly in low-skilled, low-pay sectors. The broad picture is that the average wage for workers in Northern Ireland is 9 per cent below the British average, although this disguises as much as it reveals because it includes the top earners as well as the worst paid worker. The reality is that Northern employees work longer than their British counterparts but still come out with less pay. There has also been a big increase in temporary work. The comparison is also complicated by the fact that public sector wages are broadly equivalent to those in Britain and this helps to even up the picture. In 2019 Northern Irish public sector earnings were just £7 lower than in the UK while earnings of private sector employees in Northern Ireland were £92 lower than in the UK.[47] This means that private sector wages are shockingly low – at least for those who are not in the top managerial grades. So while the category known as 'managers, directors and senior officials' are earning £800 a week, workers in call centres are getting about £360 a week and those in social care are getting £388.[48] Low wages help to increase the subvention from the British exchequer, because welfare benefits of various kinds usually make up the difference for a lot of low-paid workers, especially those with families.

The reality is that the 're-balanced' Northern economy is being built on a low-skilled workforce. A recent report on the labour market put it succinctly, 'A lack of skilled workers has long been considered one of the central weaknesses of the NI economy. The proportion of people with no qualifications in NI is almost double that of EU counterparts.'[49] The prevalence of low-skill, low-pay jobs means that far from one group of workers gaining at the expense of the other, most workers are being subjected to high levels of exploitation – a part of the brutal legacy of communal politics.

5
Protestant Workers

When Harland and Wolff workers walked off their jobs in 1994 because of the murder of Maurice O'Kane, there was a cold silence in republican quarters. The memory of a long history of sectarianism and violence against Catholic workers was simply too strong. Despite the fact that a mainly Protestant workforce was protesting over the murder of a Catholic fellow worker by the UVF, the bitterness against the shipyard workers meant that few republicans could see little positive in this act of solidarity.

Behind this lies a belief that Protestant workers are inevitably sectarian. In the past, republicans suggested that Protestant workers enjoyed privileges over their Catholic counterparts, and this bound them inevitably into supporting an Orange state. Some on the left echoed this with a claim that Protestant workers constituted a 'colon-proletariat'.[1] Michael Farrell's otherwise excellent book, *The Orange State*, is unfortunately marred by this approach because Protestant workers are presented as a 'labour aristocracy' chained to a unionist regime for as long as Stormont persists. This does not account for the fact that the majority of Protestant workers did not have well-paid skilled trades or that by 1919 skilled engineering workers were some of the most radicalised workers in Belfast. The 'labour aristocracy' approach means that attempts to unite and mobilise Northern workers on social and economic issues is dismissed as a strategy because, it is suggested, 'Unionist leaders have no difficulty in representing any challenge to the Unionist party, or any criticism of the regime, as a threat to the existence of the state.'[2] The term 'labour aristocracy' was originally used (mistakenly) by Lenin to account for the influence of reformist ideas among workers.[3] However, the concept was stretched to explain how Protestant workers directly benefitted from discrimination and might embrace semi-fascistic views.

The conclusion was that all attempts at uniting Protestants and Catholics on immediate economic issues was futile. Even if unity could be achieved, it would be short-lived as long as Britain propped up a sectarian state in the North. The ending of partition was a precondition for the unity of the working class. This underpinned the 'stages approach' which suggested that a united Ireland had to be first won on the basis of the existing economy and without the participation of Protestant workers. Achieving national unity was to take precedence over any other issue as there was no point drawing Catholics and Protestants together into a fight for immediate social and economic issues. While Sinn Féin might use a left-wing rhetoric, it was understood that talk of socialism, or distinct working-class interests, was not a practical proposition until partition had been removed. Moreover, if Protestant workers were imprisoned in an Orange ideology, republicans had to seek allies elsewhere to bring about Irish unity. Such allies eventually included Bill Clinton, Irish American entrepreneurs and, it was hoped, the Dublin government.

Today debates about the stages theory has been described by one writer as of interest only to the 'ideological cognoscenti'.[4] If by this is meant debates within large left-wing movements, this is probably correct. However, there is still a strong sense within Irish republicanism that certain issues should be parked for the future until after the national question is solved. The difference today is that Sinn Féin has shifted its rhetoric to a 'two cultures' approach. This frames the issue as promoting understanding and respect between two antagonistic cultures which are deeply embedded in Irish history. Thus, Declan Kearney, the chairperson of Sinn Féin, states that 'Orange culture, the unionist political tradition, and British identity are part of our shared history. Sinn Féin believes they should be central to the fabric of a new Ireland.'[5] Parity of esteem between the two cultures means that 'The Orange culture should indeed be respected. So too should the Irish language, Gaelic culture and Irish identity.'[6] Sinn Féin now seeks a dialogue with the Orange Order and the forging of a relationship of 'mutual respect' with the political leaders of unionism as a way of wooing Protestants to a united Ireland.

Sinn Féin's adaption to the rhetoric of respecting 'two cultures' is problematic. While the party has been historically critical of Orangeism, its new rhetoric appears patronising because it sees Protestants adhering to one culture and fails to recognise the long history of Protestant dissent. Orangeism was an historic creation, initially forged as a counter-revolutionary movement and then sustained and manipulated by a unionist elite. The use of the term 'culture' assumes that Orangeism is sustained by symbols, tradition, ritual and a way of life. This effectively plays down the ideological content of Orangeism which projects a Protestant superiority linked to support for empire and its security forces. The 'two cultures' approach also ignores the Orange Order's virulent support for right-wing politics and its misogyny whereby only a tiny number of women have been admitted to its ranks. The focus on 'identity' depoliticises the content of Orangeism and seeks to render it harmless by transforming it into a quaint series of Orangefests. Most crucially, the 'two cultures' approach ignores how Protestant workers do not just mobilise on the basis of 'identity' but also, on occasions, as a class. Far from Orangeism having an uncontested grip over Protestants, it has repeatedly had to fight to break any emerging unity between Protestant and Catholic. A brief look at that record gives us a different vantage point.

WHEN PROTESTANT AND CATHOLIC UNITED

Irish republicanism owes its origins to a Protestant radical tradition which celebrated the French revolution. Later, a different mythology developed which saw the 1798 rebellion being led by a priest, Father Murphy, with leaders like Wolfe Tone coming over to the Catholic side. The reality was somewhat different. The United Irishmen originated among the early business leaders of Belfast who saw that even though their city 'on the Scale of Commerce, Manufacturers and Revenue, contributes eminently to the prosperity of the kingdom',[7] they were not being represented in the Dublin parliament dominated by aristocratic landlords. The Protestant radicals were the Irish version of the bourgeois class in France that fought to overthrow the privileges of the aristocracy. Far from basing itself on 'the men of no property' the Belfast United Irishmen, contained an 'overwhelming presence of merchants, affluent traders and shopkeepers'.[8] Their key concern was democracy and they saw themselves standing in the tradition of the Enlightenment, challenging superstition and popery. While they began as reformers, they moved – and were pushed from below – to becoming revolutionaries, republicans and separatists. After they were driven underground, lower-class elements played a more active role in shaping their politics.

Far from being imprisoned by two inherently antagonistic cultures, the outlook of these Protestant radicals was transformed by the French Revolution because, in this mainly Catholic country, a revolution had established freedom of conscience and commerce. Wolfe Tone's genius was to persuade Protestant upper-class radicals to forge an alliance with the Catholic peasantry, urging them to 'Look at France and America; the Pope burnt in effigy in Paris, the English Catholics at this moment seceding from the church.'[9] He pointed out that the priests 'hated the very name of the French revolution'[10] and so the danger of Catholic domination and superstition was receding. If Protestant radicals and dispossessed Catholics forged an alliance, they could break the power of Britain, create a real democracy and speed up the development of their commerce.

The United Irishmen rebellion was eventually crushed with utmost brutality. While many read about the terror that followed the French revolution, few learn about a British reign of terror that involved house burnings, pitchcapping, mass executions and burning rebels alive. An estimated 50,000 perished, but in suppressing the uprising, Britain also found a mechanism for control over the Protestant population. The Orange Order was born from a crucible of sectarian tensions in Armagh, where there was a more even balance between Presbyterians, Catholics and Anglicans leading to greater conflict over land leases and piece rates for weaving. It was founded as a movement from below after what became known as the Battle of the Diamond, where Defenders – a largely Catholic secret society – were killed. The gentry, however, saw an opportunity to develop it as a counter-revolutionary force against radical ideas and so joined in significant numbers. When the United Irishmen moved to open rebellion, the British authorities forged an alliance with the Orange Order, recruiting many of them into the yeomanry to put down the rising. General Knox, the British commander for Ulster put the matter succinctly, 'As for the Orangemen, we have rather a difficult card to play... we must to a certain degree uphold them, for with all their licentiousness, on them we must rely for the preservation of our lives and properties should critical times occur.'[11] Writing to a fellow general he boasted, 'I have arranged... to increase the animosity between the Orangemen and the United Irishmen... Upon that animosity depends the safety of the centre counties of the North.'[12]

Far from Orangeism developing as an organic part of Protestant culture, it was promoted by state forces. Sectarian competition pre-dated Orangeism but the Order solidified it by suppressing radical Protestant dissent. As Belfast developed an industrial base and attracted rural dwellers into the city, the Orange Order used exclusionary tactics to discourage the recruitment of Catholics, particularly into the skilled trades. It preyed on the fact that the working class experiences both division and unity. The market forces workers to compete against each other for jobs and pay but exploitation fosters a class unity to oppose employers. Yet neither unity nor division are an inevitable feature of working-class life and depends on the social forces – unions, political parties or exclusionary organisations – that are present. By transferring sectarian hatred from the countryside to the city, the Orange Order served as an important mechanism through which the unionist elite undermined working-class solidarity. Other factors certainly assisted the Orange Order in establishing its hegemony in the nineteenth century. The shift in the Irish nationalist movement to a focus on Catholic Emancipation helped, as did a surge in Protestant evangelicalism in 1859 which challenged Presbyterian sympathy with Enlightenment ideas. Uneven economic development whereby Belfast was seen as a progressive industrial centre in contrast to a backward Catholic agrarian south, all fed into notions of Protestant superiority. Yet despite all these favourable conditions for its growth, the Orange Order's policy of sectarian division was often challenged.

Kirby Miller has produced fascinating research on Protestant emigration to the US that significantly questions the identification of Protestants with Orangeism. Between the American Revolution and the Famine, a quarter of a million people emigrated from an Ulster that, at its height, contained just over one million people. The migrants, who were mainly Presbyterian and Catholics, fled terrible economic conditions and after examining many of their letters home, Miller concludes that:

> Ulster Presbyterian radicalism in the 1790s was not – as historians have argued – naturally or inevitably diluted at home by evangelicalism or Orangeism or even by the North's much vaunted prosperity. Rather, it was largely transplanted overseas by the massive migrations of those who would not or could not adapt to the new Unionist (and capitalist) Order.[13]

In other words, just as a conservative Catholic society in the South was helped by the safety valve of emigration, so too was the supposedly natural identification of Protestantism with Orangeism.

Nor was the Orange Order successful in preventing Protestant workers joining with their Catholic counterparts in militant class struggle. In 1907, for example, Jim Larkin arrived in Belfast to recruit unskilled workers into the National Union of Dock Labourers (NUDL). Skilled workers, particularly those in the shipyards, were earning wages comparable to those in the rest of Britain, but between them and the unskilled, there was 'a yawning abyss unequalled anywhere else in the United Kingdom'.[14] Belfast employers such as Thomas Gallaher, who owned a tobacco factory and was chair of the Belfast Steamship Company, would not tolerate a militant union for the unskilled. The conflict between Larkinism and the employers became a titanic struggle with the tactic of solidarity action deployed by the unions while the employers used the police and army to protect non-union strike-breakers. Larkin united a mainly Protestant workforce with Catholics in a militant struggle that saw even members of the police, the Royal Irish Constabulary, join the strike. On 26 July, 100,000 people marched in support of the strike and socialist ideas spread with the formation of new Independent Labour branches. Larkin spelled out the political implications:

> They were that day to say the old sectarian curse had been banished forever from Ulster. Ninety percent of the strikers were members of the old Orange Institution. Dublin Castle has endeavoured in the police question to introduce the question of religious bigotry again, but they could never succeed in it in Belfast again.[15]

He was being wildly optimistic because, as a syndicalist, he thought the economic unity could translate quickly into political unity. The strike was ultimately defeated because the union bureaucracy of NUDL retreated in horror before the escalating action. With defeat came the reassertion of old identities which had briefly been submerged by a class awareness. During the strike, for example, the Orange Order split and support grew for the Independent Orange Order. While this showed that unionism could fracture on class lines, the fact Protestant workers remained within the Orange framework meant they were vulnerable to being pushed back behind Big House unionism once the drum was beating.

In 1919, a revolt of a different sort occurred when skilled engineering workers in Belfast led a strike for a 44-hour week. After they were joined by municipal workers, about 60,000 workers were involved and they effectively took control of electricity, gas and water supplies. The mainly Protestant workforce were led by a Catholic, Charles McKay, and a 'rotten prod' socialist, James Baird, while other elements of the strike leadership, who were more conservative, tended to be aligned to the Unionist Party. While the strike was part of a wider British-based movement for shorter hours, it caused embarrassment and nervousness among the Orange leadership. A document from the Grand Lodge claimed that 'the condition of affairs today had been to a great extent engineered by parties who are neither employers nor employed but have taken advantage of a trade dispute to bring discredit on the fair fame of Belfast'.[16] The unionist leader, Dawson Bates, explained to Carson that the statement was designed to get 'the decent men to secede from the Sinn Fein Bolshevik element' because, he believed, that fewer than a quarter of the strikers were 'out and out socialists and extremists'.[17] Yet despite these and other attacks from the *Belfast Telegraph*, the strike held together. In the end, it was defeated because moderate elements on the strike leadership refused to call out transport workers and others. And once again, after defeat, came demoralisation, evident in the way that many of the strike leaders were expelled from the shipyards the following year.

The 1932 Outdoor Relief riots were another occasion when Protestants and Catholics united to defend their class interests. The reason was a huge rise in unemployment which affected Protestants as well as Catholics. The unemployed were at the mercy of a Board of Guardians who gave relief for two and a half days' work, less than that in Britain and subject to more humiliating conditions. The small Revolutionary Workers' Group, led by an ex-republican Tommy Geehan, began agitating for common action for change. Marches were planned from Catholic and Protestant working-class areas and an estimated 60,000 united to demand improved conditions. When one of the marches was banned, riots broke out as police baton-charged protestors, killing two people. They concentrated their efforts on the Catholic Falls Road area in an attempt to inject sectarian division into the movement. The Ulster Protestant League, a hard-line loyalist organisation, also opposed the strike, claiming it was:

a cloak for the communist Sinn Fein element to attempt to start a revolution in our province. We also greatly deplore that some few of our loyal Protestant unemployed were misled to such an extent that they associated themselves with the enemies of their faith and principles.[18]

But their message of 'Protestants first' for a job did not succeed in dividing the movement. It had to wait a further three years before sectarian pogroms in Belfast quenched the memory of the riots.

The equation of Protestantism and loyalty to empire was also put to the test during the Second World War. While adherents of the two-culture approach now celebrate the sacrifices of the 36th Ulster Division at the Somme in the First World War, Protestants workers took a more jaundiced view. Stories of the sheer horror of two days of senseless fighting in July 1916, when 5,500 Ulster men were killed or wounded, meant there was little enthusiasm for enlisting during the Second World War. Moreover, the threat of resistance from the Catholic population, meant that conscription was not imposed on the North and so, unlike the rest of Britain, enlistment was voluntary. The result was a significant fall-off in recruitment of Protestants as well as Catholics. In the initial weeks, 2,500 were joining the British Army each month but by 1940 this had fallen to 600 – and that included some Southern Irish recruits.[19] Far from displaying an overwhelmingly loyalty to empire, Protestant workers pushed their class interests to the fore. Ferocious working hours were imposed at Harland and Wolff and one result was that absenteeism in the Belfast shipyard was twice that of any other yard in Britain.[20] As unemployment decreased, there was an explosion of industrial militancy. In 1943, three million working days were lost through strikes in Northern Ireland, a figure that led to denunciation of the workers as 'a disgrace to the British Empire'.[21] A powerful Belfast Shop Stewards movement came into being, coordinating strikes in shipbuilding, engineering and aircraft. In 1944, five shop stewards were sentenced to three months hard labour for organising strikes which the unionist Prime Minister, Basil Brooke, denounced as an act of sabotage. Some 40,000 workers, however, struck in their support, forcing a hastily organised compromise that secured the shop stewards' release. In addition, the strike won significant pay rises.

These tumultuous events indicate a strong history of class action among mainly Protestant workers and nor is it a distant historical tradition. Underneath the talk of Catholic–Protestant division, there is a continuing record of Catholic and Protestant workers striking together and Protestant workers opposing their unionist bosses. Health care staff throughout the North have come together to fight for pay parity with the rest of Britain. Civil servants have staged major strikes against low pay. Firefighters are amongst the most militant workers in pushing for better conditions. Workers at the now diminished Harland and Wolff have occupied their yard to protect jobs. Meat workers have walked off their jobs because of the lack of social distancing during Covid-19. One of the more bizarre disputes occurred in Ballymena, a unionist heartland, when Wrightbus made 1,200 workers redundant. It transpired that that its majority shareholder, Pastor Jeff Wright, had being making donations to his Green Pastures Evangelical church from the company accounts. Between 2010 and 2017, the Corner-stone Group, which controls the Wright factory, had donated €16 million to the church of Pastor Jeff Wright. Worse, even as the company went into administration, it refused to hand over the land at a price that would have allowed work to continue under a new owner. It took mass protests and even a hundred-strong picket outside the church to force the company to change its mind and help save jobs.[22]

CLASS STRUGGLE AND IDEOLOGY

This record – and we have provided only a very short description – is written out of conventional history. Working-class struggle is often assigned a marginal historical role but in Northern Ireland there is an additional reason why it is ignored – namely, the statelet is viewed through an 'ethno-national' prism. The province is supposed to be permanently divided between Catholic and Protestant 'ethnic communities' that hate each other. According to the main theorists of this approach, McGarry and O'Leary:

> Ethnic communities are perceived kinship groups. Their members share a subjective belief in their common ancestry, shared history and common culture and in specific situations such communities are prone to competition and antagonistic conflict, especially when such conflict has a national character… Since the ethno-national group regards itself as a large extended family, its members regard an attack on one as an attack on all. Explosive national conflicts arise between politically mobilised ethnic communities.[23]

The 'ethno-national community' supposedly arises from a primordial need to belong and so like a 'large extended family', internal divisions based on social class barely register because what matters is the subjective belief in a common ancestry. With the focus on how people identify psychologically with their culture, there is little appreciation of the importance of class struggle.

However, life is a little more complicated. There are, of course, traditions with which people identify, for good or ill, but these can be sometimes submerged by alternative solidarities. During a major strike, for example, new forms of brotherhood or sisterhood are established. During mass demonstrations, activists develop new connections with each other. They may not last long, but they signal new possibilities for identities that go beyond the 'ethno-national'.

Writers like Henry Patterson undoubtedly recognise this and some of his work has focused on working-class struggle. Their main point, however, is that Protestant workers are not simply duped by unionist leaders and that trade union militancy and Orangeism can 'interpenetrate' each other. The historical record clearly supports the first point, but the notion that Orangeism and class struggle can support each other is simplistic because Orangeism is not just a tradition but a supremacist ideology. By the term 'ideology', we mean an outlook on the world which articulates the interests of a particular social group or class. Not every perspective on the world, however, will help advance the interests of a social group. When black soldiers in South Africa joined the Hammer regiment of the apartheid regime to colonise neighbouring countries, their self-understanding did not support their own interests. When women in the past embraced the ideal of the housewife, their perception of themselves did not advance their freedom. Sometimes ideologies work in complex ways to lead people to align their outlook with that of their rulers and Orangeism functions in this way at many different levels. It promotes the view that Catholics are disloyal, feckless and to blame for their own poverty. It pretends that Protestantism is superior, and Catholics represent a threat to their very identity. It supports a hierarchical view of the world that inculcates respect for monarchy, the police and politicians who uphold the value of empire.

By its very nature class struggle comes into conflict with this ideology because it unites workers, bringing them shoulder to shoulder in a fight against a boss. It challenges the idea of belonging to just one community, and cuts across the notion that one section of workers can gain at the expense of the other. When struggles are intense, workers are sometimes brought into conflict with state forces and the idea of support for 'our' security services clashes with the actual experience of police or army actions. Implicit in most working-class struggles is a lack of deference and a sense of equality that challenges existing hierarchies. For all these reasons, working-class struggle comes up against the obstacle of Orangeism.

It does not follow, however, that economic struggles translate into political unity. The historic record shows that workers' unity has often been buried beneath sectarian divisions within a short period of time. The 1907 strike was followed by sectarian riots in 1911; the 1919 engineering strike was followed by pogroms a year later; the 1932 outdoor relief movement was followed by the 1935 riots. This pattern occurs precisely because Orangeism is a powerful ideology that can be deployed against workers' unity. With more than a hundred years of history behind it, the idea that Protestant interests come first does not disappear overnight. How quickly that ideology can undermine workers' unity depends on a variety of factors, crucially on the intensity, length or outcome of the struggles. In a mass bureaucratic strike called by a national union, with little grassroots activity, the challenge to Orangeism is limited. If struggle is short-lived, there is little prospect that it will create tensions with Orangeism. After defeats, the temptation to 'look after our own' also grows because right-wing ideas generally batten off working-class demoralization and the perceived inability to advance as a class.

Even in the most favourable conditions, ideologies do not simply vanish. As Gramsci pointed out, people brought up in a certain society share a 'conception of the world', which is 'mechanically imposed on them by their external environment'. This environment is made up of 'social groups with which they are automatically involved from the moment of their entry into the conscious world'.[24] These different conceptions make up their 'common sense ' – views that are taken for granted without much thought and which cause 'people to "think", without having a critical awareness, in a disjointed and episodic way'.[25] Left-wing politics challenge these conceptions of the world, with the aim of 'superseding the existing mode of thinking'[26] and so in every country left-wing movements offer 'a criticism of "common sense"'. But to be effective, the left cannot start from an abstract, dogmatic standpoint but needs to take elements of workers' own experience to produce a more critical awareness. These particular experiences will, for a period, coexist with other notions, producing what Gramsci called a 'contradictory consciousness'. By this, he meant that a worker has two ways of understanding the world: 'one which is implicit in his activity and which in reality unites him with all his fellow workers in the practical transformation of the real world; and one, superficially explicit or verbal, which he has inherited from the past and uncritically absorbed'.[27] The tension between the two conceptions of the world cannot last for ever, either there is a growth towards a full realisation of class interest, or the insights gleaned from struggle are submerged behind the normal common sense. It depends on the political forces and how they relate to workers' experiences.

Let's move from these rather general speculations to a concrete case. In the aftermath of the Outdoor Relief protests, James Connolly Workers' Republican Clubs were established in the Shankill and Newtownards districts. A small minority of Protestant workers joined an organisation they believed was going to lead the fight for socialism in Ireland. In 1934, they marched on the annual commemoration of Wolfe Tone at Bodenstown behind a very distinct banner which proclaimed 'Shankill Road Belfast Branch. Break the Connection with Capitalism.' Their presence, however, was not welcomed by the right-wing IRA leaders who ordered this 'communist banner' torn down. The next day they marched through Dublin to Connolly's grave where a Shankill man, Robert McVicker, gave an oration.

> We do not pretend to speak on behalf of the majority of Belfast workers. We are a body of Protestant workers, the vanguard of the working class… [come from Belfast] to pledge our determination at the graveside of Connolly to do all we can to carry out[his] message… to break all connection with England and to smash Irish capitalism.[28]

This minority of Protestant workers had generalised from their experience of the wider struggle to move to socialist views but Irish republicanism, however, could not accommodate those whose starting point was anti-capitalism rather than a traditional hostility of Britain. As a result, their insights were lost because there was not a political force that could give it expression. Nevertheless, it showed that Protestants could be won to a socialist anti-partitionist position but 'ultimately this was not possible within the confines of a nationalist project'.[29]

The conceptions of normal times – that Protestant workers had distinct interests that conflicted with Catholic fellow workers re-emerged. The Ulster Protestant League (UPL), which had been marginal at the height of the Outdoor Relief agitation, grew quickly in some of the poorest Protestant districts fuelled by the same anger that had led to the Outdoor Relief riots. However, while the Outdoor Relief strike pointed the finger of blame at the unionist government, the UPL accused their Catholic neighbours.[30]

Tragically, the balance of forces between the left and Protestant sectarianism was overwhelming in favour of the latter because of the implicit support of many Orange employers who could give jobs to their nominees. While the UPL represented the extreme end of popular sectarianism, they could also draw on an official state ideology to support their message that Catholics were disloyal. They knew they could gain some support from the Unionist Party, which ran the state, because prominent politicians such as Basil Brooke, the future Prime Minister, was speaking at their meetings. In brief, they could back up their claim that Protestants should get first offers for jobs with some real substance.

Ideologies are not disembodied entities but are carried by real people, embedded in networks and institutions. They give a partial account of real experiences and slant it in particular ways. In the 1930s, there was a material base, a real experience from which Orange sectarians could draw to defeat left-wing ideas. They could point to a whole series of workplaces, run by Orange bosses, where they could demand 'Protestants first'. They could act as unruly extremists, knowing that they could win support inside the ranks of the respectable Unionist Party. Above all, they operated on a terrain where they saw the state as their own and so the contest between a left-wing, class outlook and Orangeism was decidedly uneven. It was not simply that the UPL were better organised or more determined to promote their sectarian message – they had a material foundation on which to grow their message. But how secure is this today?

PROTESTANT WORKERS TODAY

After examining the data for the mid-1980s, two economists Bob Rowthorn and Naomi Wayne concluded that: 'While poverty and insecurity is widespread among the working class of each community, the situation of Catholics is considerably worse.'[31] They based this on statistical evidence that Catholics had a far higher unemployment rate; that male Catholic unemployment was higher than any other disadvantaged group in the UK; and that Catholics were 'crowded into low pay, insecure work'.[32] This data merely confirmed the level of the discrimination directed at Catholics for decades. However, even though small changes had started to occur in the 1980s, these accelerated after Rowthorn and Wayne's book was published. At that time Protestant employment in manufacturing industry had started to decline but, for a period, this was counter-balanced by jobs that Protestants found in security forces. Overall, the book provided ample evidence of a material basis for the appeal of Orangeism.

Even then, however, discrimination did not eliminate Protestant poverty nor was the gap between Protestant and Catholic workers in any way similar to that between South African whites and blacks. Despite facile comparisons, few Protestants had a swimming pool in their back garden or a Catholic domestic servant! Nevertheless, as Eamonn McCann put it, 'When tuppence halfpenny is looking down on tuppence, the halfpenny difference can assume an importance out of all proportion to its actual size.'[33]

Today these differences have almost disappeared. The restructuring of industry and the introduction of Fair Employment legislation were all factors, but there can be little dispute about the change. The Stormont Executive produces a regular Labour Force Survey which draws a comparison between both religions on a 25-year time span between 1992 and 2017. In 1992, the unemployment rate for Catholics was double that of Protestants with an 18 per cent jobless rate compared to 9 per cent, but by 2017 the unemployment rate of both groups was 4 per cent.[34] Both had almost an equal number categorised as self-employed as against directly employed – 16 per cent for Protestants and 15 per cent for Catholics.[35] When the figures are looked at in more detail, there are some surprising results.

In the skilled trades, where the Orange Order was originally most successful in its exclusionary tactics, composition is only marginally in favour of Protestants who hold 51 per cent of the jobs compared to 49 per cent for Catholics.[36] However, in the category Associate Professional and Technical Occupations, Catholics make up 57 per cent of employees compared to 43 per cent of Protestants.[37] This is a significant gap and probably reflects a pattern whereby Protestants are more likely to study in Britain – with a relatively high number staying there on completion of their studies. The overall result is that it is no longer the case that Catholics are concentrated in lower grades because the categories of Managers, Directors and Senior Officials as well as Professional Occupations are evenly divided at 50–50.[38] The biggest differential in occupation is now in Agriculture, Forestry and Fishing where Protestants make up 65 per cent of employment compared to 35 per cent for Catholics.[39]

When it comes to wages, the median wage of Protestants and Catholics is now exactly equal with workers from both denominations earning an average of £10.58 an hour in 2017.[40] However, while there is an equality between Catholics and Protestants within Northern Ireland, it is more a case of equality of poverty. Wages in Northern Ireland are less than those in Britain as a whole and are significantly worse in the private sector, bringing high levels of poverty for both sections of workers. A recent audit of education inequality shows that 100,000 young people, or one in three of the total, are entitled to free school meals. Those receiving these meals have a 17 per cent attainment gap in achieving five good GCSE grades compared to students who do not. Within those figures, young Protestant male students fare worst.[41]

All of this indicates that there has been a serious erosion of the 'halfpenny' advantage of Protestants, but alongside these changes in economic conditions there has been an important transformation in how people understand the world. Perceived images are being shattered, especially when we examine how a senior UDA figure explained why he was against Irish unity:

> I am not denying that we were sectarian, but we had our own ideas. The Republic was a backward place, no contraception, no divorce, and lots of censorship; It was hardly Disneyland. The country executed more IRA men than the Unionists. Did you know that?... the Irish state was rotten to the core... with no real welfare state like we had? Was I supposed to roll over and say OK, let's have a united Ireland and live in a more conservative country that was just as sectarian?[42]

Aside from his point the about the welfare state, there is little in this description of the Southern state that makes sense today. Huge social movements have broken though much of the conservative Catholic culture of the South, challenging both the political elite and the bishops. The Repeal movement, mainly composed of young people, forced the political elite to do a U-turn and allow a referendum which legalised abortion. Another movement carried the day on marriage equality with the country becoming the first in the world to allow, by popular suffrage, gay people to marry. Bans on contraception were ended long ago. There is still much to be done to break the power of the Catholic Church over education, but it is no longer possible to talk of a more liberal North and a deeply conservative South. More generally, the image of Orangeism as representing a progressive industrial North in contrast to a backward agrarian South makes little sense. Just 4.5

per cent of the Southern workforce is employed in Agriculture and Fisheries compared to 2.5 per cent in the North.[43] Both economies have witnessed a decline in manufacturing, and a growth in services. Both have become more dependent on foreign capital.

If the traditional image of the South no longer corresponds to reality, neither does the Orange image of 'Britishness'. According to Orange ideology, the union with Britain provided the best defence against Catholic expansionism and the focal point of its loyalty is the Crown rather than Westminster, as the monarchy is, officially, charged with protecting that Protestantism. Alongside the Crown, the Orange Order emphasises its loyalty to the security forces. At one stage, Robert Saulters, a former Grand Master of the Orange Order, cited the British army involvement in the war in Iraq as playing a part in defining contemporary Britishness.[44] However, as a not unsympathetic observer notes, this loyalty is to a 'form of national-imperial Britishness whose origins remain strongly associated with a bygone age'.[45] Modern Britain is a multicultural society – despite efforts to promote empire nostalgia – where most of the population have little relationship to the Protestant churches. As Linda Colley points out, Protestantism and even Christianity has only a 'residual influence' on modern British culture, with more Muslims living in the country than Methodists.[46] The queen is more likely to be seen as a soap opera matriarch than as a defender of the faith. In brief, the concept of 'Britishness' which plays such a central role in Orange ideology barely exists.

More fundamentally, the conditional loyalty of Protestants to the Union is now coming under strain. The original basis of the relationship was union with Britain as long as its government supported the Protestant position in the North. For decades, it did not seem to matter that Westminster had an informal custom of not discussing Northern Ireland, but once the British state became more involved, its actions and wider British attitudes came under closer scrutiny. In 1994, the Springfield Inter-Community Development Project held a 'community exploration' on the situation facing Protestant workers. A striking aspect of their report was an acknowledgement of the 'deep trauma within the Protestant psyche' which was primarily caused by British 'betrayal'. The report noted that 'most working-class loyalists now believe their "loyalty" counts for little on the mainland – Britain no longer wants them'.[47] That was over 20 years ago, and the perception has deteriorated further since because of a combination of manifest arrogance and ignorance by which the British government has treated the province. One Northern Ireland Secretary, Karen Bradley, when appointed by Westminster, admitted that she had never been there beforehand and was 'slightly scared' of the place. She said that 'I freely admit that when I started this job, I didn't understand some of the deep-seated and deep-rooted issues that there are in Northern Ireland.'[48] That, however, did not prevent her from taking up the position of Secretary of State.

The debacle over Brexit has exacerbated the sense of betrayal. The hardest elements within unionism supported a Leave position hoping that it would clarify Northern Ireland's distinctness from the Republic. To achieve this, the DUP aligned itself with the most extreme Brexiteer caucus in the Tory party but when it came to the crunch point, the unionists of Northern Ireland were sacrificed for Eurosceptic England. It became clear that they were simply used by Boris Johnson in his fight to win the leadership of the Tory party and then discarded rapidly afterwards. To reach a deal with the EU, Johnson agreed to creating a customs border down the Irish Sea – meaning that the North would be treated differently to other parts of Britain. Nothing could better summarise the real attitude of the Tory party which presents itself as the strongest defender of the unity of the United Kingdom.

The overall effect has been growing demoralisation in the ranks of unionism. This is evident in the rapid decline of the Orange Order, the glue which held together an all-class alliance. In 1968, the Orange Order was claiming 93,447 members, by 2007 it had declined to 35,000.[49] Since then the decline has probably accelerated but the full figures are not revealed. The demoralisation is also reflected in growing splits between efforts by Orange Order leaders to regain 'respectability' and younger loyalists who have joined Blood and Thunder bands. Whereas in the past the majority of bandsmen went on to become Orange Lodge members, now many do not because as one Blood and Thunder bandsman put it, 'The Orange Order to some people has taken this image of being an old man's organisation.'[50] These divisions reflect wider tensions over what exactly loyalism is loyal to? To a Protestant religious tradition or to a more secular culture which defines itself against the 'other side'? To a mythical Britain or a mythical 'Ulster'?

Overall, the shifts and changes within the Protestant working class have led to an anger which seeks out the best 'outbidder' for their community and, so far, the main beneficiary has been the DUP. Its narrative that Catholics are getting in everywhere and have gained the most from the Good Friday

Agreement has won it most unionist votes. In public, the DUP promises to stop the concessions to 'the republicans' while in private it does deals with Sinn Féin. The current consociational regime, which puts a premium on strong communal representatives, makes it easy for the DUP as they merely have to call for unionist discipline to send 'our' representatives into government. But elections are just one indicator of the public mood and in the North they often amount to a sectarian headcount. To return to Gramsci, there is a contradictory consciousness among Protestant workers and the forces that could resolve those contradictions in a sectarian direction are weaker today than in the past. They don't have the same dense institutional networks that the Orange Order once provided. They cannot look to a one-party unionist state to support them. They cannot point to a more progressive British way of life. They cannot show how Protestants will get preferential access to jobs. In brief, there is a contest under way.

LOYAL OR LEFT

But who are the contenders to give voice to working-class concerns? In the early 2000s, it looked as if a 'new loyalism' might emerge to promote social democratic politics in opposition to the right-wing politics of big house unionism and the DUP. These developments were favoured by some academic writers in the hope that working-class voices on both sides of the divide might help reduce sectarianism. Thus Pete Shirlow, who claimed that loyalists are divided between 'progressive and regressive elements', called for a break with the latter to 'create a new loyalism upon the foundations of key social justice driven principles'. They could then 'embed themselves in a community/voluntary structure that deliberately seeks to challenge socio-economic exclusion within an evolving post-conflict landscape'.[51]

The record, however, of loyalist paramilitaries creating a political wing is not particularly positive. In 1981, the Ulster Defence Association set up a party, the Ulster Democratic Party which attacked Paisley as a 'phoney politician' who worked with paramilitaries but subsequently branded them as criminals.[52] However, the UDA simultaneously embarked on a brutal sectarian murder campaign and eventually the UDP was disbanded. It was replaced by a smaller Ulster Political Research Group, but this also played a marginal role. The rival loyalist paramilitary, the Ulster Volunteer Force, set up the Progressive Unionist Party in 1979 and this initially appeared to be more promising. The PUP presented itself as a left-of-centre alternative within the unionist community and took a series of progressive positions such as pro-choice on abortion and support for marriage equality. It opposed zero-hour contracts and challenged a school system that was failing Protestant working-class students.[53]

However, there were major problems because these new loyalist parties remained closely tied to paramilitary groups that have limited popular support in Protestant areas. Despite talk of being community representatives, loyalist organisations have a long history of drug dealing and other criminality. Linked to this has been a history of feuding and the cultivation of 'hard men' images as a means to shore up a political base. Thus, Billy Hutchinson the current leader of the PUP, has expressed 'no regrets' over his murder of two Catholic workers in 1974, claiming that his actions helped to prevent a united Ireland.[54]

Aside from this history, there are deeper reasons why a 'new loyalism' cannot encompass genuine working-class radicalism. This is because it defines itself as defending a *Protestant* working-class community rather than the wider working class and assumes that this section of workers has distinct interests from Catholic workers. It promotes a tradition of loyalty to the queen and British armed forces as a condition for adherence to its party. So instead of adopting a critical perspective, for example, on how Protestants were used as 'cannon fodder' by the generals in the Battle of the Somme, it excuses the massacre. Instead of commemorating those who died by denouncing the horror of war, it demands loyalty to the armed forces as if this were an intrinsic part of Protestant culture. In brief, new loyalism seeks to compete with old unionism on the same terrain – by adding an extra class element for Protestant workers.

However, once it competes on this terrain, the 'progressive loyalists' must march to the beat of the Orange drum and every move by the 'other side' forces the PUP into a fake unity with other unionists. Thus, in 2012 the PUP had a policy which did not insist that the Union Jack be flown at Belfast City Hall every day of the year. However, in response to 'community opinion, or more precisely agitation stirred up by the DUP, it changed its views and became the most ardent flag wavers, helping to organise street protests and blockades'.[55] The pressure for communal unity grows with general elections and the 'progressive loyalists' often stand aside for a right-wing party like the DUP. How a supposedly left-wing party backs a party that kept Tories in power can only be explained by a communal loyalty that trumps class politics.

Working-class radicalism can, therefore, only find its political expression in a genuine left which starts from the common interests of all workers in their conflict with employers and the state. Such a left, however, cannot avoid advancing a clear position on the 'national question' because it will not simply be able to talk about 'bread and butter issues'. It will need to advance a distinct viewpoint that transcends existing communal frameworks and that can only occur in the context of pushing for a radical transformation of Ireland as a whole.

6
The Return of the National Question

The Belfast Agreement was supposed to settle the constitutional position of Northern Ireland for decades. Two communal parties, it was thought, would perfect the art of staging public rows while cooperating silently on business needs. That at least was the hope of its principal architects in the US administration and the governments of Ireland and Britain. However, far from the question of the border receding, it has jumped back centre stage. In the aftermath of Brexit, there are growing demands for a border poll and it is not just coming from republicans. The group Ireland's Future, for example is pushing for a border poll in 2023, and as one journalist pointed out it 'does not just comprise fervent Sinn Feiners' but instead has 'attracted a broad swathe of support [from some who] were hitherto wary of campaigns that chimed with Sinn Fein's ambition'.[1] A border poll could determine whether partition should be ended and Ireland united. However, the power to call a referendum rests with the British Secretary of State who will decide 'if it appears likely to him' that a majority of those voting would wish to leave the United Kingdom and become part of Ireland. The Belfast Agreement does not specify how he will make such an assessment and it allows the British government to pick the most opportune time to retain its sovereignty. Nevertheless, the calls for a border poll are an indication that the national question has returned. This is not the result of a grand strategy of any one party or even a broad social movement but results from developments which are reshaping the politics of the North. In this chapter, we focus on three key changes that are putting a question mark over partition.

BREXIT

Brexit is often viewed in conventional terms and explained purely in terms of the actions of leading political personalities. In the mainstream Irish press, there is a narrative that stupid British workers became Trump-style racists and rejected the progressive and liberal EU. The EU is referred to as 'our partners' who supported Ireland in its negotiations over Brexit. The subtext is that the Irish population should support their own political establishment and not be tempted by 'populists' as the British were. This narrative, however, ignores how Brexit resulted from deep contradictions between British imperialism and some of its rivals inside the EU. More poignantly, it forgets the role that the EU played in forcing people in Ireland to pay for the 're-capitalisation' of the banks. The banking sector had borrowed billions from French and German banks and, when they were unable to repay, this threatened their solvency. In response, the European Central Bank President, Jean Claude Trichet, warned that a 'bomb would go off' in Dublin if the state did not take responsibility for the debts.[2] The political elite naturally obeyed.

There is one aspect of Brexit that is rarely discussed, namely how has the long-term decline of British capitalism conditioned the response of its ruling elite? All indicators show that the country, once the workshop of the world, has fallen well behind its rivals in manufacturing. Between 1973 and 2007, the annual average growth of manufacturing output in Britain was only 0.4 per cent whereas Germany grew by 2.1, France by 2.4 and Japan by 2.2 per cent, respectively.[3] There is a major 'productivity gap' whereby the British worker produced 16 per cent less on average in 2016 than their counterparts elsewhere. In the words of the *Financial Times*, 'Britain's productivity crisis should be keeping the country's politicians and civil servants awake at night.'[4] They point out that a French worker will have produced more by the end of Thursday than their British counterpart will have in a full week. The main cause of this decline has been an historical pattern of lower levels of investment by the employer class. To gain competitive advantage, they rely instead on a low-paid, low-skilled workforce. An OECD study in 2016, for example, found that England has the highest proportion of low-skilled young workers among advanced economies. The picture, however, is not uniform and high salaries are earned in financial services in London, but this has only added to severe regional disparities.

The Conservative Party has long been the main party of big business, but it has also held the political allegiance of a minority of British workers. It promised security, reasonable living standards and stability if the population stayed loyal to queen and country. It was the party of the Union, upholding an imperial tradition that incorporated Northern Ireland, Scotland and Wales. The downward trajectory of British capitalism, however, is mirrored in the decline in size, confidence and coherence of the Tories. The Tories are an ageing, mainly male and thoroughly upper-class party where the over-65s, for example, constitute 40 per cent of their membership.[5] Many of these live off forms of rentier income and they want their dividends to flow in annually. They invest in the City of London and expect a regular income as their fund managers scour the world for profitable returns.

Initially, the EU proved to be a major boon for those who lived off finance as the City of London became the continent's centre for 'light regulation' and tax dodging. Money from all over world flowed into the coffers of its finance houses, which were then able to 'passport' their services throughout the EU. Even financial deals conducted in the Euro, a currency which Britain did not join, were 'booked' in London. Most of the EU's foreign exchange trading and hedge fund assets were held in the City of London. Only a small cut flowed into the pockets of the local dealers, but as this came from a massive amount of financial activity, it was enough to featherbed them. After the crash of 2008, however, other EU states increased pressure for greater regulation of finance. France, for example, pushed for a clearing house within the eurozone for financial transactions conducted in that currency and although this represented a threat for the City of London it was by no means a matter of life and death. However, it fed into the rage and resentment of the Tory grassroots as the EU had become a punchbag for their anger over Britain's decline. The EU was a symbol of how 'the foreigners' were taking down Great Britain, and its 'red tape' was apparently strangling their entrepreneurial spirit.

In normal times, the ruling elite have a stable support base in a right-wing party that champions private property and the market. The big business leaders rarely involve themselves in day-to-day politics but draw on an activist base of barristers, auctioneers and estate agents who, most of the time, remain deferential and loyal to their betters. In times of crisis, however, this easy fit between the economic elite and their political servants comes unstuck. This is one of the features of late capitalism and reflects its deepening instability because the base of many conservative parties is rebelling – by moving further right. This pattern of radicalisation has occurred in other countries such as the US, Brazil and Hungary and involves familiar themes. There is a call for a return to national greatness, a deep hostility to migrants, a yearning for white supremacy, a growth of conspiracy theories, a resentment against sexual openness and a return to family values. In India, it takes a somewhat different form as a secretive fascist organisation, the RSS, achieves a growing dominance in the ruling BJP party and carries out attacks against the Muslim minority. By injecting a radicalised right-wing discourse into political debates, conservative parties hope to reconnect to an electorate that has seen its living standards decline. The 'culture wars' become a substitute for the failure of the economic system to bring real benefits. But they can also have dysfunctional effects, as the British case illustrates.

The core of the British ruling class wanted to remain in the EU because they knew that many of Britain's export markets were in the EU and that the City of London – despite minor attempts to restrict its activities – was benefiting. The top brass of the civil service, of the army and of the political elite also knew that Britain's geopolitical interests were best served by Remain. In post-austerity Britain, however, the chains that linked the 'natural leaders' of British capitalism to their petty bourgeois activist base snapped. An increasingly shrill Eurosceptic wing of the Conservative Party developed a rhetoric which mixed the lack of democracy in the EU with resentment against foreign migrant labour. To their own surprise, they won because this rhetoric connected with millions of workers who were fed up with low pay and insecurity. Many wanted to give two fingers to the 'establishment', and they thought Leave was the best way to do it. Hence Brexit.

The EU faced its own problems, and this conditioned its response to the aftermath of Brexit. Before the economic crisis of 2008, its attempt to create a new constitution was spectacularly defeated in France and Holland and efforts to reframe this as the Lisbon Treaty were initially rejected in Ireland. Later, the Irish were intimidated into voting again to give the correct Yes answer. To put it mildly, the EU had a problem in terms of popular legitimacy. This intensified after the economic crash as voters in the PIIGS countries – Portugal, Ireland, Italy, Greece and Spain – watched as the rhetoric about European solidarity was replaced with a demand for austerity and calls to recapitalise banks. In this context, there was a fear that Brexit could become a trigger for a wider break-up of the EU. This was the main reason why the EU took such a hard position in its negotiations with Britain. It wanted to show other countries that leaving the EU would bring negative economic consequences and decided to drive a hard bargain on the terms of Britain's exit. This, more than any sentimental attachment to Irish interests, explains why the EU focused so much on preventing a hard border in Ireland. It knew that opposition to such a border was popular and that it could be used as a lever to try to force Britain to remain in the Single Market and the Customs Union. When this did not work, it turned the pressure up on Britain to allow the North to effectively become a special economic zone that continued to have access to the Single Market. While the EU was exerting this pressure on Britain, many Irish people thought it was acting in 'our interest'. However, many also failed to notice that the EU itself was willing to impose a hard border on the island of Ireland to protect its own interests if negotiations with Britain failed.[6]

The outcome of the conflict revealed a lot about the British elite's perception of Northern Ireland. After a long deadlock in the House of Commons, where it was impossible to achieve any coherence on Britain's negotiating position, the Tory party finally put its fate into the hands of an overconfident charlatan, Boris Johnson. His singular talent has been an ability to lie and smooth over his own contradictions with the panache of an upper-class public-school boy. His primary agenda was to 'Get Brexit Done' so that Britain could become a more deregulated, bargain basement economy with a closer alignment to the US. To do so, he had to escape from the clutches of his predecessor, Theresa May, who had agreed that Britain would effectively remain part of a customs union with the EU until it had found a way to prevent a hard border in Ireland.[7] After his election as leader, Johnson came to the DUP conference in November 2018 and told its delegates that there would not be a separate arrangement for Northern Ireland. There could be no customs border in the Irish Sea because that would leave Northern Ireland as an 'economic semi-colony of the EU'. He added:

> We would be damaging the fabric of the Union with regulatory checks and even customs controls between Great Britain and Northern Ireland... I have to tell you no British Conservative government could or should sign up to any such arrangement.[8]

Eleven months later, Johnson signed a deal that did precisely that. It gave the rest of Britain the freedom to withdraw from a customs union but at the expense of special arrangements for Northern Ireland. To get his deal, Johnson agreed to a new Protocol whereby the province would remain in closer economic alignment with the EU to prevent a hard border between both parts of the island. The result is that the North will be separated from, what unionists consider, the mainland by a border in the Irish Sea. As if to confirm this, the British government submitted applications for Border Control Posts at Northern Ireland's ports, and these will be used to check animals and food arriving in the EU's single market.[9] Subsequently, Johnson introduced an Internal Market Bill giving Britain more power to minimise the effects of this Protocol. Nevertheless, the central point remained clear – the Tories are willing to jettison the concerns of Northern unionists if they stood in the way of the needs of British capitalism.

The political effects of all this on the status of Northern Ireland are enormous because the behaviour of the British Conservative Party has demonstrated in the clearest fashion their contempt for Ireland's unionists. Historically, they have been willing to use the unionists as a social base to halt progressive change in Britain itself. Thus, the early Tory mobilisation against Home Rule was linked to an upper-class revolt against removing the veto powers of the House of Lords. In more recent times, the DUP was co-opted into supporting a Tory government led by Theresa May. During the Brexit debates, the hard-right wing of the Tory party aligned with the DUP to oppose the different proposals on a negotiated settlement with the EU. The DUP, it should be noted, had traditionally viewed the EU as a Catholic super-state or, as Ian Paisley called it, 'the greatest Catholic superstate ever known' and 'the kingdom of the anti-Christ'.[10] At one stage it was thought that winning DUP support for a withdrawal agreement with the EU was important for satisfying the Tory right. However, when it came to the final deal, the DUP and unionist concerns were simply jettisoned as the wider interests of British imperialism in restructuring itself as a global economic power took precedence. The unionist bloc in Northern Ireland was to be used for political purposes and then discarded when appropriate. The contempt was, however, not exclusively directed at unionism. In a rare display of unity, all five parties in Stormont voted to reject Johnson's deal but this had no effect on the Conservative Party.

The emergence of a customs border on the Irish Sea is set to create problems for the Northern Irish economy. Brexit will cause difficulties for agriculture and the food sector as Northern farmers are more reliant on Common Agriculture Payments than their counterparts in the rest of the UK.[11] The withdrawal of these payments after 2022 and the prospect of cheaper food imports to Britain will add to their woes. The imposition of new administrative costs associated with customs arrangements will disadvantage them further. While at the time of writing it is unclear, the chances are that a large amount of paperwork will be required as the North will remain in the UK customs zone but will, at the same time, apply EU customs legislation. To complicate matters further, it will have to apply tariffs on goods that end up in the South of Ireland even though determining the destination of goods will be a bureaucratic nightmare. So, while there is much talk of the North enjoying the best of both worlds, this also acts as a disincentive to foreign investment. One study found that the number of new jobs from foreign investment had fallen by 31 per cent after the Brexit referendum.[12] While this reflected an immediate uncertainty, this will probably continue with the new withdrawal arrangements.

The major impact of Brexit, however, will be in the political sphere. In 2018, Arlene Foster said that a border down the Irish Sea was 'totally unacceptable' to unionists and that 'our red line is blood red'.[13] Yet this is exactly what happened. The sense of betrayal was made worse by the fact that not a single Tory MP – including those on the party's hard right who had aligned with the DUP – voted against the deal. It could not have been made clearer that Northern unionists were simply an afterthought in Britain's wider interests. Unionism has frequently adopted the catch cry of 'betrayal' against Westminster but, in the past, this often came with a demand to be 'more British' or to give extra support to the unionist population. This betrayal is different. There is now physical evidence that the North is not regarded as a proper part of the UK and has been separated out to operate under different economic rules. These rules will draw it closer to the economic orbit of Dublin and Brussels and this has created a major demoralisation in the ranks of unionism as no one can now imagine that the province is as 'British as Finchley', an assertion once attributed to Margaret Thatcher. Moreover, the issue will also not go away because the new arrangements must come up for periodic votes in the Northern Ireland Assembly. The border in the Irish Sea will last until 2024 and can only be removed if a majority vote to end it. Even then, there will be a transition period for a further two years while the UK and the EU reach a new agreement. In effect, the new economic border on the Irish Sea is here to stay.

There is one other way in which Brexit is undermining the partition of Ireland. The vote to Leave was carried overwhelmingly by the English population and marginally in Wales, but Scotland and Northern Ireland voted Remain. Despite this, the Westminster parliament made no attempt to give any recognition to these divergent opinions – even at the level of taking account of their desire for a soft Brexit. The main reason is that the Tory radicalisation has brought with it a deeper immersion into English nationalism. In the general election of 2015, for example, the Tories ran a campaign to keep Scottish nationalists out of government and one of the images was a poster of Alex Salmond, then leader of the Scottish Nationalist Party, in a black turtleneck picking the wallet out of an English voter's back pocket. The whipping up of chauvinist opposition in England against the Scots led one journalist to conclude that the 'Scots were being bracketed with benefits scroungers and immigrants as undesirables'.[14] So deep is the interconnection between right-wing radicalism and English nationalism that a full 63 per cent of Conservative members told a YouGov survey that they would back Brexit even if it meant Scotland leaving the UK.[15] Thus while the rightwards shift in the Tory party was aimed at restoring its hegemony, it came at the expense of opening new fractures in the UK itself. There is a real prospect that the break-up of the UK will start with a push for independence in Scotland and as this possibility grows, it will come with demands for the reunification of Ireland.

How to assess these developments? Many on the left who take a mechanical view of history think that progress only comes from struggle over the bread and butter issues that affect working people. The implicit hope is that one day the contending classes will line up for a good clean fight on issues of economic justice. From this perspective, the demand for Scottish independence or the call for Irish unity represent an unfortunate upsurge of nationalism. However, nationalism is not some sort of ethereal spirit that invades people's souls. Instead, different forms of nationalism develop in specific social conditions and in particular historical periods. In the mid-nineteenth century, for example, German nationalism was often associated with a demand for democracy and national unification, but in the age of empire it became a cover to justify colonial oppression and racism. Rather than abstractly denouncing nationalism, it is necessary to look at its real social content and to recognise that there is the nationalism of the dominant and the nationalism of the oppressed. It makes little sense, for example, to claim that Palestinian nationalism is equivalent to a nationalism which aspires to a greater Israeli state in occupied territories. Thus, while challenging the mythology of all nationalisms that 'we are all in it together', it is necessary to distinguish between different types.

Far worse than the banal cries of Scottish nationalism is the potent mix of empire nostalgia and anti-migrant racism that lies at the heart of English nationalism. This is being stoked up by a Tory party that has little to offer its population in terms of real improvements in their lives. The bold assertion of English nationalism, particularly in the context of Brexit, is creating the conditions for Scottish independence. If that were to occur and lead to the break-up of the UK it would be a welcome development. The left would, certainly, have to work even harder to puncture illusions that Scottish millionaires and workers are in the same boat or that 'independence within the EU' would bring tangible economic gains. Nevertheless, Scottish independence would weaken Anglo-American imperialism which has been responsible for so many devastating wars. It would puncture the London establishment's self-image of 'greatness' and its natural right to rule. And it would help put an end to Britain's interference in its neighbouring island and speed the way to Irish reunification.

DEMOGRAPHY

It is not often that a census of the population has an explosive political effect yet Northern Ireland is hardly a normal society and the Census of Population, due in 2021, will probably indicate that Protestants have become a minority. As this will be published on the centenary of the official foundation of a state designed to create a 'Protestant State for a Protestant' population, it will have destabilising ideological effects. Let's look at the facts first and then examine the political implications.

In the 2011 Census, Protestants or – an important caveat – those brought up as Protestant no longer made up more than half the population. Some 48 per cent of the Northern Irish population were Protestant, or brought up Protestant, while 45 per cent were Catholic or brought up Catholic. Six per cent stated that they neither belonged to any religion nor were they brought up in any religion. However, the religious affiliation of people is not spread evenly over the province and when the geographical spread of religious affiliation was examined, it found that only two of the original six counties had a significant Protestant majority – Antrim and Down. Moreover, only Lisburn of the five official cities of Northern Ireland had a Protestant majority, while Belfast has become a majority Catholic city. As one study put it, 'In effect, a "majority Protestant Ireland" is now restricted to the suburban areas surrounding Belfast.'[16]

There are good grounds for believing that the trends will continue and accelerate into the future. If we look at the school-going population, the annual survey show that Catholics make up 50 per cent of those attending schools while the number of Protestants has dropped to 37 per cent. A similar picture of change applies to the working age population, defined as those aged between 16 and 64 years of age. In 2001, Protestants made up 60 per cent of the monitored workforce and Catholics composed 40 per cent. By 2017 this had changed so that Protestants formed 51 per cent and Catholics formed 49 per cent.[17] In general, the Protestant population is older and they form a much more stable majority in those aged over 60. In the 60+ age bracket the Protestant/Catholic ratio stands at 57:35.[18]

So much for the bare facts but what of its political importance? In a sectarian society which has historically identified with a majority Protestant culture, these changes are disturbing for unionists. One of the main rationales for their political project was the fear that if Protestants were a minority in a 32-county Ireland, they would be overwhelmed and crushed. Yet the prospect of being a minority within Northern Ireland now looms. For some this will add to a defensive siege mentality where every effort must be made to halt the advance of the 'other side'. While that is one conclusion the DUP will undoubtedly project, it is by no means the only response. There can also be aspects of republicanism that can revert to a naked sectarian headcount that was more typical of the Hibernianism of Joe Devlin, the Nationalist Home Ruler of the early part of the twentieth century. This occurred in the 2015 election when Gerry Kelly, the North Belfast Sinn Féin MLA, produced a leaflet with the census figures of Catholics and Protestants to urge voting on nationalist lines. 'Every Vote Counts' screamed a section of leaflet. Few misread the cue that Catholics should vote out 'the other side'.

The growth of the Catholic population does not equate with a demand for a united Ireland. Religious affiliation is an important marker of political identity because of the way the Northern state is structured, but the link between religion and national sovereignty is not absolute. In the 2011 census, just over half of those Catholic, or brought up Catholic, claimed an exclusive Irish identity. Added to this is that a small section of the Catholic population are migrants who have been mainly estranged from the fractious nature of the North's tribal politics. About 5 per cent of the North's Catholic population falls into this category and in the working age population it rises to 10 per cent. Given these basic facts, a 'count the Catholics' approach to politics will not yield significant movement towards a united Ireland. It depends on politics and not demography.

The most significant change in the North's demography is the growth of the category known as 'other or non-determined'. This now represents 18 per cent of the working age population which represents an incredible tripling since 1990. The sectarian lens by which the North views itself and is viewed by others is so strong that the focus is often placed on the Protestant/Catholic ratio rather than those, for whatever reason, refuse to designate themselves in this way. Yet the growth in this category is linked to an increase in youth disillusionment about the politics of the North. The British Council's *Next Generation* report found that low pay, the lack of jobs and work security worry four out of five of Northern Ireland's young people. These worries have led to major concerns about mental health and one third said they had no trust in Northern Ireland Assembly politicians.[19] The structuring of politics around the sectarian divide means that many of the concerns of young people are marginalised, leading to further alienation.

This shifting demography has started to produce interesting responses. The DUP leader, Arlene Foster, has been forthright exclaiming that if ever a united Ireland becomes a possibility, 'I would probably have to move.'[20] She was sending out a signal that every small advance by nationalists will occasion a vigorous response from her party and that everything will be done to halt any move towards a united Ireland. Her predecessor, Peter Robinson, however, took a different approach, arguing at the 2018 McGill Summer School in Donegal that unionists should prepare for the possibility of a united Ireland.[21] It was a statement that rattled his former political supporters but they seemed to have misread his intention. Using an analogy, Robinson was declaring that unionists needed an insurance policy lest the unlikely happen and his purpose was to encourage his former party colleagues to think strategically. They had to make a positive case to win over those who did not identify with a Protestant state and, if having done that they failed, they needed to make sure that they got the best deal possible in a united Ireland. It was a move designed to alert unionists to the new possibilities that were emerging in the future.

THE SOUTHERN WIND OF CHANGE

The partition of Ireland rested on two states which were mirror images of each other. The Northern state was Protestant and the Southern was Catholic and this binary divide enabled conservative politicians to dominate their own electorates by pointing to the threats from the other. Nationalist politicians in the South warned against alien pro-British influences coming from Belfast while unionist politicians warned against Papist culture that would swamp their liberties. Yet while they expressed great hostility to each other, they were united in marginalising the left and developing deeply conservative cultures. At almost every Orange parade there were denunciations of 'communism', meaning any sort of independent working-class politics. In the South, the bishops made every effort to inoculate the population against the same left-wing ideas, denouncing even mild social democratic measures such as a national health service. Unionism, in particular, needed the image of an aggressive Catholic Church that controlled a backward population to uphold partition. Today, however, there is a powerful wind of change blowing through the South.

The scale can be captured by two referenda. In 2015, Ireland became the first country in the world to vote for same-sex marriage by popular suffrage. If there was any doubt about the defeat inflicted on the Catholic Church, one only had to look at its response. Archbishop Eamon Martin said the Catholic Church felt a sense of 'bereavement', while the Vatican secretary of state, Cardinal Pietro Parolin, declared it a 'defeat for humanity'.[22] In 2018, the Catholic bishops intervened strongly in a referendum to repeal a ban on abortion, with one, Bishop Doran, claiming it was a sin to vote in favour and urging those voting Yes to go to confession. Yet the population voted by a landslide, a two-thirds majority, to legalise abortion. If there was any doubt that the Southern population were still in thrall to the Catholic Church, these two referenda dispelled that myth.

Irish Catholicism is, in fact, declining even though, nominally, 78 per cent of the population declared themselves Catholic in the census published in 2016. This data is, however, often completed by the 'head of the household' who defines the religion of their teenage sons and daughters. It does not pick up on how religious practice has fallen dramatically with only one third of declared Catholics attending mass on a regular basis, while in the Dublin area the figure is even lower at 14 per cent.[23] Vocations have almost collapsed with just six people training for the priesthood at Maynooth in 2017. At the high point of Irish Catholicism, every respectable family hoped that one of its sons would enter the priesthood and, possibly, join the great missionary project of converting 'Godless' Russia or the 'black babies' of Africa. During the 1940s and 1950s there were over 20,000 members of religious orders but today there are fewer than 2,000 priests and their average age is 65 and rising.

The rapidity of the change is even more remarkable because the Catholic Church has never faced sustained political opposition and the contrast with the French left and liberal secular tradition could not be more pronounced. The Catholic Church in France was identified with the *ancien régime* of feudal privilege and, throughout most of the nineteenth century it was seen as a supporter of the aristocracy and a defender of the worst form of reaction, including anti-Semitism. As a result, republicans knew that they had to combat its influence if they were to hold political power. In a major speech in 1900, for example, the French premier, Waldeck-Rousseau, warned about how church representatives were 'doing their best to make their pupils hostile to the Republic and to republican ideals'.[24] As a defensive measure, republican governments enacted a series of laws to create a more secular society. In 1882, religious education was banned from French schools; in 1886 priests were banned from schools, and in 1905 the formal separation of church and state was declared in France.

In Ireland no major political force opposed church control. The main reason was the ambiguous role that the Catholic Church had historically played in a colonised country. Until the end of the eighteenth century, the Catholic religion was targeted in a series of penal laws imposed by the Protestant Ascendancy. Catholics were barred from inheriting Protestant land; excluded from occupying public office; forbidden to marry Protestants; banned from entering Trinity College. As a result, the Catholic Church took on all the appearance of an oppressed church and adherence to Catholicism became a sign of resistance to colonialism. However, British colonial strategy in Ireland changed after the French Revolution and it sought to incorporate the Catholic hierarchy by supporting the training of priests in Maynooth and promoting denominational control of schooling. One result was an increase in the size and strength of the institutional church and while previously Irish Catholicism had a much looser structure, this changed dramatically. The Catholic Church grew in power, and even though it received support from Westminster it continued its verbal opposition to 'Protestant England'. Even as the bishops denounced 'secret societies' like the Fenians, some of the lower clergy joined movements like the Land League or supported the Irish language revival movement Conradh na Gaeilge. One result of this ambiguous legacy was that after independence there was no sustained political opposition to the church role in Irish society.

Twentieth-century Irish republicanism differed from French republicanism in refusing to challenge the Catholic Church. The United Irishmen had originally called for the 'unity of Catholic, Protestant and Dissenter' and the Fenian movement declared in favour of 'absolute liberty of conscience', and complete separation of church and state.[25] But latter-day Irish republicanism became increasingly imbued with a Catholic ethos and culture. Faced with condemnation of its armed struggle, republicans typically responded with anti-clericalism – rather than outright opposition to the role of the Catholic Church in Irish society. Republican leaders remained devout Catholics and, even while they were condemned by bishops and cardinals, found sympathetic individual priests as their confessors. Throughout its history Sinn Féin ensured that its politics did not challenge the Catholic Church in any fundamental way. In 1931, for example, the IRA Army Convention adopted a radical Saor Eire programme written by Peadar O'Donnell, but after a ferocious assault by the bishops, a subsequent Sinn Féin Ard Fheis, disassociated the movement from 'anti-Christian principles' and promised a social order based on the ideals of Popes Pius V and Leo XIII.[26] In the early 1950s, Sinn Féin adopted a 'national unity and independence programme' which 'promised a reign of social justice based on Christian principles'.[27] The republican fighter Sean South is celebrated in song for his attack on an RUC barracks, but less well known is his membership of the Catholic fundamentalist movement Maria Duce and his activities in chasing courting couples out of cinemas. The early Provisional IRA often said the rosary at its funerals. More recently, former Sinn Féin leader Martin McGuinness stated that his party was opposed to abortion 'on demand' but its support for abortion in certain limited circumstances was not 'incompatible with Catholicism'.[28]

Irish social democracy has taken an even more supine relationship to the Catholic bishops as leaders of the Irish unions and the Labour Party proclaimed their loyalty to the Catholic hierarchy for decades. In the 1940s, for example, the Irish Transport and General Workers' Union formed an alliance with Fianna Fáil and the *Catholic Standard* to attack Larkinism and communism. It encouraged a split in the Labour Party and helped to create a National Labour Party which 'was clear and definite on fundamentals intertwined with Faith and Nationality'.[29] The official Labour Party, from which it had split, was hardly less loyal to the same principles. In the early 1950s, it joined the bishops in opposing Noel Browne's Mother and Child scheme which would have given them free medical care.[30] Even when Labour shifted left in the late 1960s and proclaimed that 'the seventies would be socialist' its leader Brendan Corish was a member of the Knights of Columbanus, an elite and secretive Catholic organisation. He stated that he was a Catholic first, an Irishman second and a socialist third. He added, 'If the hierarchy gives me any direction as regard to Catholic social teaching or Catholic moral teaching, I accept without qualification in all respects the teaching of the Hierarchy and the Church to which I belong.'[31]

Given this extraordinary history, the question arises as to why the Catholic Church declined so rapidly. When Pope John Paul visited in 1979 a staggering 2.5 million people or half the population turned out to greet him. Even as late as 1983, when Catholic fundamentalists were able to push through the Eighth Amendment to the Irish constitution to equate the life of a woman to that of a foetus, active opposition came only from the radical left and a handful of liberals. In 1986, the Catholic Church was able to stop the removal of a ban on divorce from the constitution. Although the proposal was to only allow divorce after five years of separation, it was defeated by 63 to 37 per cent. Yet just over a decade later the Catholic Church had entered a period of crisis and decline.

One possible cause of its decline was a series of revelations concerning the number of priests and bishops who were implicated in sexual scandals and child abuse. Key figures, such as Bishop Eamonn Casey and Fr Michael Cleary, who preached a morality of sexual abstinence outside marriage, were discovered to have fathered children which they then hid away. In hindsight, these transgressions were fairly innocent compared to what followed. By the 1990s, there came a slew of child abuse cases involving priests and clear evidence that the Church hierarchy had colluded in cover-ups. At first it was a 'few bad apples' but as the numbers multiplied, it became obvious that there was a subterranean culture within the Catholic clergy that facilitated such shocking activity. One researcher pointed out the social context was 'a sexual underworld for the "normal" clergy and the unhealthy organisational culture, in which problems of sexuality arise'.[32] However, clerical child abuse did not start in the 1990s. In schools many, but tragically not all, children had long learnt, often through word of mouth, how to avoid potential abusers.

While the scandals rocked the Catholic Church, there was a deeper cause for its decline, namely that its morality came into conflict with the lived experience of the mass of people in a rapidly industrialising society. The rural idyll which the Church and the Southern state held up as a model was in decline long before scandals broke, as the working class had expanded massively and there was a huge exodus from the land. In 1951, 38 per cent of the Irish labour force worked on farms but by 2019 this had declined to 4.6 per cent. Moreover, a very high proportion of the population identify themselves as workers with some 42 per cent regarding themselves as working class, a figure just below the British figure.[33] Ireland has also become an increasingly urbanised society, with 40 per cent of the population living in the greater Dublin area.

In most societies, industrialisation undermines the bonds which link individuals to church and tradition. In Ireland, communal ties were deeply rooted in rural Ireland and produced a particularly strong variant of Irish Catholicism. Brinsley McNamara captured this intense form of conformity in his novel *The Valley of the Squinting Windows* which tells a story of a fictional village, Garradrimna, most probably based on Devlin in Co. Westmeath. It is a tale of shame, gossip and tragedy based on sexual relations stigmatised by Catholicism. However, as Irish people moved off the land in vast numbers, belief systems slowly changed. There is a German expression that 'the city air makes free' and it could not be more appropriate to Ireland, but the process was highly uneven and contradictory. Irish people began, in practice, and often in secret, to break free of Catholic values in their personal lives. In 1971, for example, 63 per cent of the population agreed in a survey that 'contraceptives should be forbidden by law'[34] but at the same time importation of contraceptives grew and younger people began to use them more frequently. Sometimes this occurred under the guise that the pill was a 'cycle regulator' but packets of condoms were also secretly imported from England and the North.

At the heart of these changes was the position of working women. Traditionally, Ireland had one of the lowest numbers of married women in the official workforce, second only to Greece in the EU. However, the multinationals, which spearheaded industrialisation, favoured a disproportionate employment of women and between 1971 and 1991 the number of economically active women increased by 50 per cent while the number of men increased by 10 per cent.[35] With economic independence came a greater desire for free expression of sexuality and control of childbirth.

Writing in 1994, for example, Dympna McLoughlin suggests that there were three main characteristics of the traditional 'respectable Irish woman': 1) an overwhelming desire to marry and to remain faithful, dependent and subordinate; 2) an unquestioning readiness to regard the domestic sphere as her natural habitat and to engage in reproduction rather than production; and 3) a willingness to accept that women's sexuality was confined to marriage. By the time she was writing, all three of these self-definitions had been blown apart.[36]

The growing involvement of women in the paid workforce utterly transformed the image of what constituted a traditional 'respectable woman'. Women began using contraception in greater numbers and planned the number and spacing of children. Fertility rates were halved as the number of births per woman fell from 4 to 1.9 between 1960 and 2000. More and more women left unhappy marriages and had children born outside of marriage. The age of marriage increased and no longer came to be regarded as the only 'legitimate' framework for sexual relations. In 1980, the average age of marriage for the bride was 24 but by 2005 this had risen to 30. The proportion of first births outside marriage grew from 15 per cent in 1980 to 44 per cent in 2005. The number of abortions to women with an Irish address grew from 261 in 1970 to 6,672 by 2001.[37] Despite the bans on abortion, Irish women in the age group 18 to 23 were having the same number of abortions as women in other countries; the difference was that they had to travel to Britain. These dry but quite dramatic figures indicate that the lived experience of tens of thousands of Irish women put them into direct conflict with the values of Catholic Ireland.

First came the practice, then came the anger. Initially, the changes occurred at a subterranean level and they found little expression at a political or institutional level. The conservative parties continued to speak of the dangers of a 'permissive society' and the liberal elements within the elite expressed themselves in the most cautious way possible. The lack of an organised political expression for the changed morality only made spontaneous explosions more likely. The first came in 1992, when tens of thousands mobilised to demand that a 14-year-old rape victim be given the right to travel to Britain for an abortion after a ban on her movement had been imposed by an attorney general who was a member of the Catholic Marriage Advisory Board. It was a glaring example of how the fundamentalists tried to use their institutional positions to stop the tide of liberalism – and how it backfired so spectacularly. Since then the mobilisations have grown in organisation and expression. In 1983, for example, fewer than 200 people marched in a gay rights' demonstration after a homophobic murder in Fairview Park in Dublin. Within two decades, tens of thousands were participating in the annual gay pride events and as the mobilisations increased, so too did the level of anger. Why, many asked, had the Catholic Church a right to interfere in our personal lives? On one level this question dovetailed with an emerging neoliberal discourse of individual choice but at a deeper level, it brought greater numbers into conflict with the power structures of society. Further questions began to be asked which were never even formulated before. Why had the Catholic Church a right to exclude children without a baptismal certificate from schools? Why do young teenagers have to attend religion classes in secondary schools if they do not want to? What right does the Catholic Church have to impose its ethics on medical procedures in hospital?

The political elite have been forced to respond to this anger. The movement for Repeal, for example, was able to mobilise over 20,000 people for its annual demonstrations and was overwhelmingly young. Similarly, the movement for the right to same-sex marriage garnered huge support, forcing political leaders to change their stance. Nothing better symbolises this popular pressure than the figure of Leo Varadkar, often held up as the symbol of a modern progressive Ireland. In 2009, he expressed his distaste for a more moderate Civil Partnership Bill in the following terms:

Two men cannot have a child, two women cannot have a child… That is a fact, nobody can deny otherwise. Every child has a right to a mother and father, and as much as possible, the state should try and vindicate that right, and that the right of a child to have a mother and father is much more important than the right of two men, or two women, to have a family.

However, as anger with the Catholic Church grew and the radical dynamic behind demands for change increased, Varadkar changed his tune. He came out as gay and campaigned for same-sex marriage in the name of individual freedom.

If evidence was ever needed for the potential of social movements then Southern Irish society provides it. Not only did a movement from below bring change, but it also brought with it an implicit challenge to an Ireland that is divided into two states – one for Catholics and one for Protestants. And it was not just implicit. On the very day that a huge crowd gathered in Dublin Castle to hear the official results of the Repeal referendum, the cry went up 'The North is next'.[38] It was a reference to the failure of the Stormont Assembly to enact legislation to give women abortion rights. Buses were organised from across the South for a Belfast demonstration that demanded the repeal of the Offences against the Person Act and free safe and legal abortions. The same spontaneous 32-county attitude was in evidence in response to a horrific rape trial that occurred in Belfast earlier that year when two Ulster rugby players and two of their friends were acquitted on a charge of rape. The woman's evidence which provided harrowing details of her ordeal was not accepted. In response, thousands in Dublin as well as throughout the North joined street protests. These are small but important signs that a 32-county consciousness is developing amongst many young people that see little sense in a partitioned country built around religious identities.

Social movements are by their very nature diffuse and sometimes lack a solid permanent organisational expression. They often burst into the open and then appear to melt away just as quickly. It would be a mistake, however, to think that the movements that gathered around Repeal or Marriage Equality have gone away because they scored victories. There is a strong sentiment against any attempt by the Catholic Church to exert an influence over Irish society and it surfaces periodically. A proposal, for example, to locate the National Maternity Hospital on the grounds of the church-run St Vincent's Hospital met with vigorous opposition. The Sisters of Charity were forced to issue a statement that operations which contravened a Catholic ethos could occur there – and even then anger has not disappeared. Similarly, when a government composed of Fine Gael, Fianna Fáil and the Greens tried to seal away the records of an inquiry into a Mothers and Babies Home scandal, they met a ferocious wave of opposition. Young people will simply not allow the memory of how the Catholic Church used unmarried mothers as slave labour and then stole their babies to be erased. These continuing protests come up against the limits of the new 'progressive' image of Southern politicians but also point to something deeper: namely, that a generation is growing up which is in open rebellion against the conservatism in which the whole island of Ireland was enchained for decades. When social movements arise, they naturally adopt a 32-county outlook because many see that the evangelicals in the DUP and Catholic fundamentalists are mirror images of each other. They offer a different vision of a united Ireland that goes far beyond traditional nationalist images of 're-taking a fourth green field'.

All of these factors contribute to why the question of the Irish border is re-emerging in the twenty-first century. Brexit is destabilising the United Kingdom and raising real possibilities of its future break-up. Even before this occurs the British elite have displayed their contempt for unionists by drawing a customs border in the Irish Sea. Within the North, there has been significant demographic change that unsettles the notion of a Protestant state for a Protestant people. Yet demography does not translate into politics and there can be different reactions to such a change. If the issue is posed in terms of the North joining, or being forced to join, a conservative Catholic South, there would be an all-class Protestant mobilisation to prevent it but, fortunately, these are no longer the only choices on offer. The social movements which have changed the South of Ireland offer new possibilities of a very different Ireland to the one envisaged by Carson or de Valera. Whether or not that will occur will depend on political forces and it is in that contestation that the left can play a major role, provided it knows how to approach the national question from a distinct socialist viewpoint.

7
The Left and Irish Unity

When the issue of partition or Irish unity is discussed, most people think of Sinn Féin. The party wants a 32-county republic and although their tactics and policies have changed, this remains their overriding goal. After the IRA armed struggle ended, Sinn Féin switched its emphasis to a border poll, and this was quite logical. After all, if it is legitimate to aspire to a united Ireland, there needs to be a mechanism through which this could occur. As republicans were told repeatedly that the armed struggle was undemocratic, they, and many in the wider nationalist population, want an alternative route to Irish unity. Yet more than 20 years after the Belfast Agreement, a border poll is resolutely opposed by the political establishment in Britain and Ireland.

The main argument deployed is that such a poll would be 'divisive' and no doubt it would be – but so too are all referenda because they divide an electorate into Yes and No camps. A similar argument was used to stop a referendum on repealing the Eighth Amendment to the Irish Constitution for many years. In 2015, for example, Clare Daly TD moved a bill in Dáil Éireann to give women with a fatal foetal abnormality a right to abortion. It was voted down as 'unconstitutional' but her opponents claimed there was no mandate to hold a referendum to change the constitution.[1] It took a further three years of intense pressure to force the political establishment to grant that referendum. One of the arguments about 'divisiveness' caused by a border poll is that loyalists would kick up a stink if it were allowed, including the threat of violence. There may indeed be some element of truth to this. However, the issue is rarely posed the other way: if Britain refused a border poll, despite agreeing to it 20 years ago as a carrot to entice republicans to end armed struggle, what would the consequences be on the nationalist end? All movements for progressive change divide people because they upset those who want to maintain the status quo and embolden those who want change. A border poll is no different and is a basic democratic right.

However, do Sinn Féin have the policy and strategies to bring about a united, non-sectarian Ireland? While the republican leadership are sometimes seen as shrewd strategic thinkers, the actual record is not so clear. Over the course of a 30-year history in which the IRA emerged as armed guerrillas within the Catholic ghettoes, it deployed four major strategies. The first phase from 1972 to 1975 was an economic bombing campaign aimed at forcing Britain to the negotiating table and extracting a declaration to withdraw. Such was the level of optimism about this purely military strategy that in 1974 *An Phoblacht* ran the headline 'Brits Get Ready to Pull Out'.[2] The Sinn Féin President Ruairí Ó Brádaigh told his Ard Fheis that he was concerned about the possibility of a 'secret or sudden withdrawal' and did not want them to leave 'without proper plans or precautions'.[3] Yet far from the British intending to withdraw, they only entered negotiations with the IRA to divide, scope and marginalise them.

The second strategic phase lasted from 1976 to 1987 and was led by a new Belfast-based leadership around Gerry Adams. This involved a long war with the reorganisation of the IRA around a cell structure, accompanied by a militant and leftist rhetoric as this speech from Jimmy Drumm in 1977 indicates:

We are not prepared even to discuss any watering down of our demands. We can see no future in participating in a re-structured Stormont, even with power sharing and a Bill of Rights. Nor certainly will we ever accept the legitimacy of the Free State, a fascist state designed to cater for the privileged capitalist sycophants.[4]

The current involvement of Sinn Féin in the Stormont Executive and its call for inclusion in the government of the South would indicate that the party has done an about-turn on this stance. This strategy was also a failure as the British managed to contain the long war.

The third strategic phase, which lasted from 1987 to 2005, was based on pan-nationalism and decommissioning. The strategic aim was to 'construct an Irish nationalist consensus with international support' and as it was believed that this helped broker the Belfast Agreement, the IRA agreed to decommissioning.[5] But while this led to growing electoral support for Sinn Féin, it also contained 'bitter pills' that republicans had to swallow. Danny Morrison, the party's talented propagandist, acknowledged that they had to accept 'the implicit recognition of the principle of unionist consent on the constitutional question'.[6] Later he added to the list:

Republicans sit in an assembly they never wanted. The British government never gave a declaration of intent to withdraw. There is still a heavy British army presence in nationalist areas. The police have not been reformed. The equality and justice issues have yet to be resolved.[7]

The fourth phase from 2005 to the present has been to focus on building in the South and here the party has had some success. In 1997, it won 2.7 per cent of the popular vote in a general election but the peace process and a change of leadership has led to major expansion since. In the 2020 election it won 25 per cent of the vote and made even more substantial gains among young people. Its rhetoric of directly appealing to workers caught a mood of opposition to the domination Fine Gael and Fianna Fáil have incredibly exercised over Irish politics for over seven decades. The party is now the main opposition in the Dáil and, depending on the circumstances, could be leading the next Southern government. How it will deal with this situation is still an open question, as its leadership has on several occasions stated their willingness to go into government with either of the two conservative parties.[8] It is a tribute both to the loyalty of its support base and the strong desire for change that Sinn Féin has grown despite its past strategic failures. The question, however, remains, how exactly does the party see that it will advance towards a united Ireland.

An insight can be gleaned from a series of articles and statements from its former leader Gerry Adams, who remains a key advocate of its united Ireland strategy. Adams claims that his 'core argument' is the 'need to move those parties (Fianna Fail, Fine Gael and Labour) which aspire to Irish unity beyond their traditional republican rhetoric and to get them involved in the real work of planning for unity'.[9] He reminds them that 'The Irish government has a duty and a constitutional obligation to make preparations for unity'.[10] The Irish government has, therefore, become the main agent in ending partition and the duty of all nationalist parties is to unite with them in bringing this about. Adams states this explicitly, 'The Irish government has a key leadership role in this. There is a need for the rest of us – whatever our electoral differences and competitiveness on other issues – to work together for unity'.[11] Lest anyone think that this represents a change in Sinn Féin's position, Adams quotes from a keynote speech he made in 1998, where he spelled out his desire for 'an alliance of Irish political parties, with the Irish government playing a leadership role and with a common position worked out between Dublin, the SDLP and Sinn Féin.[12] How such a pan-nationalist alliance led by the Irish government could attract unionists into a united Ireland is not explained. Adams merely outlines that a 'plan' needs to be developed which would outline the economic, cultural and political changes needed. One crucial new element, however, is the appeal to the EU. Whereas previously Sinn Féin took a critical stance, Adams now believes there is a need to 'engage with our friends and neighbours in Europe'.[13] Referring to the growing conflict between Britain and the EU, he notes that the EU has already promised that in the event of unity, the North would be automatically admitted to the EU.

This is a strategy to build an 'agreed Ireland' from above and it is not a plan for radical change as the main levers are the Irish political establishment and their allies in Europe. A useful way of illustrating this might be to look at Antonio Gramsci's concept of the 'passive revolution' as applied to the Risorgimento or the Italian unification of 1861. The unity of the peninsula might have occurred from below if Garibaldi and the Action Party had been able to galvanise the peasantry and link the cause of unity with real improvements to their lives. Italy, however, was united from above by an existing state, Piedmont, and a conservative politician, Cavour. Drawing a sharp contrast with the Jacobin spirit of the French Revolution, Gramsci borrowed the concept of a passive revolution from a Neapolitan conservative, Vincenzo Cuoco, to denote a process whereby there is a compromise with an older ruling class rather than a radical transformation. It meant that:

> It was possible to preserve the political and economic position of the old feudal class, to avoid agrarian reform and especially to avoid the popular masses going through a period of political experience such as occurred in France in the years of Jacobinism, in 1831 and in 1848.[14]

The point is not to draw a direct analogy between the unification of a major European country in the nineteenth century and modern Ireland. Left-wing writers have too often a weakness for trying to impose categories drawn from historical cases onto current specific situations. Nevertheless, as a general sensitising concept, there is an insight to be gleaned from Gramsci. We can state this simply – if Irish unity is to pioneered by an Irish government and its nationalist allies, there is little prospect of radical change because a Southern elite who espoused Irish unity is hardly likely to give up their privileges. There is little prospect, for example, that they will dismantle the tax haven they have carefully constructed and as a consequence, there is little hope that they will fund proper public services that give citizens high-quality support. Moreover, despite their current image as 'progressive', the Southern state still relies on a school system that is run by the Catholic Church and there is little prospect that they will take over these schools and jettison a church that served them so well. Even in the context of the Italian Risorgimento, quite significant changes took place: albeit with the privileges of the old ruling class intact. It might have been a passive revolution but there was still a major period of political turmoil. The 'agreed Ireland' perspective could amount to much less: in other words, not even a passive revolution that leads to a unitary state and an end to the Northern state but rather a continuation of two existing regimes.

This, of course, is assuming that the Southern political establishment is persuaded to try to end partition. There are good grounds for thinking otherwise – notably, their record over the hundred years of partition which indicates that their primary goal was to inculcate in their population a loyalty to the Southern state – in other words, to generate a quasi-26-county nationalism. Historically, Northern Ireland was projected as an alien place, subject to outside influences. Nationalist rhetoric about partition was deployed periodically but this was only to suggest a memory of an historic wrong caused by the 'old enemy' and was designed to unite the Southern population. Even when Fianna Fáil was articulating a desire to retake its fourth green field, it was engaged in covert arrangements with security forces in the North to harass, intern and arrest republicans. At a most basic level, the Southern elite understood that the removal of partition could destabilise their state and open possibilities for the type of unification from below discussed by Gramsci. Given a choice between stability and ending partition, they would choose the former.

Assigning to the Southern state the role of the prime mover for Irish unity, therefore, faces considerable difficulties. But what if Sinn Féin managed to persuade the Southern establishment to live up to their constitutional duty? They might have to join a government with Fianna Fáil or Fine Gael, or even the Labour Party, to move them along on this path. However, what would such a government say to the Protestant population? No doubt, they could offer guarantees to respect Protestant rights and culture in a new Ireland but what exactly constitutes such a 'culture'? In one of his less publicised predictions, Gerry Adams suggested that there would be 'continued devolution to Belfast within an all-island structure' and because 'Orange is one of our national colours' and 'there will be Orange parades in a united Ireland'.[15] While this might be interpreted as an attempt to offer a hand of friendship across the sectarian divide, it also assumes that the divide will still exist. The new Ireland, it would appear, might contain elements of the old, not least a tradition of bigotry and sectarianism. The much-vaunted motto of Wolfe Tone 'to unite Catholic, Protestant and Dissenter under the common name of Irishman' has been replaced with one of holding on to sectarian identities on an island that has only achieved territorial unity. Even this assumes such inducements would elicit a positive response from Protestants. But why would 884,000 Protestants want to join with a Southern state that cannot offer its own population a decent health service? Would they not assume that in the new Ireland the boot would be on the other foot and they would face discrimination? Would they really believe sweet words about 'respect for diversity' from former IRA operatives and their allies in a Southern nationalist government? To put matters mildly, there are problems with Sinn Féin's concept of a 'passive revolution' forged by the Southern state. All of this indicates that there is a need for a different vision of how partition can be ended – one that is not based on loyalty to the Southern state but is rooted in the tradition of James Connolly.

THE CONNOLLY TRADITION

The radical left in Ireland is comparatively small but it is growing, with People Before Profit, for example, holding elected positions in both the Dáil and Stormont. Its future progress will depend on its ability to advance a distinctive socialist position on the national question and one of the ways of doing this is to recover much of the politics of Ireland's first Marxist leader, James Connolly.

Connolly was both a fervent socialist and a committed anti-imperialist. While his involvement in the 1916 rebellion brought him into the pantheon of Irish nationalist heroes, his socialism was largely forgotten. Shortly after his arrival in Ireland, however, he proclaimed his disdain for simple-minded nationalists who just wanted either political independence or Home Rule:

Ireland without her people is nothing to me, and the man who is bubbling over with love and enthusiasm for 'Ireland', and can yet pass unmoved through our streets and witness all the wrong and the suffering, the shame and the degradation wrought upon the people of Ireland, aye, wrought by Irishmen upon Irishmen and women, without burning to end it, is, in my opinion, a fraud and a liar in his heart, no matter how he loves that combination of chemical elements which he is pleased to call 'Ireland'.[16]

This class anger was combined with a belief that socialists could not simply abstain from the national question. Prior to his arrival in Belfast, socialists tended to take different stances, with most of those from a Protestant background supporting the Union while those who came from a Catholic background backed Home Rule. One's identity shaped the response to the empire, while, as a socialist, one united on economic issues. Connolly regarded this abstention as cowardly and insisted that all socialists – no matter where they came from – should oppose empire and advocate independence. Against the Tories and unionists, they should defend measures to grant Home Rule, inadequate as it might be. However, they should do so from a distinct position.

They should oppose the 'union of classes' which was inherent in nationalist politics and by this Connolly meant calls for national unity that cut across the class divide. He pointed out that when people revolted against oppression, they rarely confined themselves to one injustice and so a revolt against empire would widen out into a full-scale cry for liberation. It is ridiculous, he wrote, to 'talk of revolting against British rule and refuse to recognise the fact that our way to freedom can only be hewn by the strong hand of labour and that labour revolts against oppression of all kinds'.[17] Attempts to bring the privileged into a national movement could only come at the expense of restraining the poor. To illustrate the fallacy of the all-class movement approach, Connolly wrote his masterpiece, *Labour and Irish History*. By looking at the different revolts in Irish history, Connolly sought to show that the wealthier elements of Irish society were more frightened of the poor and when they led a fight against the empire, they did so timidly and with an eye to maintaining a garrison that protected their interests. Given this class dynamic, Connolly argued that the fight for national freedom needed to culminate in the establishment of a socialist republic.

It may be pleaded that the ideal of a Socialist Republic, implying, as it does, a complete political and economic revolution would be sure to alienate all our middle-class and aristocratic supporters, who would dread the loss of their property and privileges.

What does this objection mean? That we must conciliate the privileged classes in Ireland! But you can only disarm their hostility by assuring them that in a free Ireland their privileges will not be interfered with. That is to say, you must guarantee that when Ireland is free of foreign domination, the green-coated Irish soldiers will guard the fraudulent gains of capitalist and landlord from 'the thin hands of the poor' just as remorselessly and just as effectually as the scarlet-coated emissaries of England do today. On no other basis will the classes unite with you. Do you expect the masses to fight for this ideal?[18]

While these views represented his general orientation, his appointment as a union organiser in Belfast forced him to confront the reality of working-class division as sectarian rioting became more common. In July 1912, for example, 3,000 workers were expelled from their jobs in Belfast after Carson stoked up his violent opposition to Home Rule. Connolly's approach was to regard Orangeism as a reactionary and sectarian ideology – even when held by thousands of Protestant workers. In an article written in 1913, he reported on how a union excursion was attacked by shipyard workers because the Irish Transport and General Workers had their headquarters in Dublin 'and [were] therefore what is known in Belfast as Fenians'.[19] Sectarian hostility translated into a wider opposition to left-wing ideas so that even socialists who did not support Home Rule were prevented from holding meetings in any 'exclusively Orange district'. Far from ducking the issue of Home Rule, Connolly denounced the 'political ruffianism of Edward Carson' which had 'broken whatever class solidarity ever existed in the city'.[20] Recognising that his own position would arouse 'passions immensely more bitter' than had ever been met by socialists in Dublin, he still concluded that 'a real socialist movement cannot be built by temporising in front of a dying cause as that of the Orange ascendancy, even though in the paroxysms of its death it assumes the appearance of health'.[21] Here Connolly was drawing a distinction between an *ideology* held by many workers and their *interests*. Workers could support ideas propagated by their rulers, even when these ran contrary to their interests and socialists had to challenge them, no matter how unpopular that might be. Connolly's central point was that by dividing workers and aligning some of them behind the Tory party, Orangeism was an anti-working-class ideology. An analogy from today might be how US socialists respond to the fact some white workers attack the Black Lives Matter movement and support Trump. Generally, they oppose any form of white supremacism, even if a substantial number of workers in some states adhere to such views. They see this ideology as the primary cause of division between black and white workers.

Connolly's reference to the 'paroxysms of death' of the Orange ideology proved to be false. He predicted also that Home Rule would be implemented and a united working class could then emerge. By 1914, however, after the leaders of Ireland's nationalist movement agreed to partition, Connolly had a dark sense of foreboding. The division of Ireland would bring about a 'carnival of reaction'[22] and he suggested that:

Filled with the belief that they were after defeating the Imperial Government and the Nationalists combined, the Orangemen would have scant regards for the rights of the minority left at their mercy. Such a scheme would destroy the Labour movement by disrupting it. It would perpetuate in a form aggravated in evil the discords now prevalent and help the Home Rule and Orange capitalists and clerics to keep their rallying cries before the public as the political watchwords of the day. In short, it would make division more intense and confusion of ideas and parties more confounded.[23]

Connolly proposed two ways to address the rupture between the ideology of Protestant workers and their class interests. First, he called for special propaganda 'for the conversion to socialism of Orangemen' with special emphasis on challenging the myth that the Orange Order stood for civil and religious liberty.[24] However, forging workers' unity was not simply a matter of words. He encouraged Catholic and Protestant workers to fight alongside each other in their day-to-day economic battles. While openly opposing Orangeism, Connolly's union, the ITGWU, recruited workers from the Larne aluminium plant even though the town was a bastion for these ideas. He did so because of its reputation for militancy. However, while Connolly often had a syndicalist outlook which assumed that economic unity translated into political unity, he also had a vision of what type of

Ireland might attract Protestant workers. There had to be a break from an economic policy based on low wages to attract foreign capital:

> When the Sinn Feiner speaks to men who are fighting against low wages and tells them that the Sinn Fein body has promised lots of Irish labour at low wages to any foreign capitalist who wished to establish in Ireland, what wonder if they come to believe that a change from Toryism to Sinn Feinism would simply be a change from the devil they know to the devil they do not.[25]

From this brief excursion into the writings of James Connolly, it should be clear what he saw as his legacy for the Irish left. There was, firstly, an invitation to combine a revolutionary socialist outlook with a militant rejection of imperialism. Far from socialists waiting, standing aside or seeing a fight against empire as a distraction from economic battles, they needed to engage in that struggle and offer a distinct perspective. Second, there was a suggestion that the national question would not be solved within a capitalist framework but would need a radical transformation of society. This, however, did not mean that Connolly was indifferent to any change short of socialism. Connolly was for a workers' republic, but that did not stop him from supporting Home Rule despite the fact it would be limited and decidedly not socialist. Sometimes Connolly came at his wider argument by linking the cause of political freedom to economic freedom, suggesting that undoing the conquest involved a break with an economic system imposed by the empire. More substantially, however, Connolly posed the question of radical transformation as a way of overcoming working-class division. By suggesting that partition would bring about a 'carnival of reaction', he implied that its undoing involved a challenge to both states.

This legacy would indicate that socialists who belong to the Connolly tradition are not neutral on the question of the break-up of the union with Britain. Nor is support for that break-up *contingent* on it being done exclusively on a socialist basis. Rather the best way to overcome partition is by promoting a policy that openly asserts the need to abolish both states which are products of partition. It should not be a matter of inviting Protestant workers into a pre-existing Southern state but of creating a new and more radical Ireland from which all workers benefit. Linked to this approach there is also in Connolly a fundamental opposition to the idea of Orangeism. Far from adopting a neutral stance between republicanism and Orangeism, Connolly defined the latter as inherently reactionary because of its support for monarchy, ascendancy and empire. It was not a matter of evenly balancing between two traditions but pointing to the one that he perceived as the cause of division. In this sense, there is a thoroughly modern ring to his arguments. Few radicals today, for example, would suggest a 'balance' between racist and black nationalist views but would rather point to racism as the cause of divisions.

The impact of Connolly's ideas on the Irish left has varied over time and with the different tempos of the Northern struggle. In the early period, which was dominated by the civil rights agitation from 1968 to 1972, Connolly was viewed as the main touchstone of Irish radicalism. Thousands of people sported a metallic badge with his image and songs projecting alternative versions of him as 'the hero of the working man' or a 'brave son of Ireland' were popular. There was an instinctive recognition that the battle against the Stormont regime would also involve a challenge to the Southern state. In the words of one historian, Ireland looked like a 'boiling volcano' with even the political correspondent of the *Irish Times* declaring that 'something deep was stirring in the whole of Ireland'.[26] The then President of Sinn Féin, Tomás Mac Giolla, put matters succinctly, when he stated that 'we are witnessing what we hope is the beginning of the disintegration of two old and corrupt parties'.[27] This period also saw the birth of a new left with individuals such as Bernadette Devlin, Eamonn McCann and Michael Farrell becoming household names. In his book *Northern Ireland: The Orange State*,[28] and in his more general writings, Michael Farrell located himself firmly within the Connolly tradition arguing that 'the border must go because it is a relic of imperialism and in order to root out imperialism, we have to root out the neo-imperialist set up in the South and the neo-colonial one in the North'.[29] In a similar vein, Farrell also argued that 'only the concept of a socialist republic can ever reconcile Protestant workers, who rightly have a very deep seated fear of a Roman Catholic republic, to the ending of the border'.[30]

THE BREAK WITH CONNOLLY

This strand of Connollyite politics persists in Irish society as a vague rebellious spirit that often resurfaces on occasions of mass resistance. During a water charges protest in 2014, for example, thousands listened with rapt attention to the singer Damian Dempsey deliver 'The Ballad of James Connolly'. It was a deeply symbolic moment as Dempsey stood on a podium outside the GPO, the focal point of the 1916 rising, connecting that rebellion to a present-day fight against water charges. And it is precisely because it is a living tradition that Connolly's ideas have come in for explicit criticism.

There is a wider context to the attacks on the Connolly tradition. After the Bloody Sunday murders in 1972, there was a huge upsurge in opposition to the British army with tens of thousands involved in the burning of the British embassy. The Southern political establishment were very fearful but got ahead of the anger by calling a 'national day of mourning' for the Bloody Sunday victims. Later, however, they set out systematically to turn the population towards a concern with the security and peace of their own state. They used a terrible car bombing in Dublin organised by loyalist paramilitaries and British intelligence to frighten people and to present the IRA as a threat to their security. The guerrilla army tactics also played into the hand of the Southern establishment – car bombings in city centre streets were viewed with disgust. The Southern population had – and still has – an historic memory of a 'war of independence' but by the 1970s, there was a massive difference between their experience and that of those living in the Catholic ghettoes of the North. In Belfast or Derry, many people disliked the IRA tactics, but they still excused or continued to support them because they saw how the British army were oppressing their areas. In the South, it was very different and so the car bombs helped to alienate people from the struggle. The Provos refused to recognise this elementary fact – and resorted to moralistic attacks on 'the free state mentality'. The difference in experience between Southern workers and Northern nationalists could never, however, be overcome by moralism.

This shift in the political atmosphere in the South was echoed and amplified by intellectuals who had previously been associated with the left. The main target of their attacks was the Connollyite tradition. The most dramatic volte-face came from Conor Cruise O'Brien, who had previously praised Connolly's role in the 1916 rebellion and was identified with opposition to the US war in Vietnam.[31] In 1969 he was still praising 'the courage, determination and tactical skill of the Bogsiders' for establishing a no-go area for the RUC. By 1972, however, in his influential book *States of Ireland* he was claiming that left-wingers who used 'language and gestures which are subjectively revolutionary, but have appeal only within one sectarian community, are objectively [using] the language and gestures of sectarian civil war'.[32] As violence increased in Northern Ireland, O'Brien located its source in an emotional, irrational form of Catholic nationalism which pervaded Ireland. This 'holy nationalism', he claimed, was built on the cult of martyrs of the 1916 rebellion and transmitted from generation to generation through memory, tradition and myths. It led to an implicit support for a sectarian and fascistic IRA campaign.[33]

O'Brien became a leading ideologue in the Irish Labour Party and helped to shift it into a coalition government with Fine Gael in 1973. He acknowledged that Connolly's call for a workers' republic became 'the accepted corpus of doctrine for the revolutionary left in Ireland' and set out to dismantle that influence.[34] His main charge was that Connolly had written Protestant workers out of Irish history and supported the use of force to incorporate them into a united Ireland. The evidence he produced was patchy but O'Brien wanted to appear as an iconoclast who was tearing down the martyrs of 1916. His attacks on the Connollyite tradition had a vague radical tinge as they appeared to offer a challenge to the dominant role of Catholicism and the anti-communist ethos of the Provisional IRA at the time. This had a certain appeal to centre-left activists of the Labour Party who supported the Southern state's efforts to crush the 'fascist' tendencies in Irish republicanism. Given the supposedly irrational and dangerous ambivalence inherent in Irish nationalism, O'Brien, however, went further and advocated censorship for any republican sentiment. As a government minister he became the main advocate of Section 31 of the Broadcasting Act which banned any republican voices from the Irish radio and television. Despite his original left veneer, O'Brien was essentially arguing from a conservative perspective, equating the nationalism of the oppressed with an irrational emotion. If a similar argument was applied to the Vietnamese during their conflict with the US, then the cause of all their suffering was an 'irrational' nationalist tradition that abhorred domination by foreign forces. O'Brien's point of contrast with these 'holy nationalisms' was Western liberal democracy, unblemished by violence, inspired by Enlightenment ideas and thoroughly rational in its domination of non-European countries.

A more sophisticated attack on the Connolly tradition was undertaken by intellectuals associated with Sinn Féin–The Workers' Party, later renamed simply the Workers' Party in 1982. In 1979, Paul Bew, Peter Gibbon and Henry Patterson published their book, *The State in Northern Ireland*,

1921–72 aiming to plot a new course for Irish Marxism which, they claimed, was on the 'verge of extinction'. The main culprit was the Connolly tradition which had absorbed socialism into 'national irredentism'.[35] Bew, Patterson and Gibbon deployed an image of rigorous, serious Althusserian Marxists to debunk the unsophisticated Connolly. Interestingly, Althusser was also the framework for ideologues sympathetic to republicanism such as Ronnie Munck and Bill Rolston who utilised his structuralist framework to argue that class politics could not overcome sectarianism. The relative autonomy that Althusser afforded the structures of economics, politics and ideology allowed for a Marxism of both green and orange variety, that effectively conformed with the status quo. Let's look at some of the arguments of Orange Althusserians.

Their first claim was that Connolly – and the wider Marxist tradition – had failed to recognise the material basis for partition in the uneven development of Irish capitalism. Ulster had an industrial base, linked to the core regions of Britain and had a direct interest in maintaining those links. Southern Ireland was a backward agrarian economy whose indigenous capitalists needed protectionism to expand. Because of this economic divergence, both Protestant employers and Protestant workers developed a direct interest in partition.

There can be little doubting the different roads to economic development in the North and the South, but acknowledging this does not imply partition was an inevitable outcome. As we have seen, the issue of partition was bound up with a Tory strategy to defend the empire and initially Carson's aim was not control of a six-county state but the retention of the link with Britain for the whole island. Bew, Gibbon and Patterson play down the political contestation involved in the pro-imperialist mobilisations, the Curragh mutiny and pogroms designed to intimidate the Catholic population into submission. Their focus is on internal economic factors that leaves aside the strategies of the British ruling class. They accord 'primacy' to internal class relations in Ireland and suggest that the British state did not have a unity of purpose.[36] They conclude that partition arose for mainly Irish developments. This argument, however, has a distinct teleological character equating 'Ulster's' political economy with the actual Northern state which emerged. They can offer no explanation for why it needed to include a substantial Catholic minority. Bizarrely, they suggest that Belfast Catholic attitudes to the Northern state was 'a product of a specific conjuncture of events' rather than 'an expression of a deep-seated ideological attitude'.[37]

Arguing that Protestant workers had an *interest* in supporting partition is to confuse an immediate desire for employment and job security with a wider class consciousness. If the same method were applied to other cases, one could argue that specific groups of workers had an interest in supporting their sector of the economy. It is undoubtedly the case, for example, that bank workers will on occasion defend the profits of banks because they think it will lead to more stable jobs. Car workers will occasionally join with their employers in opposing restrictions on the use of cars because of a narrow sectional viewpoint. They will do so because they assume that what is good for their company is good for their jobs. However, you cannot equate the immediate 'interest' of a group of workers within a capitalist economy with their wider class interests. Or rather, you can if you think that there is no possibility of an alternative to capitalism. You could then argue that there is a certain logic in workers responding to its competitive dynamic by backing employers in their own sector of the economy. However, that would also mean that 'class consciousness' could never exist.

Their second claim is that Connolly had a crude pre-Marxist concept of ideology, seeing it primarily as an illusion. By this, Bew, Gibbon and Patterson meant that Connolly saw the ideology of unionism as a 'stage managed' ruling class fabrication.[38] They attack him for thinking that 'Orangeism and trade union militancy were... mutually exclusive' and instead, the authors argue that Orangeism and proletarian class ideology 'interpenetrated' each other.[39] Moreover, far from workers being dominated by an alien ideology, the unionist leadership 'had been obliged to concede a proportion of its power to the Orange section of the working class'.[40] Protestant workers had a democratic, secular but pro-imperialist ideology which contrasted the industrial North and the backward agrarian South. This, it is suggested, arose from their lived experience rather than false consciousness. However, while Connolly did suggest that support for empire was promoted by the upper class, he also pointed to a certain material base for Orangeism. He noted that:

> At one time in the industrial world of Great Britain and Ireland the skilled labourer looked down with contempt upon the unskilled and bitterly resented his attempt to get his children taught any of the skilled trades;

the feeling of the Orangemen of Ireland towards the Catholics is but a glorified representation on a big stage of the same passions inspired by the same unworthy motives.[41]

This suggestive remark needs some elaboration. The expansion of the industrial base around Belfast drew in many Catholic migrants from the rural hinterland and one of the features of the uneven development of the Irish economy was a more intense competition for jobs between skilled or in situ Protestant workers and Catholic newcomers. When the older traditions of settler versus native are overlaid with competition for jobs, one can see how Orangeism could gain a certain hold. This, however, does not mean that the ruling class played no role in fomenting reactionary ideas.

Far from 'conceding a proportion of its power to the Orange section of workers', the early Stormont regimes were dominated by big landowners and business leaders who set out to crush left-wing ideas. Carson and J. M. Andrews, a well-connected businessman, became the president and chairman of the Ulster Unionist Labour Association (UULA). This was an organisation which played an active role in combating 'Bolshevism, Syndicalism and Socialism' amongst Protestant workers and was created precisely to tie Protestant workers to their Orange bosses.[42] The UULA opposed the 1919 engineering strike and, after Labour candidates scored victories in Belfast's municipal election in 1920, Carson deliberately targeted socialists in his infamous speech on the twelfth. He claimed that the enemy was deploying an 'insidious method' of 'tacking on the Sinn Fein and Irish Republican question to the Labour question' and so 'these men who come posing as friends of Labour care no more about Labour than the man in the moon'.[43] The consequence of Carson's attack became clear when 'rotten Prods' – or genuine trade unionists – were expelled from the Belfast shipyards alongside their Catholic workmates.[44] One can acknowledge that Orange ideas were popular but how could they be described as 'democratic' if it entailed opposition to strike leaders, union activists and a Catholic minority?

The last major claim of the three authors is to deny the impact of British imperialism through two main strategies. The first is to use the criteria enunciated in Lenin's *Imperialism. the Highest Stage of Capitalism* to define a Marxist definition of imperialism. So Bew, Gibbon and Patterson elucidate features such as export of capital; domination by finance capital, industrial cartels over which banks have a predominant influence, which Lenin argued, helped to explain the drive to subject developing countries to control from a metropolis. They then show how these features do not exist in Northern Ireland. By outlining a Leninist concept of imperialism as a specific stage in global capitalism, Bew, Gibbon and Patterson draw sharp distinction between Marxist and nationalist concepts of imperialism. With this apparent sophistication, they can then dismiss attempts to link partition to the interests of British imperialism.

However, while appearing to adhere to Lenin's schema, the writers miss out on its essence. If they were to apply the same checklist – such as the export of surplus capital or the role of finance in organising industrial cartels – they could equally conclude that the US was not involved in an imperialist intervention in Vietnam or Iraq. Yet Lenin's central argument was that in an uneven world where individual corporations dominate major sectors of production, they look to individual states to protect their interests through economic and military expansion. In other words, the drive to conquer and establish territorial hegemony does not arise simply from arbitrary foreign policy decisions but is intrinsically linked to the dynamic of capitalist competition. As we have seen, in the modern age Britain has aligned itself with the US to promote and protect the distinct interests of its corporations. The British state uses its credibility as a military power on a global basis to extract concessions favourable to its corporations. It cannot be seen to be beaten either by an IRA campaign or a mass movement that drives them out of Ireland.

The second strategy of the authors is to claim there was a lack of unity of purpose in British policy. However, there has always existed divisions in the ruling class about how best to advance their interests. Marx called them a 'warring band of brothers' by way of a reference to capitalist competition but this also finds its expression within competing tendencies in the state. No doubt there have been sections of the British ruling class who proposed a softer approach to Ireland, perhaps even accepting, in different periods, the possibility of Home Rule or a united Ireland or troop withdrawals. That does not, however, change the fact that the hegemonic force around the British ruling class, particularly around the Tories and powerful sections of the military, have had a consistently imperialist approach to Ireland, that has invariably led them to support unionism. Sections of the ruling class in the

US disagreed on whether the invasion of Iraq was the right thing but it did not make the invasion any less imperialist.

The focus on internal elite division leads to a familiar trope whereby Britain is presented as reluctantly stumbling into control of an empire that, at one stage, had a landmass of 13 million square miles, nearly a quarter of the planet. Thus, Sir David Canadine claims that even in the 'climatic years of high imperialism... traditional hostility to additional annexations remained deeply embedded in most parts of Whitehall'.[45] Bew, Patterson and Gibbon use a similar approach to argue that the partition of Ireland was primarily a response to local conflicts but their methodology of focusing on internal Cabinet papers exaggerates divisions within the British elite. One of the ways a ruling class develops a united strategy is by first assessing their various options, off camera. This sometimes takes the form of internal polemical debates before arriving at a decisive course of action. Rather than examining their internal discussions, it is more useful to assess the result of their actions.

We have dealt at some length with the arguments of Bew, Gibbon and Patterson as they offer the most explicit refutation of the Connolly position from an apparently left-wing position. In reality, the writers were gravitating to a pro-unionist tradition, symbolised rather dramatically in the trajectory of the former Workers' Party member, Paul Bew, who became Lord Bew and now sits in the House of Lords. While Bew, Gibbon and Patterson's books had a limited appeal outside intellectual circles, a more popular version of their arguments had an influence on certain strata of Irish life. This did not arise from the vigour or sophistication of their argument but from the way in which it was embedded in networks that promoted a 'revisionist' outlook. These included two political parties, the Labour Party and the Workers' Party, and through them, a section of the trade union leadership. It also found an audience in university history departments and in many complex ways, through the role the Workers' Party played, in the national broadcasting network RTE.[46] All of this gave rise to what became colloquially known as a 'D4 attitude' where support for liberal causes was often associated with rejection of 'atavistic' attitudes towards the North. The more one despised republicanism and opposed any attempts to undermine or coerce unionism, the more progressive and liberal you were.

The arguments of Ireland's foremost public intellectual, Fintan O'Toole, illustrate the extent of the break with the Connolly tradition. O'Toole writes from a liberal or progressive tradition but like the above-mentioned writers sees partition as 'an inevitable product of Irish political, economic and religious division' and suggests that the only alternative to it was 'a bloody civil war'.[47] The Northern state is not deemed to be the cause for the maintenance of sectarian division because, as he argued, 'sectarian prejudice did not cause the violence. It was to a great extent the violence that caused the prejudice.'[48] While O'Toole acknowledges the role played by loyalist paramilitaries and the British state, the main culprit for the violence is the IRA, 'which has functioned at times as purely a Catholic sectarian murder squad seeking slaughter of Protestant people because of their religion'.[49] O'Toole's particular focus has often been – like Conor Cruise O'Brien's – on the irrational traditions of 'inherited hatreds' which enable individuals to maim and kill. At the core of this fanaticism is a 'habitual view of Protestants as people who have been bribed and duped into believing they were British'.[50] Failing to recognise the deeply felt political identity of Protestants, he claims, is itself sectarian.

THE CONNOLLY TRADITION TODAY

Much of the political charge that animated these arguments came from a revulsion against the IRA's tactics. With the ending of this campaign it has become more possible to question some of the fundamental assumptions of the left liberal approach – namely the view that British imperialism plays a marginal or absent role; or the view that partition is simply an inevitable product of Irish division; or the description of loyalism as a depoliticised 'identity' which needs to be respected. By questioning these assumptions, it is possible to restore much of the Connolly approach. There are, however, some ambiguities and confusions in this tradition, particularly as it was developed. Some of these are to be found in Connolly's own writings and others have been added on as socialists grappled with the Northern conflict.

Connolly's involvement in the 1916 rebellion has helped to construct him as occupying a common ground shared by socialists and republican traditions. This legacy has meant that he sometimes becomes the inspiration for a 'socialist republicanism' which maintains all the trappings of a republican organisation while speaking of the working class in general terms. This ignores an elementary fact that Connolly saw himself as a Marxist and did not join Sinn Féin, even when other left-leaning trade unionists became members. Aside from his participation in the 1916 rebellion, there are deeper reasons why Connolly can be seen to have played this role. He broke with the dominant tradition of Second International Marxism in recognising that colonised countries did not have to wait a long period of industrial development before challenging capitalism but he also wrote in a period before any anti-imperialist movement had come to power. He never had the benefit of seeing how a radical nationalist movement like the National Liberation Front in Algeria or Robert Mugabe's ZANU-PF were transformed into ruling parties that managed capitalism once they took power; or how a section of the republican movement became Fianna Fáil and presided over a corrupt and conservative state. As a result, he sometimes tended to equate anti-imperialism with anti-capitalism or at least imply there was an inherent dynamic to move in that direction. More specifically, he regarded the Irish bourgeoisie as a class wedded to an 'alien' social system and therefore to empire. He significantly underestimated how this class could change its outlook and how variant forms of Irish republicanism could become the vehicle for its rule in an independent Ireland. There is much that is of value in the republican tradition – not least its tenacity in opposing empire and its democratic ethos. Nevertheless, the tradition is encased in a nationalist outlook that seeks its place within the conventional order of global capitalism. While some of the best elements can be recovered for the left, it is necessary to build a different tradition.

After Connolly's execution, a strand of thinking developed on the Irish left which saw the road to fundamental change lying through a call to 'complete the national revolution'. When this referred to how the revolutionary process that developed between 1918 and 1922 was truncated by conservative elements and by partition, it made perfect sense. 'Completing the national revolution' can also mean, however, that the struggle against the Northern state becomes the lever to prise open a wider social transformation in Ireland as a whole. This is often underpinned by a view that while the North is a direct colony, the Southern state remains a 'neo-colony'.[51] This characterisation was deployed by Gerry Adams, when writing in his more left-wing phase. He claimed that:

> while maintaining the symbols of political independence, [the South] is in reality a neo-colony. The British government by its direct control of a part of Ireland exerts a political influence over all of Ireland, ensuring

through partition that Irish politics are neutralised and distorted with British political influence maintained.[52]

If nothing else Brexit showed how utterly nonsensical is this characterisation. If the 26 counties, according to this republican schema, is a British neo-colony, then how was it that throughout the entire Brexit crisis the Dublin ruling class sided with Brussels? If the Irish ruling class were simply a British-backed caste, why did they go against their colonial leaders? If it is claimed that the 26 counties are no longer a neo-colony of Britain but of the EU, this only begs the question: when exactly did that historic transfer take place? The whole 'neo-colony' theory severely understates how the Southern state functions as a representative for a weak but independent ruling class.[53] Moreover, the hundred years of relative capitalist stability in the South has produced a host of issues, around which people mobilise, that are not directly linked to a national question, still less British domination.

When young people mobilise over climate change, for example, their focus is not on 'completing a national revolution' but rather dealing with a global problem and the lack of action of the Irish elite. The issues on which people struggle, therefore, cannot be simply refracted through the lens of the national question. Mass mobilisation develops on issues that confront people in their immediate lives – rather than emerging according to any pre-existing schema. The task of socialists is to politically make connections between these issues and the wider nature of Irish society which has been so shaped by two conservative states.

Shorn of some of these ambiguities, there is much to recommend in Connolly's writings for the modern-day left. He was a worker-intellectual who wrote in a clear style and an excellent propagandist, capable of reaching a wider audience. This is in marked contrast to a type of leftist academicism which produces supposedly sophisticated analyses that are only addressed to other academics. More importantly, Connolly was a brilliant exponent of socialist ideas – challenging those who refused to think in international terms or outlining why the drive to war was an intrinsic part of a brutal system. While he famously proposed the formation of an Irish Labour Party at the Irish Trade Union Congress in Clonmel in 1912, he did so because he thought there was a need for a broad party to represent Irish workers after the introduction of Home Rule. He never believed in a purely parliamentary strategy and always stressed the self-activity of working people. Connolly's brilliance as a revolutionary, however, was to link the fight for Irish freedom with a plan to uproot capitalism – to strive not just for a republic, but a workers' republic. This enabled him to see that any conventional 'solution' to Ireland's national question involving partition would produce a carnival of reaction. As the issue of the border re-emerges, he provides a vision of how opposition to an Irish border must be linked to radical change on the island.

8
What Kind of United Ireland?

It began as a game between former pupils of Eton over who should lead the Tory party. Boris Johnson thought that advocating leaving the EU would be enough to catapult him into the leadership, while David Cameron thought that a referendum would quickly settle matters. But both sides failed to take account of the sheer anger in British society and so, Brexit came to be. Since its passing in 2016, the referendum has reopened the question of Irish reunification and, even though it is not the sole cause, has destabilised the North. Before Brexit the province was settling in for a long period of haggling over what constituted 'parity of esteem' as identity politics replaced talk of anti-imperialism and British sovereignty. Sinn Féin and the DUP looked like they would jointly rule Stormont for decades to come – and then it changed.

Talk of Irish unification has suddenly grown amongst the wider public opinion and even amongst establishment opinion leaders. An IPSOS/MRBI exit poll conducted after voting for the general election in the South in 2020 revealed that 57 per cent of respondents thought there should be a border poll within the next five years; amongst younger voters this reached 74 per cent.[1] A Lord Ashcroft poll conducted in September 2019 revealed that a slight majority of respondents in Northern Ireland favoured Irish unity, 51 to 49 per cent. As this lies within the bounds of a margin of error, it still leaves uncertainty. However, the poll also found that 60 per cent of those aged between 18 and 24 wanted Irish unity. More significantly, while a majority felt that a border poll would not deliver Irish unity if conducted at present, this was reversed if it was held in ten years' time. Most believed that the vote would then be for unification, with only three in ten believing voters would choose the UK.[2]

Between reality and dreams there are possibilities and Irish unity is becoming a feasible option according to key organs of the global establishment. The *Economist* magazine ran a headline 'Irish Unification Becoming Likelier: Time to Start Thinking About What It Might Mean'.[3] The *New York Times* had 'No Deal Brexit: Could Open Path to Irish Unity'.[4] The

Financial Times had a think-piece from David McWilliams on 'Why the Idea of a United Ireland is Back in Play'.[5] Capital Consultancy Services, which produces long-term reports for investors, stated that 'We do not think that Irish unification should be high up investors' list of near term risks in Ireland or Europe. But it is a plausible event in five to ten years' time'.[6] The prospect of Irish unity is beginning to enter the mainstream.

This has only added to the nervousness of the Southern political establishment because, while they officially support Irish unity, they want to keep it to the distant future. They know that their decades-long domination of Southern politics – whereby Fianna Fáil and Fine Gael swapped turns in government office – would be put in danger. Unification would create instability and, for them, that is reason enough to continually postpone it. Neale Richmond, a Fine Gael TD, captures this attitude well: 'The heart says: yes. The head says: not yet, just 21 years into the generations-long process of healing sectarianism. Does the Republic really want to import several hundred thousand hard-core Unionists, some of whom may kill for their identity?'[7]

One of the standard discursive techniques of the Southern establishment is to reduce political choices to a question of money. Expert economists regularly appear to calculate the precise costs so that the voter-consumer can choose with their wallet. When it comes to Irish unity, the question becomes, 'How could we afford €9 billion subvention from the British Exchequer?' This lies at the core of a paper produced by two mainstream economists, John Fitzgerald and Edgar Morgenroth. Their method is to give the reader different scenarios and assign exact costs for each one. Rhetorically, the reader is pushed into choosing the least worst of a set of unity scenarios which are all disastrous. Thus, in one example:

the deficit would in the order of €9.8 billion... about two thirds of the deficit in Ireland (excluding support for the banks) at the height of the financial crisis. Based on the experience of dealing with the financial crisis in Ireland, this would require a fiscal adjustment in Ireland amounting to cuts or tax increases of €20 to €30 billion.[8]

Lest anyone has doubts about what this means, this is translated into costing €2,000 a year for the average person in the Republic.

However, behind this spurious exactitude lies an unreliable set of figures. Fitzgerald and Morgenroth indicate that for 2016 there was a Northern deficit of £9,347 million which is then plugged by a British subvention. This derives from a gap between the spending of the Northern state and revenue it takes in, but it happens to be €450 million less than the £9.8 billion figure above.

Each year the British Office of National Statistics publish their 'Country and Regional Public Sector Finances', which outlines the financing of Northern Ireland. It breaks expenditure down into 'identifiable' and 'non-identifiable' transfers from the British exchequer. The former refers to expenditure which benefits individuals in a region such as spending on health, education and social protection while the latter refers to the region's share of wider UK spending on items such as public debt, defence, BBC, UK border protection and the Foreign Office. Bizarrely, Fitzgerald and Morgenroth do not take this distinction into account even though if Northern Ireland were to break from the rest of the UK it could hardly be deemed responsible for continuing to pay for these UK-wide 'non-identifiable' services.

If we take the most recent year, 2018–19, as an example, we can see the weakness of their argument. In this period, Northern Ireland raised £18.5 billion in revenue.[9] However, the total public sector expenditure was £27.9 billion, giving us a £9.4 billion deficit, which is made up by a British government subvention. However, if we look at the spending on *identifiable* services, we find that this amounts to £21.8 billion, shrinking the deficit considerably to £3.3 billion. Even this more modest figure, however, is exaggerated because of a number of difficulties in calculation. Thus, for example, the tax receipts of a corporation located in Northern Ireland but with a head office in London may not appear in its accounts.

Beyond the figures, the argument that 'we could not afford' the subvention makes little sense because most countries have imbalances between regions, leading to fiscal transfers. So, London makes a transfer to the North East of England and Dublin transfers resources to the Border, Midlands and Western (BMW) region. The 'we' in 'we cannot afford it' might equally be applied to Dubliners who object to transfers to the BMW region as its growth rates and ranking are similar to the North. Moreover, while Fitzgerald and Morgenroth point to weakness in the Northern economy, they fail to draw relevant conclusions from their analysis. Almost every commentator who examines the issue has noted that the North is falling behind most of the UK economy. Thus, in the period 2000 to 2014, while regions in the UK such as London, Scotland and the North West grew by 23 per cent, 25 per cent and 19 per cent per capita respectively, Northern Ireland had the second lowest growth rate of just 7 per cent.[10] It is not just one of the poorest regions of the UK but the gap with the wider UK economy is increasing. The link with Britain is not serving the Northern economy particularly well and there is little evidence that it is closely integrated into the UK's regional economies.[11]

Mainstream economists point to two main factors which have created a structural weakness in the North's economy. There is, first, a lower level of productivity because of a limited level of investment. While both the North and South have become more reliant on multinationals, these have focused more on low wages in the North rather than capital investment. The second recognised factor is that the Northern economy has also suffered from lower educational attainments compared to the South. In brief, there is a need for structural change based on much higher levels of investment in industry and education but, as Michael Burke points out, this is more likely to occur if the two Irish economies are integrated. A unified Ireland would create a larger domestic market leading to a 25 per cent increase for the South and a fourfold increase for the North.[12] Whether that investment becomes reliant on private capitalists or from public control of resources is a matter for political choice.

There is, therefore, no overriding economic case that rules out Irish unity in the foreseeable future. Attempts to do so mainly arise from those motivated by a concern for the stability of the Southern state. At the very least, the election arithmetic would endanger the hold that Fine Gael and Fianna Fáil have on governmental office. More importantly, a united Ireland would draw in 1.9 million people who have no loyalty to their state. Many would regard the creation of a united Ireland as an opportunity for radical change throughout the island. They would demand a national health service and an array of social rights which the Southern state has not granted. The instinctive hostility of the Southern establishment to any short-term prospect of Irish unity is evident in their repeated rejections of a call for a border poll by implying that it is simply a Sinn Féin ruse. However, while this is the current position of the political elite, there are already some establishment outliers who have started contemplating what a united Ireland might look like – not now, but in the more distant future. Their primary concern is to preserve the existing structures with a newly unified Ireland.

THE MORE THINGS CHANGE, THE MORE THEY STAY THE SAME

The call for a united Ireland has traditionally been associated with a radical tradition that challenged the Southern state. The hope was that unity would end the carnival of reaction and fulfil the original ideal of the 1916 proclamation to 'cherish all of the children equally'. However, in recent years a small number of conservative and liberal voices have emerged to present their vision of a united Ireland.

Michael McDowell is a former leader of the Progressive Democrats, Ireland's first openly neoliberal party which has since disappeared, though many of its policies have been embraced by Fianna Fáil and Fine Gael. McDowell is the grandson of Eoin McNeill, who famously issued the countermand order to stop the mobilisation of Irish Volunteers for the 1916 rebellion. Less well known is that McNeill was a minister in the pro-Treaty government that adopted a policy of violent repression against his republican opponents, which tragically led to the death of his own son, Brian. It is from this more conservative nationalist tradition that McDowell draws his inspiration.

In a paper entitled 'What Exactly Do We Mean by Irish Unity', he argues that there are two fundamentally different concepts. One is that the North would leave the UK and become part of a republic under an existing or a new constitution, while the other is that the North leaves the UK to become part of an agreed confederation between the two states – Northern Ireland and the Republic. McDowell strongly favours the second option because the first would represent a more fundamental change and, by contrast, 'a confederal form of unity would leave both jurisdictions largely intact and in which... only limited powers [would be] devolved by each part of the confederation to its institutions'.[13] The confederal institution which binds the two jurisdictions together would be made up of 'a balanced form of joint ministry' and some elected body to which it might be accountable.[14] However, its scope for decision-making would be very limited as it would mainly deal with relations with the EU and other international issues.

This is the most explicit position on how Irish unity could involve minimal change where the Stormont Executive and the Dáil would stay in place. The existing civil service, police and judiciary would continue and, over time, differences between both parts of the island might even grow as 'Each part of the confederation would have its own constitution, parliament, government, laws and institutions including local government, and its own social welfare system, educational system and police force.'[15] The North could have some continuing connection to the Crown and the South would not. The main rationale for this option is that by proposing the most minimal of change, McDowell believes that it would be the least threatening to voters and so would be more likely to win acceptance. In addition, it would demonstrate to those who value their 'Britishness' that there is no threat to their identity.

A somewhat similar but not identical approach comes from a High Court judge, Richard Humphries. A former member of Young Fine Gael, he defected to join Labour and won a council seat for the party in Dun Laoghaire. In a time-honoured tradition, he was then appointed a High Court judge by a coalition government composed of his two former parties, Fine Gael and Labour. While acting as a government advisor, Humphries attended talks which contributed to the Belfast Agreement – albeit in a somewhat marginal role. Nevertheless, it sparked an interest and he has written two books on Irish unity. The first was *Countdown to Unity: Debating Irish Unification* published in 2008 and the more recent *Beyond the Border: The Good Friday Agreement and Irish Unity after Brexit* in 2018. Humphries offers a legal perspective on the implications of the Belfast Agreement, not just as they concern the current institutional arrangements within the North but as they might apply to a united Ireland. His starting point is that there is no end date for this agreement as the Stormont institutions are not transitional but are a 'permanent feature of the constitutional landscape'.[16] This means – and he claims this on legal authority – 'they would remain in place even in the event of a united Ireland'.[17] Like McDowell, he is at pains to argue that 'very little would change on the ground if a majority for unity emerged, MPs would go to Dublin as TDs rather than Westminster but beyond that day to day governance of Northern Ireland would continue to be at local level'.[18] Sovereignty would be transferred from London to Dublin but would occur in an almost frictionless way that would not disturb existing arrangements. In this context, Humphries suggests that relations between Britain and Ireland could improve with further legal changes. Thus, Britain might remove its ban on a Catholic becoming its monarch, while the South might consider joining the Commonwealth. Humphries' overall approach is shaped by gradualism and in *Countdown to Unity* he proposes 30 years of joint authority to reduce tensions 'commencing under the aegis of British sovereignty and gradually moving towards a transition to Irish sovereignty'.[19]

Brendan O'Leary tackles Irish unity as a social scientist and deploys a rhetoric of careful prediction based on evidence and analysis so that his own political preferences appear as a muffled voice behind a screen of objectivity. O'Leary began as a 'man of the left', writing for the *New Left Review* and engaging in discussion on historical materialism and then moved to more conventional grounds, concluding that 'Marxism is no longer a vibrant ideology amongst Western leftist intelligentsia'.[20] He became an advisor to the British Labour Party during discussions on the Irish peace process and has since promoted consociational forms of government for ethnic conflicts in different parts of the world. O'Leary produced a large three-volume study in 2019 called *A Treatise on Northern Ireland* with the last volume subtitled 'Consociation and Confederation'.

O'Leary distinguishes between a confederation which he defined as 'a union of states that delegate their revocable sovereignty to shared confederal institutions and retain the right of succession'[21] and a federation. A federation is defined as an arrangement between states where the right to secession is removed and where a federal authority gains more power over its constituents. O'Leary believes that the confederation option is the more likely to emerge through negotiations.[22] The North–South Ministerial Council which arose from the Belfast agreement, could, he thinks, prove a stepping stone to this confederal Ireland.[23] As this implies an arrangement between two states, Northern Ireland would need to be granted the status of a state and once that occurred there could be 'incremental and reversible re-unification'.[24] By reversible, O'Leary means that Northern Ireland would have a right to secession after a particular interval if it had a negative experience of unity. Like McDowell and Humphries, he thinks this, plus membership of the British Commonwealth, might help to allay unionist fears. While O'Leary acknowledges that there could be a possibility of Irish unity based on the dissolution of Northern Ireland, the main thrust of his writing is to suggest two other institutional formats. These are:

- A decentralised Irish unitary state that preserves Northern Ireland with a devolved legislature, with internal consociational arrangements, as long as these are preferred by a majority of former unionists.
- An Irish confederation with two states, that may allow for the formation of one state, one of which will probably be internally consociational.[25]

In both cases, Stormont would continue with its current communal arrangements. The differences would come down to whether sovereignty is shifted to Dublin in the short term or whether it would emerge through confederation. More generally, these differing proposals are geared to the political elites who will undertake future negotiations. The assumption is that with gradual, minimal change and recognition of 'Britishness', all can eventually agree some type of Irish unity. The 'stepping stones' of the original Anglo-Irish Treaty of 1921, that Michael Collins thought would lead to a 32-county Irish Republic have, therefore, become a lot longer and a different form of unity has emerged. There are, however, significant objections to this approach.

The first is that in all essentials it preserves the original British imposed solution of the Irish question. In 1921, in order to curtail an Irish revolution and prevent the unravelling of its then empire, the British administration imposed partition on Ireland although it went against the democratic wishes of its people as expressed in the only all-island ballot in the 1918 election. One consequence was the fossilisation of sectarian identities and the consequential conflict that arose between unionists and nationalists. An Irish unity from above, in the manner proposed, sustains these structures into future generations.

Connolly's 'carnival of reaction', therefore, continues in a host of ways. Politics in the North will still be organised on sectarian lines with Catholics and Protestants encouraged to vote for the strongest communal representatives. Two dominant parties would continue to publicly fight over what exactly constitutes 'parity of esteem' while in private they can do deals over the distribution of patronage. To add to this already fractured dynamic, there will be repeated disputes over the 'right to secede' from, what some unionists will argue, is an expensive cumbersome confederation. In the South, the conservative parties will feel their current arrangements are not disturbed and they will be able to cloak their defence of class privilege with a claim they have achieved Irish unity – while still promising to move it on further. Denominational forms of education will continue throughout the island whereby Catholics and Protestants are educated separately. The Catholic Church will remain in control of the majority of schools in the South and most of the schools in nationalist areas of the North. State-run schools in the North will retain their 'British' ethos and draw their student cohort from the Protestant population. Little will have changed in people's day-to-day lives.

If the motivation is to cause the least disturbance, we may ask – why would working-class Protestants vote for it? The three writers assume that 'identity' is the most important feature of their lives and that concerns about jobs, wages and living conditions form only a residual element of their consciousness. However, if identity is that important why would Protestants not stick with the existing union with Britain rather than vague promises of respect in a united Ireland? If people are so locked into a conflict over identity, would Protestant workers not fear that 'the boot will be on the other foot' – that is, that they will face discrimination and lose out in this united Ireland? In reality, as we have argued, people view the world from a class prism even as they identify as Catholic or Protestant. From a class point of view, neither Catholic or Protestant workers will gain job security or better wages and they will fear the loss of even a depleted national health service. The waiting lists and the two-tier Southern health system act as disincentive to anyone contemplating a united Ireland under existing arrangements. This was confirmed by a poll carried out by LucidTalk which showed that one quarter of the electorate said that a national health service would make them more likely to vote for the Union.[26]

However, the invitation to a confederal Ireland may not be directed to Protestant workers at all because O'Leary, for example, suggests that 'liberal unionists' might be attracted to this type of united Ireland if Brexit goes badly. He suggests that if nationalists construct 'durable alliances with liberal unionists' who support the EU, they could win support for unity in a border poll.[27] However, the heartland of 'liberal unionism' lies in North Down which Sylvia Hermon once represented as an Independent Unionist MP. It is a constituency with a high number of upper professionals who live on the 'gold coast' and where, as the old joke goes, the main difference is between the 'have and have yachts'. It is possible that their pro-Remain passions are so strong that they might look to a united Ireland as the only way back into the EU, but it is neither certain nor highly likely. The social base of liberal unionism rests on stronger direct connections with Britain than many Protestant workers have. The upper professional strata often occupy important positions within the UK state and its local iteration in Northern Ireland and their expertise and occupational culture are derived from a familiarity with that state. Their sons and daughters are more likely to attend British universities – and stay on the mainland. While they might despise the crudities of DUP fundamentalism or the rage of working-class Brexit voters, their support for the EU may not be enough to embrace sovereignty from Dublin.

Finally, the pledges to respect 'Britishness' is problematic because, as we have seen, 'Britishness' denotes a particular type of imperial culture that belongs to a bygone age. It is not a reference to the type of multicultural identities found in a vibrant city like London, nor does it make much room for the celebration of working-class struggles. Embedding 'Britishness' into the institutional framework of a united Ireland could become a cover for drawing the country into a closer relationship with Anglo-American imperialism. Thus, O'Leary suggests that a British Irish Council 'could become a (renamed) forum in which post UKEXIT co-ordination would develop among partner governments'.[28] However, the majority opinion in Ireland as a whole wants little to do with modern or past British imperial adventures. This became clear, when in the name of respecting two cultures, a Fine Gael Justice Minister attempted to organise a commemoration for the RIC and, by extension, the Black and Tans. It was met with a huge outrage and his government was forced to cancel the event. Respecting the best traditions of 'Britishness' in terms of working-class struggle, irreverence towards religion and modern multiculturalism does not equate with quashing the anti-imperialist legacy of Ireland.

A UNITED TAX HAVEN

Alongside the literature on possible political institutions, two recent economic reports suggest that a united Ireland would have economic benefits. The lead researcher on both reports is Kurt Hubner, Professor of Political Science at the University of British Colombia who also holds a Jean Monnet Chair for European Integration and Global Political Economy. In addition, he participates in a Vancouver-based consultancy, KLC, which was commissioned to do the reports by the Knights of the Red Branch Inc. The registered agent for this somewhat mysteriously named organisation is an activist with the Friends of Sinn Féin in the US.[29] As Hubner's reports are frequently quoted by Sinn Féin, we can reasonably assume that the party supports its argument. Hubner's first report appeared in 2015 and was entitled *Modelling Irish Unification*. In the aftermath of Brexit, he updated his figures to produce a new report, *The Costs of Non-Unification: Brexit and the Unification of Ireland*.

Both reports adopt the conventional economist's method of creating models, which it is acknowledged, are an 'abstraction of reality, embodying many assumptions'.[30] There is nothing particularly unusual in this – we simply need to examine what the assumptions are. Hubner contrasts the economic model of the South, which he suggests is very successful, with that of the North. He suggests that economic unification would mean integrating the North into the Southern economy in order to derive the predicted benefits. One way this would occur is through a change in currency from sterling to the euro because this would bring about an effective devaluation and give the North a competitive trade advantage. Another way would be through a 'shift in the tax structure to one compatible with the South'.[31] In practice this means a cut in corporation tax to a headline rate of 12.5 per cent but as, we shall see later, the Southern tax regime also contains many loopholes to lower this further. Hubner's suggestion is that these tax cuts will attract foreign direct investment in sufficient quantities to overcome the low productivity of Northern industry.

Alongside adopting the Southern model of economic development, *Modelling Irish Unification* also indicates that considerable savings might be made by eliminating duplication. Clearly, there is some sense in this as one government department rather than two is more likely to avoid unnecessary waste, but the report goes much further in suggesting that public spending in the North will decline over time. In other words, any savings from duplication will not necessarily be transferred to other areas of public spending but could ultimately go the private sector. After making these types of assumptions, the report claims that:

> unification positively impacts output per capita across the two-island region by €1,497 in the year the policy is implemented. This impact, largely centred on the Northern economy accumulates to €17,168 within 8 years.[32]

Here then is an optimistic prediction about the benefits of Irish unification on a wholly conventional basis. The North would simply leave the UK and become integrated into the Southern economy to reap substantial rewards.

A subsequent report from the same team, *The Costs of Non-Unification*, built on the first report by factoring in the negative effects of Brexit. It noted that its prediction about devaluation was no longer relevant as investors had taken a negative view of Brexit and sterling. This meant that the economic benefits for the North that would flow from a devaluation of currency would no longer occur, as originally thought. Nevertheless, Hubner still predicted a 'surge' in foreign direct investment in a united Ireland leading to consider-able economic benefits. By contrast, Brexit, even if the North stayed in a Single Market, would lead to major losses, with per capita GDP declining by 4 per cent between 2017 and 2025.[33]

These reports have dovetailed with a major shift in Sinn Féin thinking. In 2014, the party endorsed a campaign to devolve powers to set corporation tax rates in the North. This became a key clause in the Stormont House Agreement. Its intention was to reduce corporation tax to the 12.5 per cent levied in the South by April 2018 but subsequently difficulties emerged as it became unclear how the cut would be funded. In a *United Ireland – Better for Jobs, Enterprise and Research*, Sinn Féin took up Hubner's ideas with its particular emphasis on 'attracting' foreign direct investment. This policy discussion document noted that:

Foreign Direct Investment is an important part of Ireland's export potential. The current system whereby the North and South compete with each other for the same investment both increases costs and reduced the benefits accruing from FDI. Unity would provide a competitive boost across the economy, particularly in sectors that are complementary and would develop the existing strengths, North and South, thus reducing an overreliance on FDI.[34]

The document added that a United Ireland could become 'a global leader in attracting FDI in sectors with good growth prospects'. Clarifying what was meant by 'overreliance on FDI', the document suggested that there should be a 'complementary strategy to develop indigenous business in these same sectors'.[35]

This indicates that the current stance of Sinn Féin is to promote Irish unity on the existing capitalist arrangements. The model of looking to foreign direct investment and attracting it via tax cuts will not change but, as Hubner suggests, be extended to deal with the North's economic problems.

Unity on the basis of the status quo is also increasingly evident in the party's proposal for future political arrangements which have moved closer to the liberal and conservative nationalists discussed above. In *Towards a United Ireland* Sinn Féin states that it is now open to 'transitional arrangements' which could include a confederal Ireland.[36] This could entail 'continued devolution to Stormont and a power-sharing executive within the North within an all-Ireland structure'.[37] Even within this all-Ireland structure, the party suggests there could be 'weighted majorities in relation to legislation on fundamental issues'.[38] In line with the emphasis on respecting 'British-ness', the party suggests that 'expression be given to the relationship between Unionists and the British monarchy'[39] and they also propose 'recognition of the loyal orders (including the Orange Order) in the cultural life of the nation'.[40] This represents a considerable shift within the republican tradition and shows that its change in economic thinking is being mirrored in how it views the political arrangements in a future united Ireland. Essentially, it is an Ireland where there are no fundamental changes on an economic level and where existing sectarian arrangements remain in place.

There are, however, huge problems with the economic model proposed because cutting taxes to attract foreign direct investment would have a detrimental effect on Irish democracy – as the experience in the South demonstrates. It creates a secretive culture where the political elite develop a close relationship with corporate leaders, acceding to their demands and representing their views on international forums and appearing on their boards of directors after retirement. This relationship has become institu-tionalised in the South but operates outside public view, through informal networks. On a formal level, the close relationship between the Irish state and the leaders of corporate finance was exemplified by the Irish Financial Services Clearing House Group which operated within the Department of the Taoiseach. This was an embedded lobby group composed of executives from the bigger banks and finance houses, located inside a key government department. When a scandal broke over its influence, it was simply renamed as the Industry Advisory Group, but the corporate leaders still maintained their influence. Thus, without any discussion with the wider Irish public, the Irish state has become the key opponent of any moves to impose an EU-wide digital tax or even the ultra-modest Tobin tax on currency speculation. Informal relationships are also evident in the way the American Chamber of Commerce influences politicians or the manner in which the Industrial

Development Authority functions as a voice for multinationals inside the state machinery. The close 'frictionless' relationship between the corporate and political elites is buttressed by an official culture which stresses how 'the multi-nationals give us jobs'. This is a peculiar way of framing the issue – no less strange for the countless times it is repeated. 'Giving us jobs' suggests that multinationals are benefactors heaping generosity on Irish workers, when it would be more accurate to suggest that 'Ireland gives them tax-free profits and they employ Irish workers to make even more money.'

Hubner's reports use anodyne language about the need for 'tax harmonisation' and many assume that this means dovetailing the North's headline tax rate with the South's rate of 12.5 per cent. However, this fails to acknowledge that that South's 'success' is based on deliberately contrived loopholes which reduce the actual tax rate well below this figure. Thus, many of the vulture funds who bought up Irish property after the crash of 2008, used clauses in the tax acts such as Section 110 to get away with paying minimal rates of taxes. Goldman Sachs, for example, who bought €200 million of property loans, paid no tax on the cash repayments.[41] Another 'loophole' uses allowances for internal company loans, interest payments and the cost of 'buying' a brand to reduce taxable profits. These mechanisms, for example, allowed Starbucks to pay just €45 in taxes in 2016.[42] The political elite excuses these scandals by claiming that, unfortunately, clever accountants outwitted the tax authorities but, in reality, the political elite work with clever accountants to create the very loopholes that reduce taxes. This is most evident in those sectors of the economy with 'good growth' prospects. The revelation, for example, that Apple paid an annual tax rate of less than 2 per cent in its entire existence in Ireland is shocking enough but the real scandal is that they are not the only multinational to benefit from such rates. They are the rule rather than the exception.

Some suggest that Ireland's history of poverty provides it with an excuse to operate as a tax haven. However, tax dodging is not a victimless crime and has harmful effects on Irish society itself. On a mundane level, the 'onshoring' of US profits into Ireland artificially inflates its GDP. In 2015, for example, Ireland's economy grew by an unbelievable 26 per cent, an event that had never before occurred in human history. This type of 'leprechaun economics',[43] as Paul Krugman termed it, brings its own cost because an artificially higher GDP requires Ireland to make a larger contribution to the EU budget. More directly, when the state grants such tax subsidies to foreign direct investors, the burden of financing falls on PAYE workers. In 2017, for example, Irish workers paid €22.5 billion out of €136 billion in wages – the corporate sector paid €8.1 billion in taxes on gross earnings of €167 billion.[44] Or to put this another way, workers paid an effective tax rate that was more than three times higher than the bosses that employ them. One reason for this, is the low level at which Irish workers hit the highest rate of income tax compared to other OECD countries.

Even though Irish workers pay higher tax rates, they receive less benefit from the public purse than their counterparts elsewhere. Thus, Irish hospital waiting lists are the worst in Europe, while Irish primary school classes are the largest and worst funded. Ireland has the highest level of university fees in the EU. Provision of public housing is woefully inadequate and cities like Dublin have astronomical rents. Childcare costs are a scandal with fees that pass €1,000 a month in Dublin, while a much poorer country like Bulgaria can provide childcare for just €18 a month. Given this disastrous record, the question arises where is the economic benefit for working people from an Irish unity built on the present economic model? Conventional economists, like Hubner, miss out on this simple question because their analysis is focused on categories such as 'per capita GDP'. However, GDP is no longer a real measure of the scale of the Irish economy because it has become so distorted by tax dodging. And 'per capita' or 'per head' disguises how Irish society is divided on class lines. Those from the lower end of the social spectrum experience Ireland's 'economic success' far differently from the tiny elite who benefit most.

THE CONNOLLY WAY

The proposals up to now have assumed that a united Ireland will emerge through negotiations between political elites who have a vested interest in preserving current political and economic structures. It is thought that Britain might facilitate such a move as it would be assured that there would be no threat to its interests, and relations with the Irish Republic might improve even more. It is also believed, in somewhat of a contradictory fashion, that the EU would become involved in supporting Irish unification with special funds. However, all these scenarios imply that Irish unity will be delivered from above with minimal prospect of radical change. Fortunately, this is not the only option.

If, as Connolly argued, partition produced a 'carnival of reaction', Irish unity needs to emerge in *opposition* to the political elites through a social movement that challenges the structures built up during partition. It would need to challenge some of the direct effects of partition such as church control or discriminatory practices, but it would also have to oppose the truncated forms of capitalist development on both sides of the border. The distinguishing feature of this type of movement is that it should be independent and critical of the 26-county state. While it favours a 32-county Ireland, it should not promote the incorporation of the North into a corrupt, 26-county tax haven.

The elements that might compose a movement for unity from below are coming into place, particularly in the South. Partition gave the Catholic Church almost unlimited power, able to shape the constitution, to control the schools, and to run many of the hospitals. They used this control to enforce a hypocritical morality on the mass of people. As the South industrialised, this morality came into direct conflict with the lived experience of people and it produced a deep opposition to their power. Vibrant social movements emerged to challenge the Catholic Church on many fronts. Against their morality most people wanted contraception to plan their families; they did not want to stay locked in unhappy marriages and demanded divorce. Most recently, a generation of young people found it totally unacceptable that aging bishops could have any say over their fertility or their sexuality. In most cases, the political elite had to be forced, through mass pressure, to accede to demands for change and it is only in recent years that they try to cultivate an image being 'progressive' rather than conservative.

However, while the Catholic Church is in full-scale retreat, the Southern state has no intention of uprooting its institutional grip. This is evident in the way that the political elite let the Catholic Church continue to control 94 per cent of primary schools and most 'voluntary' hospitals. They allow 'ethics committees' to ban certain medical procedures in hospitals because they conflict with their Catholic ethos. They do little to stop schools forcing young people to attend Catholic religion classes and have watched as school principals outsourced sex education to Catholic agencies. Bizarrely, they have not even forced the religious orders to make their contribution towards the compensation costs for their legacy of child abuse. Under a deal negotiated in strange circumstances by a Fianna Fáil minister, Michael Woods, the Catholic Church was required to pay only €128 million in return for state indemnity against all future actions by those who, as children, had been abused in religious-run institutions. Yet even though compensation has so far cost the state more than €1.4 billion, it has still not collected the puny €128 million owed by the religious orders.

The bishops have served the political establishment well in the past by inculcating a spirit of obedience among the population and denouncing any form of leftism as 'communism'. Today the elite may prefer to use more modern methods of ideological control – the mass media, the universities and their PR machines – but the Fianna Fáil and Fine Gael leaders have no intention of cutting loose sections of their conservative base. They still need networks of 'respectable' Catholic conservatives to combat the growing tide of left-wing ideas. And even after some of these elements move further right, the conservative parties will seek an accommodation with them. More directly, the state has continued the old Catholic doctrine of 'subsidiarity' – whereby the state does not replace social supports from voluntary or family groups – in a new neoliberal form. Far from encouraging the view that citizens have social rights, the state continues to promote voluntary effort. There are still over 10,000 charities in the South but now most of their funding comes from the state.[45] Typically, the state enters into 'service level agreements' with voluntary organisations, which sometimes originated around Catholic networks, to provide social services.

The desire to uproot Church control over education, health and social services has, therefore, not reached its end goal. It will repeatedly clash with a state dominated by skin-deep liberals and this will bring into being new social movements. Experience already shows that activists in these movements rapidly develop a spontaneous 32-county perspective because the idea that a struggle is over once gains have been won in the South is no longer deemed acceptable. As soon as marriage equality was won in the South, many in the movement turned their focus to the restrictions in the North. The very day the vote for Repeal in the South was announced, a cry went up 'the North is next'. The challenge to the conservative structures on both parts of the island was already in evidence when busloads of Northern activists joined their Southern counterparts in canvassing for Repeal. These small signs indicate that there is an instinctive understanding that some key political transformations in Ireland must occur together. The ignorance and indifference towards the North that was subtly promoted by the Southern political elite is breaking down.

A 32-county perspective in social movements is not confined to opposition to the Catholic Church. The Covid-19 crisis has brought into sharp focus the need for a one-tier, all-island health service where people are treated according to their medical need and not the size of their wallet. The presence of two states on a small island with different strategies for dealing with Covid-19 has helped to illustrate the absurdity of partition. More than 30,000 people cross the Irish border every day and five times as much freight moves across the Irish border than between Northern Ireland and Britain. Yet the two states could not develop a uniform policy on lockdowns or wider strategies for tackling Covid-19. Instead the political establishment used the border as an excuse for not adopting a zero-Covid strategy whereas in reality, they were responding to business pressure. The border, however, does not stop the Southern state paying private health providers in the North exorbitant fees to treat patients that its own system has failed. Most people instinctively recognise that the Irish health system discriminates against the poor in terms of longer waiting lists and access to the most qualified medical staff. They know that it makes perfect sense to have an all-island national health service.

A growing environmental movement will also challenge both states who have done so little to quell global warming. The South is one of the worst performers for reducing emissions in the EU, because it chooses to do nothing to tackle the agrifood sector who are determined to increase beef and dairy herds. In the North the climate-deniers of the DUP have a strong presence in government and use that to hinder serious initiatives to curb climate change. When one company, Tamboran Resources, sought a petroleum licence to start fracking in Fermanagh, a spontaneous movement emerged on the other side of the border to help the opposition. Many environmental activists recognise there is a need to fight on a 32-county basis.

Beyond all that, the strongest movement that can transform Ireland has yet to flex its muscles. The Irish labour movement has been shackled by an ethos of social partnership and a trade union leadership that has little experience of conducting militant struggles. Social partnership strategy is designed to give union leaders an influence on the 'inside track' of the state but the price paid has been a lack of resistance to wage cuts and a worsening of workers' conditions. Jack O'Connor, a former leader of SIPTU, acknowledged as much when he noted that a recent Croke Park agreement 'took the best organised section of the workforce out of the equation of social protest'.[46] While social partnership has been institutionalised in the South for more than 30 years, it operates at a more informal level in the North. Sections of the union leadership are developing a relationship with Sinn Féin and, while promoting some struggles over issues like wage parity with the UK, have failed to launch an all-out defence of working-class interests. The result has been a decline in union density, more noticeable in the South where it has fallen to 24 per cent, compared to 35 per cent in the North.

However, if the older methods of trade union struggle have met an impasse when faced with an aggressive, confident management, the elements of a potential union revival are already present. Young workers are experiencing low wages, long-term insecurity, greater work intensity and grievances are mounting in an age group that is more educated and more attuned to questioning society. It may not be too long before the tens of thousands of young people who marched for bodily autonomy or who shout 'System Change not Climate Change' look at their own workplaces and the many injustices there. If and when this labour movement revives, it is more likely to embrace a 32-county outlook of solidarity because that has been the most recent experience in key struggles. When workers at Harland and Wolff faced the shutdown of their yard, they occupied it for nine weeks, eventually securing its reopening under a new owner. However, the key to winning was solidarity from across the whole island as the UNITE official Susan Fitzgerald explains:

> Solidarity also came in from across the island of Ireland, with workers in the South coming to visit the occupation. UNITE construction and energy workers were visited, bringing thousands of euros with them for the hardship fund. The UNITE construction branch T-shirts were seen everywhere at the yard. Waterford Crystal workers travelled up to speak and to share their occupation experience, and again came with a fantastic donation.[47]

Similarly, when the Debenhams' workers were fighting for better redundancy pay, they also reached across the border to protest outside the shops and to receive solidarity donations from Harland and Wolff.

These examples are only embryos of a 32-county awareness that arises directly from struggles. By themselves, they do not lead to opposition to the border or to a vision for a new Ireland. For that to happen, they need to find a political expression that can articulate a Connolly-style vision for the twenty-first century. In practice, there needs to be a substantial political party that promotes a radical Irish unity movement from below which challenges both states, one that recognises that the Northern state is built on institutionalised sectarianism and that underneath the public, communal divisions lies massive social inequality and class privileges. And, as we have argued, one that recognises that, consciously or not, the two main parties who now run Stormont have become agents in administering a model of capitalism that relies on low wages and insecurity. Opposing that model will require a cross-community movement that challenges the division of the working class on ethnic identities by targeting the new elite who sit at the top of the Northern state. No two societies are similar, but an interesting comparison can be made between the North and Lebanon in this regard.

Like the North, Lebanon has a consociational form of governance with official politics organised on a sectarian system, where cabinets are formed according to communal divisions. The political elite are drawn from warlords who fought in a previous civil war but who now cooperate with each other in government. Prior to 2019, they were able to jointly implement neoliberal politics even while keeping their supporters locked into sectarian enclaves. However, a revolt began as the government proved incompetent in addressing issues such as wildfires ravaging the country or shortages of gas and bread. A rage against the regime was unleashed when the government announced highly regressive taxes, including one of the messaging service WhatsApp. The two best known slogans of the protests were 'The People want the downfall of the regime' which was the well-known chant of the Arab Spring uprising of 2011. The other was 'All of them means all of them' a reference to the particular form of Lebanese sectarianism.[48] The people were not fighting against one ruler but a number of sectarian rulers who govern through consociational power-sharing. For a period, Lebanon became almost ungovernable because the mass of people was no longer willing to be locked into their ethnic identities while watching their living standards decline. The example shows that consociational arrangements may not be as durable as some expect.

If there needs to be a challenge to the Northern state, there must also be a fight against the model of tax haven capitalism in the South. Recent years has helped dispel the myth of a conservative, Church-ridden population and most commentators now agree that the old 'two and half party system' – whereby the conservative parties dominated both the government and opposition with the help of a weak Labour Party – has broken down. The initial beneficiary of the popular slogan 'Break the Cycle' of FF–FG rotation has been Sinn Féin because it articulated a pro-working class and anti-austerity rhetoric. However, their declared intention is to enter government with, if necessary, one or other of the conservative parties. The party, will no doubt, view this government as a strong platform to move forward their agenda for a federal or confederal Ireland. Their problem is that managing, or part managing, Southern capitalism could clash with the rising aspirations of working people.

The best hope is that a strong radical left emerges which pushes a different vision of Irish unity. It will agree with Sinn Féin on occasion – but it will challenge it when it moves to the centre ground. It should neither be politically sectarian towards Sinn Féin, nor become its junior cheerleaders. A debate between Sinn Féin and the radical left will emerge on whether a united Ireland can be achieved through an 'agreed Ireland' that leaves most of the existing political structures intact or whether it will need a fundamental opposition to them. So far, this debate is conducted at a symbolic level such as whether republicans should be welcoming and shaking the hands of the queen. Yet behind these symbols lies a matter of much greater importance – will a united Ireland be anti-imperialist and true in the best elements of the Irish revolutionary tradition? That tradition has its touchstone in the 1916 rebellion and is somewhat diffuse but it has survived decades of reaction. It provided, and still provides, a focal point to critique the failures of two societies produced by the counter-revolution of 1921–23. The 1916 Proclamation claimed the right of the people of Ireland to the ownership of Ireland and promised to cherish all the children of the nation equally. For Connolly especially, but even for Patrick Pearse to a much lesser extent, that meant that the nation had to take control of the natural resources and subordinate private ownership to public control.

The best elements of Irish republicanism have embraced this tradition and been its main exponents for decades. Their core message was building a society that was fit for 'Catholic, Protestant and dissenter' in a unitary state which was not segmented into competing identities. This ideal arose at the high point of a revolutionary wave that spread from France to the most advanced democrats in Ireland. Yet no tradition survives unsullied for centuries and into this radical vision of republicanism came figures like Arthur Griffith, the original founder of Sinn Féin. Griffith's main passion was the creation of a 'Gaelic Manchester' or an Irish capitalism that could trample underfoot the rights of workers. He promoted an 'Irish-Ireland' but did not care if was run as a dual monarchy – as long as profits for Irish business kept rolling in. Modern-day Irish republicanism rarely mentions Griffith and instead plays due respect to the revolutionaries of 1916. But when you have been part-running a Stormont regime for two decades and aspiring to enter a Southern government with one of the conservative parties, the ghost of Griffith returns. Not because anyone subjectively wants it, but the structures that underline those governments – a weak form of capitalism dependent on multinational investment – force you to adapt to its needs. An 'agreed Ireland' that accepted a confederation of two existing regimes would be a betrayal of the radical legacy of republicanism.

Those debates will have greater significance in the future but in the present, there is one issue on which republicans and the radical left can unite. This is the elementary democratic demand for a border poll so that people can choose their own future. By right, such a poll should be conducted on an all-island basis and, if it were, there would be little doubt about its outcome. Yet even the minimal demand for a poll within Northern Ireland is being resisted by the British government with the connivance of the Southern establishment. The wording of the Belfast Agreement is not helpful as it requires a British Secretary of State to conduct such a poll if it appears likely that a majority want a united Ireland. But how can he or she know that in advance? How can they determine whether the opinion polls which indicate a slim majority desire for united Ireland are mistaken? The very fact that only a *British* minister can decide on such a poll is an affront to those who have, the Belfast Agreement acknowledges, a legitimate aspiration to a united Ireland. It will require huge public pressure across the island to force the Irish government to come out in favour of a border poll and to force the British government to conduct it.

A border poll will not automatically bring about an end to both states, as the conservative option of confederation or a federal Ireland could come into play. There is no guarantee even that a vote in favour of a united Ireland will be accepted by the British government or the DUP. Nevertheless, a successful outcome of a border poll would lift the aspirations of people and open up all sorts of possibilities. Many would see it not just as an opportunity to remove a border but to finally bring about an ideal where the children of the nation are cherished equally. In other words, to bring to fruition the aspirations of Ireland's revolutionary tradition.

Before such a poll and even more importantly, during a referendum campaign, socialists will need to carve out a distinct space that is capable of winning some support across the sectarian divide. It will only be able to do this if it refuses to be part of an alliance with any section of the Irish elite. Instead of accepting an outcome that preserves the Stormont regime or the corrupt regime of the South, it should promote a vision of a unitary state. This will require a totally new constitution to the one drafted by Éamon de Valera and the arch conservative John Charles McQuaid in 1937. The founding document for a unitary state will require the convening of a constituent assembly from across the whole island, in which will be represented every part of Irish society from the traveller in west Cork to migrant worker in Gort to the industrial worker in Belfast and lots more besides.

Ireland has entered a new era where the national question is returning centre stage. No matter how hard they try to resist, the pressure for a border poll will grow and, if successful, there will be an opportunity to reshape politics on the island. The radical left, particularly in People Before Profit, will push for real gains for all workers in a united Ireland. It will openly challenge the idea of integrating the North into the Southern tax haven because if the corporations and the wealthy are facilitated in dodging taxes, working people pay with poor public services. There is simply no way around this conundrum. If on the other hand, there is a determined effort to share out the wealth, a decent life for all becomes entirely possible.

A radical united Ireland could create a top-class national health service where personal wealth does not determine the quality of treatment. It could abolish university fees and open up third-level education to those who are excluded. It could launch a major house-building programme and establish proper rent controls. It would reorientate Irish agriculture away from control by beef barons by creating green jobs and sustainable agriculture. It could provide childcare for free or very cheaply for parents who are now crucified with huge costs. It could create genuinely democratic structures which would allow for the recall of elected representatives. It could stop the judiciary being selected from the upper crust of society and those in the orbit of the conservative parties. It could build an economy that relies on public investment rather than being beholden to multinationals. It could create thousands of green jobs by seriously tackling climate change. And much more. In brief, it could take seriously the socialist vision of James Connolly.

Notes

1 'A CARNIVAL OF REACTION': THE ORIGINS OF PARTITION

1. G. Lewis, *Carson: The Man Who Divided Ireland*, London: Hambledon Continuum, 2005, p. 14.
2. Hansard, HC vol 123, cols 1168–233 (22 December 1919).
3. K. Rankin, 'The Search for a Statutory Ulster', *History Ireland*, www.historyireland.com/revolutionary-period-1912-23/the-search-for-statutory-ulster/.
4. J. Kendle, *Walter Long: Ireland and the Union, 1905–1920*, London: McGill-Queen's University Press, 1992, p. 12.
5. R. Murphy, 'Walter Long and the Making of the Government of Ireland Act, 1919–1020', *Irish Historical Studies*, Vol. 25, No. 97 (May 1986), pp. 82–96.
6. A. O Day, *Irish Home Rule 1867–1921*, Manchester: Manchester University Press, 1988, p. 295.
7. Murphy, 'Walter Long and the Making of the Government of Ireland Act'.
8. D. Ferriter, *The Border: The Legacy of a Century of Anglo-Irish Politics*, London: Profile Books, 2019, p. 8.
9. F. McCluskey and B. Kelly, 'A "Carnival of Reaction": Partition and the Defeat of Ireland's Revolutionary Wave', *Irish Marxist Review*, Vol. 4, No. 14 (2015), pp. 59–71.
10. Quoted in H. McDonald and J. McCusker, *UVF: The Endgame*, Dublin: Poolbeg, 2008, p. 30.
11. A. Morgan, *Labour and Partition: the Belfast Working Class 1905–23*, London: Pluto Press, 1991, p. 267.
12. C. Townsend, *The Republic: The Fight for Irish Independence*, London: Allen Lane, 2013, p. 149.
13. A. Parkinson, *Belfast's Unholy War*, Dublin: Four Courts Press, 2004, p. 33.
14. J. Gray, 'Belfast General Strike', *Rebelnews*, www.rebelnews.ie/2019/01/29/belfast-general-strike-of-1919/.
15. Quoted in McCluskey and Kelly, 'A Carnival of Reaction'.
16. B. Probert, *Beyond Orange and Green: The Northern Crisis in a New Perspective*, Dublin: Academy Press, 1978, p. 57.
17. E. McCann, *War in an Irish Town*, London: Pluto Press, 1993, p. 211.
18. M. W. Heslinga, *The Irish Border as a Cultural Divide: A Contribution to the Study of Regionalism in the British Isles*, New York: Humanities Press, 1962, p. 78.

19. M. Chamberlain, 'Imperialism and Social Reform', in C. C. Eldridge (ed.), *British Imperialism in the Nineteenth Century*. Problems in Focus Series. London: Palgrave, 1984, pp. 148–67.

20. A. Aughey, *Nationalism, Devolution and the Challenge to the United Kingdom State*, London: Pluto Press, 2001, pp. 71–2.

21. Ibid., p. 69.

22. Lewis, *Carson: The Man Who Divided Ireland*, p. 48.

23. A. T. Q. Stewart, *The Ulster Crisis: Resistance to Home Rule, 1912–1914*, London: Faber, 1969, p. 62.

24. T. P. Coogan, *The Troubles: Ireland's Ordeal and Search for Peace*, New York: Palgrave, 1996, pp. 16–17.

25. P. Farrell, *Ireland's English Question*, London: Batsford, 1971, p. 249.

26. R. Saunders, 'Breaking the Parliamentary Machine: Lesson of the 1914 Crisis', *New Statesman*, 4 September 2019.

27. See K. Allen, *1916: Ireland's Revolutionary Tradition*, London: Pluto Press, 2016, chapter 4.

28. M. Farrell, *Northern Ireland: The Orange State*, London: Pluto Press, 1980, pp. 90–1.

29. Quoted in B. Manning, *The English People and the English Revolution*, London: Bookmarks, 1991, p. 416.

30. Ferriter, *The Border: The Legacy of a Century of Anglo-Irish Politics*, p. 37.

31. J. Knirk, 'After-Image of the Revolution: Kevin O Higgins and the Irish Revolution', *Eire-Ireland*, Vol. 33, Nos 3 and 4 (2003), pp. 212–43.

32. Ibid., p. 43.

33. M. O Callaghan, 'Religion and Identity: The Church and Irish Independence', *The Crane Bag*, Vol. 7, No. 2 (1983), pp. 65–76.

34. B. Kissane, *Explaining Irish Democracy*, Dublin: UCD Press, 2002, p. 162.

35. J. Whyte, *Church and State in Modern Ireland, 1923–1979*, Dublin: Gill and Macmillan, 1980, pp. 45–6.

36. *Constitution of Ireland*, www.irishstatutebook.ie/eli/cons/en/html.

37. *Irish Press*, 24 January 1933.

38. *Dail Debates*, Vol. 56, cols 2114–15, 1 March 1933.

39. J. Connolly, 'Labour and the Proposed Partition of Ireland', *Irish Worker*, 14 March 1914.

40. *Quadragesimo Anno*, www.vatican.va/content/pius-xi/en/encyclicals/documents/hf_p-xi_enc_19310515_quadragesimo-anno.html.

41. J. Cooney, *John Charles McQuaid, Ruler of Catholic Ireland*, Dublin: O'Brien Press, 1999, p. 258.

42. G. Bell, *The Protestants of Ulster*, London: Pluto Press, 1976, pp. 26–7.

43. Ibid., p. 26.

2 REPUBLICANS AND LOYALISTS

1. B. Purdie, *Politics on the Street: the Origins of the Civil Rights Movement in Northern Ireland*, Belfast: Blackstaff Press, 1990, chapter 4.

2. S. Prince, 'The Global Revolt of 1968 and Northern Ireland', *The Historical Journal*, Vol. 49, No. 3 (2006), pp. 851–75.
3. B. Rowthorn, 'Northern Ireland: an Economy in Crisis', *Cambridge Journal of Economics*, Vol. 5, No. 1 (March 1981), pp. 1–31.
4. D. McKittrick and D. McVea, *Making Sense of the Troubles*, Belfast: Blackstaff Press, 2000, p. 51.
5. 'Struggle or Starve: Interview with Sean Mitchell', *Jacobin*, www.jacobinmag.com/2017/09/ireland-dup-brexit-outdoor-relief-riots-sectarianism.
6. P. Bishop and E. Mallie, *The Provisional IRA*, London: Heinemann, 1987, p. 31.
7. R. Seymour, 'The Last Gasp of Northern Ireland', *New York Times*, 2 November 2018.
8. M. Unwin, *A State in Denial: British Collaboration with Loyalist Paramilitaries*, Cork: Mercer Press, 2016.
9. L. Bosi, 'Explaining Pathways to Armed Activism in the Provisional Irish Republican Army 1969–1972', *Social Science History*, Vol. 36, No. 3 (2012), pp. 347–90.
10. D. Finn, *One Man's Terrorist: A Political History of the IRA*, London: Verso, 2019, p. 1.
11. B. O'Leary, 'Mission Accomplished: Looking Back at the IRA', *Field Day Review*, 2005.
12. B. O'Leary and J. McGarry, *The Politics of Antagonism – Understanding Northern Ireland*, London: Athlone Press, 1993, p. 26.
13. P. Grant, *Imperfection*, Edmonton, AB: AU Press, 2012, p. 45.
14. I. Wood, *Crimes of Loyalty: A History of the UDA*, Edinburgh: Edinburgh University Press, p. 12.
15. Ibid.
16. Bishop and Mallie, *The Provisional IRA*, p. 390.
17. M. Davis, *Buda's Wagon: A Brief History of the Car Bomb*, London; Verso, 2007, pp. 53–60.
18. E. Mallie and D. McKittrick, *The Fight for Peace: The Secret Story Behind the Irish Peace Process*, London: Heinemann, 1996, p. 168.
19. R. W. White, 'The Irish Republican Army: an Assessment of Sectarianism', *Terrorism and Political Violence*, Vol. 9, No. 1 (1997), pp. 20–55.
20. K. Kelley, *The Longest War: Northern Ireland and the IRA*, London: Zed Books, 1988, p. 129.
21. Quoted in R. English, *Armed Struggle: The History of the IRA*, London: Pan Books, 2004, p. 237.
22. H. Patterson and E. P. Kaufmann, 'From Deference to Defiance: Popular Unionism and the Decline of Elite Accommodation in Northern Ireland', in P. Carmichael, C. Knox and R. Osborne (eds), *Devolution and Constitutional Change in Northern Ireland. The Devolution Series*, Manchester: Manchester University Press, 2007, pp. 83–95.
23. E. Moloney and A. Pollock, *Paisley*, Dublin: Poolbeg, 1986, p. 25.

24. Ibid., pp. 89–90.
25. Quoted in R. Perry, *Revisionist Scholarship and Modern Irish Politics*, Farnham: Ashgate, 2013.
26. Ibid.
27. C. Keneally, *War and Peace: Ireland since the 1960s*, London: Reaktion Books, 2010.
28. NIPSA, *The Daylight Robbery of Privatisation*, Belfast: NIPSA, 2013, p. 29.
29. 'NI First Minister Received Assurances from Cerberus on Treatment of NAMA Borrowers', *Irish Independent*, 7 October 2015.
30. 'Inside the DUP: Domination by Free Presbyterian Church and Orange Order Laid Bare', *Belfast Telegraph*, 4 June, 2014.
31. 'Most in UK Want to Decriminalise Abortion in N Ireland, Poll Shows', *Irish Times*, 10 October 2018.
32. F. Bloomer and L. Hoggart, 'Abortion Policy – Challenges and Opportunities', *Knowledge Exchange Seminar Series*, Northern Ireland Assembly, 2015–16.
33. '17 Quotes from DUP that are Actually Real', www.indy100.com/article/dup-theresa-may-tory-deal-alliance-minority-government-quotes-arlene-foster-lgbt-abortion-religion-7783241.
34. 'Let's Take a Closer Look at the DUP's Climate Science Denial', www.desmog.co.uk/2017/06/11/let-s-take-closer-look-dup-s-climate-science-denial.
35. 'Flying the Flag: DUP MPs Under Fire Over Donald Trump Re-election Banner', *Belfast Telegraph*, 3 September 2020.
36. J. Tonge, M. Braniff, T. Hennessey, J. W. McAuley and S. Whiting, *DUP: From Protest to Power*, Oxford: Oxford University Press, 2014, p. 90.
37. 'Paisley Says Belfast Agreement Must Be "Destroyed"', *Irish Times*, 29 April 2003.
38. DUP, *Towards a New Agreement*, Belfast: DUP, 2003, p. 5.
39. Ian Paisley speech to North Antrim DUP, 27 November 2004, https://cain.ulster.ac.uk/issues/politics/docs/dup/ip271104.htm.
40. E. Moloney, *Paisley: From Demagogue to Democrat?*, Dublin: Poolbeg, 2008, p. 503.

3 BRITISH IMPERIALISM

1. '$1m an Hour to Schmooze Sheiks? No Wonder Mr Blair's Preening Like the New Peacocks on his Country Estate', *Daily Mail*, 15 September 2012.
2. G. Adams, *The Negotiators Cookbook: Best Kept Secret of the Peace Process*, Dublin: Sinn Féin, 2018.
3. 'Peace Foundation Launched in Memory of Martin McGuinness', *Belfast Telegraph*, 28 October 2019.
4. RTE Archives, www.rte.ie/archives/2018/1019/1005269-workers-unite-for-peace/.

5. BBC News, 18 January 2002, http://news.bbc.co.uk/2/hi/uk_news/northern_ireland/1767064.stm.
6. J. McGarry and B. O'Leary, 'Consociational Theory, Northern Ireland's Conflict and Its Agreement: Part 1 What Consociationalsist Can Learn from Northern Ireland', *Government and Opposition*, Vol. 41, No. 1 (2006), pp. 43–63.
7. Ibid.
8. Belfast Agreement 1998, p. 3.
9. Sinn Fein Discussion Paper, 'The Nature of the Problem and the Principles Underlying Its Resolution', www.sinnfein.ie/contents/16340.
10. A. Lijphart, 'Northern Ireland Problem: Cases, Theories and Solutions', *British Journal of Political Science*, Vol. 5, No. 1 (1975), pp. 83–106.
11. C. Coulter, 'Northern Ireland's Elusive Peace Dividend: Neoliberalism, Austerity and the Politics of Class', *Capital and Class*, Vol. 43, No 1 (2018), pp. 123–38.
12. E. Mallie and D. McKittrick, *The Fight for Peace: The Secret Story Behind the Irish Peace Process*, London: Heinemann, 1996, p. 107.
13. N. Ferguson, *Empire*, Harmondsworth: Penguin, 2004.
14. B. Anderson, *Imagined Communities*, London: Verso, 2006, p. 93.
15. Mallie and McKittrick, *The Fight for Peace*, p. 83.
16. Ibid.
17. V. Lenin, *Imperialism, the Highest Stage of Capitalism*, Moscow: Progress Publishers, 1963.
18. D. Harvey, *The New Imperialism*, Oxford: OUP, 2003, p. 33.
19. V. Kiernan, *America: The New Imperialism: From White Settlement to World Hegemony*, London: Verso, 2005, p. 364.
20. M. Kitson and J. Michie, 'The De-Industrial Revolution: The Rise and fall of UK Manufacturing, 1870–2005', Centre for Business Research, University of Cambridge Working Paper No. 459, 2014, p. 3.
21. C. Hill, *The English Revolution of 1640*, London: Lawrence and Wishart, 1940, www.marxists.org/archive/hill-christopher/english-revolution/.
22. Kitson and Michie, 'The De-Industrial Revolution', p. 3.
23. E. J. Hobsbawm, *Industry and Empire from 1750 to Present Day*, London: Penguin, 1970, p. 146.
24. World Bank Data, https://data.worldbank.org/indicator/NE.GDI.FTOT.ZS?locations=GB.
25. M. Roberts, 'UK: A Big Business Budget', 9 July 2015, https://thenextrecession.wordpress.com/2015/07/09/uk-a-big-business-budget/.
26. House of Commons Briefing Paper, 'Manufacturing Statistics and Policy', House of Commons, 2020, p. 7.
27. M. Roberts, 'UK: Full Employment but Falling Incomes', 13 September 2017, https://thenextrecession.wordpress.com/2017/09/13/uk-full-employment-but-falling-incomes/.
28. TUC, 'Britain 17 Year Real Wage Squeeze Will Be the Worst in Two Centuries', TUC, 2018.

29. Quoted in A. Eagle and I. Ahmed. *The New Serfdom: The Triumph of Conservative Ideas and How to Defeat Them*, London: Biteback, 2018.

30. Office of National Statistics, 'Exploring Foreign Investment: Where Does the UK Invest and Who Invests in the UK', 1 November 2018.

31. UK Balance of Payments, The Pink Book, 2010, figure 17.

32. T. Norfield, *The City: London and the Power of Global Finance*, London: Verso, 2016.

33. Office of National Statistics, 'International Trade in Services UK: 2018', figure 4.

34. P. Savona and G. Sutija, *Euro Dollars and International Banking*. London: Macmillan, 1985.

35. Norfield, *The City*, p. 49.

36. R. Palen, R. Murphy and C. Chavagneux, *Tax Havens: How Globalization Really Works*. Ithaca, NY: Cornell University Press, 2010, p. 139.

37. N. Shaxson, *Treasure Islands. Tax Havens and The Men Whole Stole The World*, London: Vintage, 2012, p. 252.

38. Addicted to Tax Havens – The Secret Life of The FTSE 100 @, www.actionaid.org.uk/sites/default/files/doc_lib/addicted_to_tax_havens.pdf.

39. Campaign Against Arms Trade, Export Credits, www.caat.org.uk/issues/ecgd.

40. 'The Army's Secret Opinion', *New Statesman*, 13 July 1979.

41. E. Maloney, *Voice from the Grave: Two Mens' War in Ireland*, London: Faber and Faber, 2011.

42. Republican Movement, 'TUAS Document', 1994, https://cain.ulster.ac.uk/othelem/organ/ira/tuas94.htm.

43. M. Whiting, *Sinn Fein and the IRA: From Revolution to Moderation*, Edinburgh: Edinburgh University Press, 2018, p. 103.

44. Ibid., p. 101.

45. Ibid., p. 111.

46. P. Dixon, 'Performing the Northern Ireland Peace Process on the World Stage', *Political Science Quarterly*, Vol. 121, No 1 (2006), pp. 61–91.

47. J. Dumbrell, 'The United States and the Northern Ireland Conflict 1969–1994: From Indifference to Intervention', in *Irish Studies in International Affairs, Reflections on the Northern Conflict and Peace Process*, Dublin: Royal Irish Academy, 2018, p. 125.

48. 'Blair Unveils Bold Intervention Doctrine', *Chicago Tribune*, 23 April 1999.

49. Quoted in C. O'Clery, *The Greening of the White House*, Dublin: Gill and Macmillan, 1997, p. 8.

50. T. Byrne, *Understanding the Drivers of Foreign Direct Investment from the USA*, Department of Economy, 2017, p. 27.

51. Ibid., p. 49.

52. Ibid., p. 50.

53. 'Where and Why Does NI Invest in Northern Ireland', Northern Ireland Assembly research paper, 2018.

54. 'Brexit and English Nationalism', *Economist,* 30 January 2020.

55. 'Is Caledonia Catalonia?', *Economist*, 8 August 2020.

4 MANAGED SECTARIANISM

1. *Sectarianism in Northern Ireland a Review*, 2018, www.ulster.ac.uk/__data/assets/pdf_file/0016/410227/A-Review-Addressing-Sectarianism-in-Northern-Ireland_FINAL.pdf p.23.
2. Ibid, p. 13.
3. Padraig O'Malley, 'Religion and Conflict: The Case of Northern Ireland', John M. McCormack Graduate School of Policy and Global Studies Publications, Paper No. 29, 1995.
4. J. Nagle, '"One Community, Many Faces": Non-Sectarian Social Movements and Peace-Building in Northern Ireland and Lebanon', in L. Bosi and G. Fazio, *The Troubles in Northern Ireland and Theories of Social Movements*, Amsterdam: Amsterdam University Press, 2017, p. 189.
5. J. McGarry, 'Northern Ireland, Civic Nationalism and the Good Friday Agreement', in R. Wilford (ed.), *Northern Ireland and the Divided World*, Oxford: OUP, 2001, p. 124.
6. B. Barry, 'Political Accommodation and Consociational Democracy', *British Journal of Political Science*, Vol. 5, No. 4 (1975), pp. 477–505.
7. C. McGlynn, J. Tonge and J. McAuley, 'The Party Politics of Post Devolution Identity in Northern Ireland', *British Journal of Politics and International Relations*, Vol. 16, No. 2 (2014), pp. 273–90.
8. Henry Jackson Society, Statement of Principles, https://henryjacksonsociety.org/statement-of-principles/.
9. 'Working Class Catholics were "Anti-Everything", Said Cathal Daly, Records Reveal', *Belfast Telegraph*, 30 December 2016.
10. E. Moloney, *A Secret History of the IRA*, Harmondsworth: Penguin, 2007, p. 187.
11. Quoted in D. Finn, 'The Adaptable Sinn Fein', *Jacobin*, 14 April 2016.
12. E. McCann, Why the Agreement Failed, *Rebelnews*, 21 May 2018, www.rebelnews.ie/2018/05/21/why-the-agreement-failed/.
13. '20% of NI Adults Now Consider Themselves to Have "No Religion"', *Belfastlive*, 21 June 2020.
14. 'Police in Northern Ireland are Raiding Women's Houses for Abortion Pills', *Grazia*, 13 March 2007.
15. 'Prosecution of Northern Ireland Mum for Buying Daughter Abortion Pills "did Not Breach Human Rights," Court Rules', *Belfast Telegraph*, 16 December 2019.
16. 'Sinn Fein and DUP Defeat Belfast City Council Abortion Motion', *Irish News*, 3 October 2019.
17. Northern Ireland Life and Times Survey, 2017, www.ark.ac.uk/nilt/2017/Minority_Ethnic_People/RACPREJM.html.
18. 'Northern Ireland's Increasing Problem with Racism', www.amnesty.org.uk/blogs/belfast-and-beyond/northern-irelands-increasing-problem-racism.
19. 'Defending the Bedrock of Protestant Culture', *Irish Times*, 26 September 1998.

20. Quoted in Michel Savaric, 'Conflicting Symbols, Symbols of Conflict and Symbolical Conflict – The Drumcree Crises', CAIN 1998, https://cain.ulster.ac.uk/issues/parade/savaric98.htm.

21. DUP Leaflet, 'A Shared Future for Who'.

22. 'Belfast City Council Debate on Inviting the ROI & NI Football Teams to City Hall', Slugger O Toole, 5 January 2016, https://sluggerotoole.com/2016/01/05/belfast-city-council-votes-to-invite-the-ni-and-roi-football-teams/

23. 'Sinn Fein Block Cartoonist Sketching Councillors – Party Accused of "Censorship"', *Belfast Telegraph*, 10 January 2019.

24. 'Addressing the Legacy of Northern Ireland's Past', The Commission for Victims and Survivors, Belfast, 2019, p. 1.

25. K. McEvoy, D. Holder, L. Mallinder, A. Nyson, B. Gormley and G. McKeown, *Prosecutions, Imprisonment and the Stormont House Agreement*, Belfast: Committee for Administration of Justice, 2020, p. 5.

26. Northern Ireland Council for Voluntary Action, 'State of the Sector', www.nicva.org/stateofthesector.

27. Building Change Trust and University of Ulster Final Report, 'Independence of the Voluntary, Community and Social Enterprise Sector in Northern Ireland', November 2016, p. 37.

28. Northern Ireland Audit Office, 'The Social Investment Fund: A Report by the Comptroller and Auditor General', November 2018, p. 4.

29. J. Barry, 'Northern Ireland: Hardening Borders and Hardening Attitudes', *Soundings*, 2017, pp. 48–564.

30. 'Adams Basket Case Economic Theory', *Irish Independent*, 1 March 2007.

31. J. Fitzgerald and L. W. Morgenroth, 'Northern Ireland Economy, Problems and Prospects', TEP Working paper No. 0619, July 2019, figure 5.

32. *Northern Ireland Economic Strategy: Priorities for Sustainable Growth and Prosperity*, Belfast: Northern Ireland Executive, 2012, p. 10.

33. 'Silos, Secrecy and Quiet Deals: How Dysfunction Became Stormont's Norm', *Irish Times*, 13 January 2019.

34. Ibid.

35. K. Allen, *Reasons to Vote No to Lisbon Treaty*, Dublin: Bookmarks, 2008, chapter 4.

36. Quoted in S. McVeigh, 'Sinn Fein in Government', *Irish Marxist Review*, Vol. 1, No. 1 (2012).

37. Fresh Start Agreement, NI Executive Financial Reforms and Context, Sections 1.16 to 1.19.

38. S. McBride, *Burned: The Inside Story of the 'Cash for Ash' Scandal and Northern Ireland's Secretive New Elite*, Newbridge: Merrion Press, 2019, p. 294.

39. 'Bombardier Aircraft Programme "Critical" for NI Operation', *Irish Times*, 12 September 2017.

40. 'Bombardier Secures £15m Research Grant for Belfast Site', *Belfast Telegraph*, 19 July 2019.

41. *Re-Balancing the Northern Economy 2019 Report on Social Enterprise*, Belfast: Social Enterprise Economy, 2019, p. 3.
42. P. Stewart, T. McKearney, G. O Machail, P. Campbell and B. Garvey, *Between Sectarianism and Neo-liberalism, The State of Northern Ireland and the Democratic Deficit*, Glasgow: Vagabond Voices, 2028.
43. Ibid.
44. Fitzgerald and Morgenroth, 'Northern Ireland Economy', p. 24.
45. S. McBride, *Burned*, pp. 31–2.
46. 'Northern Ireland Notches Up 1,000 More Millionaires in the Past Year as Economy Bounces Back', *Belfast Telegraph*, 5 September 2017.
47. NISRA, *Northern Ireland Annual Survey of Hours and Earnings Geographical Area: Northern Ireland*, Belfast: NISRA, October 2019, p. 11.
48. Ibid., p. 8.
49. R. Russell, 'Census 2011: Detailed Characteristics of Ethnicity and Country of Birth at the Northern Ireland Level', Northern Ireland Assembly, Research and Information Paper, 21 November 2013.

5 PROTESTANT WORKERS

1. R. Munck, 'A Divided Working Class: Protestant and Catholic Workers in Northern Ireland', *Labour, Capital and Society*, April 1980, pp. 104–40.
2. M. Farrell, *Northern Ireland: The Orange State*, London: Pluto Press, 1980, p. 327.
3. T. Cliff, 'The Economic Roots of Reformism', *Socialist Review*, Vol. 6 (1957), www.marxists.org/archive/cliff/works/1957/06/rootsref.htm.
4. D. Finn, *One Man's Terrorist: A Political History of the IRA*, London: Verso, 2019, p. 179.
5. D. Kearney, 'Orange Culture is Being Undermined by "Project Fear"', *An Phoblacht*, 16 July 2018.
6. Ibid.
7. P. Bew, *Ireland: The Politics of Enmity 1789–2006*, Oxford: OUP, 2007, p. 11.
8. N. Curtain, 'The Transformation of the Society of the United Irishmen into a Mass Based Revolutionary Organisation, 1794–6', *Irish Historical Studies*, Vol. 24, No. 96 (1985), pp. 463–92.
9. Bew, *The Politics of Enmity*, p. 4.
10. Ibid.
11. T. Bartlett and K. Jeffrey, *A Military History of Ireland*, Cambridge: Cambridge University Press, 1996, p. 262.
12. L. De Paor, *Divided Ulster*, Harmondsworth: Penguin, 1973, p. 27.
13. K. Miller, '"Heirs of Freedom" or "Slaves to England": Protestant Society or Unionist Hegemony in Nineteenth Century Ulster', *Radical History Review*, 104 (Spring 2009), pp. 17–40.
14. J. Gray, *City in Revolt*, Belfast: Blackstaff, 1985.

15. Quoted in H. Patterson, 'James Larkin and the Belfast Dockers and Carters Strike of 1907', *Saothar*, Vol. 4 (1978), pp. 8–14.
16. Quoted in C. Kostick, *Revolution in Ireland: Popular Militancy 1917–1923*, Cork: Cork University Press, 2009, p. 64.
17. A. Morgan, *Labour and Partition, The Belfast Working Class 1905–23*, London: Pluto Press, 1991, p. 239.
18. Farrell, *Northern Ireland: The Orange State*, p. 131.
19. P. Ollerenshaw, 'War Mobilisation and Society in Northern Ireland, 1939–1945', *Contemporary European History*, Vol. 16, No. 2 (2007), pp. 169–97.
20. Ibid.
21. Ibid.
22. 'Hundreds of Laid-off Wrightbus Workers Protest Outside Church Over Donations', *The Journal*, 29 September 2019.
23. J. McGarry and B. O'Leary, *Explaining Northern Ireland*, Oxford: Blackwell, 1995, pp. 354–5.
24. C. Harman, 'Gramsci, The Prison Notebooks and Philosophy', *International Socialism Journal*, No. 144 (2007), http://isj.org.uk/gramsci-the-prison-notebooks-and-philosophy/.
25. Ibid.
26. Ibid.
27. A. Gramsci, *Selection from Prison Notebooks*, London: Lawrence and Wishart, 1971, p. 327.
28. M. Millotte, *Communism in Modern Ireland: The Pursuit of the Workers' Republic since 1916*, Dublin: Gill and Macmillan, 1984, p. 153.
29. S. Mitchell, *Struggle or Starve: Working Class Unity in Belfast's 1932 Outdoor Relief Riots*, Chicago, IL: Haymarket, 2017, p. 138.
30. Ibid., p. 132.
31. B. Rowthorn and N. Wayne, *Northern Ireland: The Political Economy of Conflict*, Cambridge: Polity Press, 1988, p. 119.
32. Ibid.
33. E. McCann, 'The Protestant Working Class', *Socialist Review*, No. 89 (July–August 1986).
34. 'NISRA Labour Force Survey Religion Report 2017', NI Executive Office, January 2019, p. 37.
35. Ibid., p. 47.
36. Ibid., p. 47.
37. Ibid., p. 47.
38. Ibid., p. 50.
39. Ibid., p. 49.
40. Ibid., p. 55.
41. Education Authority, 'Audit of Educational Inequalities', March 2018.
42. Quoted in P. Shirlow, *The End of Ulster Loyalism*, Manchester: Manchester University Press, 2012, p. 12.

43. 'Labour Force Survey Annual Report 2018', NISRA, 2019, figure 4.
44. A. Mycock, J. McAuley and J. Tonge, 'Loyalism, Orangeism and Britishness: Contemporary Synergies and Tensions', in J. McAuley and G. Spencer (eds), *Ulster Loyalism after the Good Friday Agreement*, Basingstoke: Palgrave, 2011, p. 127.
45. Ibid., p. 122.
46. L. Colley, 'Britishness and Otherness: An Argument', *Journal of British Studies*, Vol. 31 (1992), pp. 309–29.
47. *Ulster's Protestant Working Class*, Belfast: Island Pamphlets, 1994, p. 7.
48. 'Things Karen Bradley Never Knew', *Belfast Telegraph*, 10 September 2018.
49. 'Loyal Orange Lodge in Stark Decline', *Evangelical Truth*, www.evangelicaltruth.com/loyal-orange-lodge.
50. D. Diamond, *Blood and Thunder: Inside an Ulster Protestant Band*, Dublin: Mercer, 2010, p. 239.
51. P. Shirlow, *The End of Ulster Loyalism*, Manchester: Manchester University Press, pp. 199 and 202.
52. J. McAuley, 'Whither New Loyalism? Changing Loyalist Politics after the Belfast Agreement', *Irish Political Studies*, Vol. 20, No. 3 (2005), pp. 303–40.
53. Ibid.
54. 'My Murder of Two Catholics Helped Prevent a United Ireland', *Belfast Newsletter*, 19 March 2014.
55. S. Long, 'Billy Hutchinson and the Development of the PUP', on Slugger O Toole, 14 August 2015, https://sluggerotoole.com/2015/08/14/billy-hutchinson-and-the-development-of-the-pup/.

6 THE RETURN OF THE NATIONAL QUESTION

1. 'Shared Island: Northern Ireland is Still a Society on a Sectarian Edge', *Irish Times*, 5 September 2020.
2. 'Trichet Warned Me a "bomb" Would Go Off, Says Noonan', *Irish Independent*, 11 September 2015.
3. M. Kitson and J. Michie, 'The De-Industrial Revolution: The Rise and Fall of UK Manufacturing, 1870–2010', Centre for Business Research, University of Cambridge Working Paper No. 459.
4. 'Britain's Productivity in Eight Charts', *Financial Times*, 13 August 2018.
5. 'Tory Leadership: Who Gets to Choose the UK's Next Prime Minister?', *BBC News*, 23 June 2019, www.bbc.com/news/uk-politics-48395211.
6. 'No-Deal Brexit Would Mean Hard Irish Border, EU Confirms', *Guardian*, 22 January 2019.
7. 'Theresa May's Brexit Deal: Everything You Need to Know', *Guardian*, 15 November 2018.
8. 'DUP Conference Cheered Boris Johnson in Titanic-Themed Speech on Brexit', *Belfast Telegraph*, 17 October 2019.

9. 'Brexit: Application for Border Posts at Ports Sent to EU', *BBC News*, 7 July 2020, www.bbc.com/news/uk-northern-ireland-53320065.

10. B. Nelsen and J. Guth, 'European Union or Kingdom of the Antichrist? Protestant Apocalyptic Narratives and European Unity', *National Identities*, Vol. 19, No. 2 (2017), pp. 251–67.

11. M. Allen, 'Northern Ireland's Agri-Food Sector – Background and Possible "Brexit" Considerations', NI Assembly Research and Information Service Briefing Paper 66/16, p. 5.

12. I. Siedshlag and M. Koecklin, 'The Impact of Brexit Uncertainty on FDI-related New Jobs in Northern Ireland', Department of Economy, Northern Ireland, October 2019.

13. 'DUP Leader Arlene Foster: "Our Red Line is Blood Red"', *Irish Times*, 3 October 2018.

14. 'In the Face of Anti-Scottish Sentiment Stirred by the Right-Wing Press and the Tory Party, the SNP Must Stay Calm and Put the Welfare of Every Scottish Citizen First', *The Herald*, 10 May 2015.

15. 'Majority of Tory Members Would Give Up Northern Ireland for Brexit, Poll Shows', *Irish Times*, 18 June 2019.

16. D. Morrow, *Sectarianism in Northern Ireland: A Review*, Belfast: George Quigley Fund, 2018, p. 10.

17. 'Labour Force Religion Report, 2017', Executive Office, Stormont Assembly, 2019, p. 13.

18. 'United Ireland May Be in the Gift of "Others"', *Belfast Telegraph*, 19 June 2018.

19. 'What Northern Ireland 18 to 30s are Most Worried about 20 years after the Troubles', *Belfast Line*, 17 January 2019.

20. 'Arlene Foster Says "I Would Probably Move" If There was United Ireland', *Irish News*, 14 July 2020.

21. 'North Should Prepare for United Ireland Possibility – ex DUP Leader', *Irish Times*, 27 July 2018.

22. 'Catholic Church "Bereavement" after Same-Sex Marriage Vote', *Irish Times*, 2 June 2015.

23. 'Dublin Mass Attendance Drops to All Time Low of 14 percent', *Irish Central*, 14 December 2011.

24. C. D. Hazen, *Modern European History*, New York: Henry Holt, 1917, pp. 400–01.

25. 'Fenian Declaration of an Irish Republic 1867', https://theirishrevolution. wordpress.com/2017/04/19/fenian-declaration-of-an-irish-republic-1867/.

26. H. Patterson, *The Politics of Illusion: Republicanism and Socialism in Modern Ireland*, London: Hutchinson Radius, 2010, p. 53.

27. Ibid.

28. 'Sinn Fein Abortion Policy Compatible with My Catholicism, says Martin McGuinness', *BBC News*, 16 January 2015, www.bbc.com/news/uk-northern-ireland-30855440.

29. Letter from J. P. Patterson to W. O Brien, 12 February 1944, O'Brien Papers, National Library of Ireland.
30. N. Browne, *Against the Tide*, Dublin: Gill Books, 2007.
31. N. Puirseil, *The Irish Labour Party*, Dublin: University College Dublin Press, 2007, p. 213.
32. M. Keenan, 'Sexual Abuse and the Catholic Church', in T. Inglis (ed.) *Are the Irish Different?*, Manchester: Manchester University Press, 2014, p. 105.
33. J. Goldthorpe and C. Whelan. *The Development of Industrial Society in Ireland*, Oxford: OUP, 1992, p. 389.
34. B. Girvin, 'Contraception, Moral Panic and Social Change in Ireland, 1969–1979', *Irish Political Studies*, Vol. 23, No. 4 (2008), pp. 555–76.
35. B. Walsh, 'Labour Force Participation and the Growth of Women's Employment, Ireland 1971–91', *Economic and Social Review*, Vol. 24, No. 4 (1993), pp. 369–400.
36. Cited in Tom Inglis, 'Origins and Legacies of Irish Prudery: Sexuality and Social Control in Modern Ireland', *Eire-Ireland*, Vol. 40, Nos 3–4 (2005), pp. 9–37.
37. A. Punch, 'Marriage, Fertility and Family in Ireland – a Statistical Perspective', *Journal of the Statistical and Social Inquiry Society of Ireland*, Vol. XXXVI (2007), pp. 193–227.
38. '"North is Next": Fresh Fight for Grassroots Power that Beat Ireland Abortion Ban', *Guardian*, 1 June 2018.

7 THE LEFT AND IRISH UNITY

1. 'Leo: We've No Mandate for Abortion Referendum, Mick Wallace: That's Horseshit', *The Journal*, 6 February 2015, www.thejournal.ie/abortion-debate-horseshit-1923833-Feb2015/.
2. K. Kelley, *The Longest War: Northern Ireland and the IRA*, London: Zed Books, 1988, p. 210.
3. Ibid., p. 225.
4. 'Bodenstown Oration', *Republican News*, 18 June 1977.
5. TUAS Internal Document of IRA in 1994, https://cain.ulster.ac.uk/othelem/organ/ira/tuas94.htm.
6. Quoted in L. O Ruairc, *Peace or Pacification: Northern Ireland After the Defeat of the IRA*, Winchester: Zed Books, 2018, p. 63.
7. Ibid.
8. '"We Talk to All Parties": Sinn Fein Amends Motion Stating that It Can Only Go into Power with Left Wing Parties', *The Journal*, 16 June 2018.
9. 'Planning for the Future – Gerry Adams', 28 June 2019, www.sinnfein.ie/contents/54230.
10. Ibid.
11. Ibid.
12. Ibid.
13. Ibid.

14. A. Gramsci, *Selection from the Prison Notebooks*, London; Lawrence and Wishart, 1971, p. 119.

15. 'Gerry Adams: There Will Be Orange Parades in a UNITED IRELAND', *Irish News*, 18 September 2015.

16. J. Connolly, 'The Coming Generation', *Workers' Republic*, 15 July 1900, www.marxists.org/archive/connolly/1900/07/comingen.htm.

17. D. Ryan (ed.) *Socialism and Nationalism*, Dublin: Three Candles, 1947, p. 29.

18. Ibid., p 34.

19. J. Connolly, 'Belfast and Dublin Today', *Forward*, 23 August 1913, www.marxists.org/archive/connolly/1913/08/beldub.htm.

20. Ibid.

21. Ibid.

22. J. Connolly, 'Labour and the Proposed Partition of Ireland', *Irish Worker*, 14 March 1914, www.marxists.org/archive/connolly/1914/03/laborpar.htm.

23. J. Connolly, 'Industrial Unity and Political Division in Ireland', *Forward*, 21 March 1914, www.marxists.org/archive/connolly/1914/03/iupoldiv.htm.

24. J. Connolly, 'A Forgotten Chapter of Irish History', *Forward*, 9 August 1913, www.marxists.org/archive/connolly/1913/08/forgot.htm.

25. J. Connolly, 'Sinn Fein, Socialism and the Nation', *Irish Nation*, 23 January 1909, www.marxists.org/archive/connolly/1909/01/sfsoclsm.htm.

26. Quoted in B. Hanley, *The Impact of the Troubles on the Republic of Ireland 1968–79: Boiling Volcano?*, Manchester: Manchester University Press, 2018, p. 8.

27. Ibid.

28. M. Farrell, *Northern Ireland: The Orange State*, London: Pluto Press, 1976.

29. 'Interview: Discussion on Strategy of People's Democracy', *New Left Review*, Vol. 1, No. 55 (May–June 1969), pp. 4–19.

30. Ibid.

31. C. C. O'Brien, 'The Embers of 1916', *New Left Review*, Vol. 1, No. 37 (May–June 1966), pp. 3–14.

32. C. C. O'Brien, *States of Ireland*, London: Panther Books, 1974, p. 19.

33. M. McNally, 'Conor Cruise O'Brien's Conservative Nationalism: Retrieving the Postwar European Connection', *European Journal of Political Theory*, Vol. 7, No. 3 (2008), pp. 308–30.

34. C. C. O'Brien, *States of Ireland*, p. 89.

35. P. Bew, P. Gibbon and H. Patterson, *The State in Northern Ireland, 1921–72: Political Forces and Social Classes*, Manchester: Manchester University Press, 1979 edition, p. 1.

36. P. Bew, P. Gibbon, H. Patterson, *Northern Ireland: 1921–2001, Political Forces and Social Classes*, London: Serif, 2002, p. 41.

37. Ibid.

38. Bew, Gibbon, Patterson, *The State in Northern Ireland*, 1921–72, p. 6.

39. Ibid., pp. 6 and 9.

40. Ibid., p. 19.

41. J. Connolly, 'North East Ulster', *Forward*, 2 August 1913, www.marxists.org/archive/connolly/1913/08/neulster.htm.
42. A. Morgan, *Labour and Partition: The Belfast Working Class 1905–23*, London: Pluto Press, 1991, chapter 10.
43. Ibid., p. 267.
44. Ibid., p. 265.
45. D. Cannadine, *Victorious Century: The United Kingdom, 1800–1906*, New York: Viking, 2017, p. 442.
46. B. Purcell, *Inside RTE: A Memoir*, Dublin: New Island Books, 2014.
47. F. O'Toole, 'The End of the Troubles', *New York Review of Books*, 19 February 1998.
48. F. O'Toole, 'Are the Troubles Over?', *New York Review of Books*, 5 October 2000.
49. F. O'Toole, 'The End of the Troubles', *New York Review of Books*, 19 February 1998.
50. F. O'Toole, 'Guns in the Family', *New York Review of Books*, 11 April 2002.
51. See K. Allen, *Is Southern Ireland a Neo-Colony?*, Dublin: Bookmarks, 1990, www.marxists.de/ireland/neocolony/index.htm.
52. G. Adams, *A Pathway to Peace*, Cork: Mercier, 1988, p. 32.
53. Allen, *Is Southern Ireland a Neo-Colony?*

8 WHAT KIND OF UNITED IRELAND?

1. 'Exit Poll Shows Support for Irish Unity Referendum, Especially Among 18–24 Age Group', *The Journal*, 9 February 2020, www.thejournal.ie/ge2020-border-poll-4999083-Feb2020/.
2. Lord Ashcroft, 'My Northern Ireland Survey Finds the Union on a Knife-Edge', 11 September 2019, https://lordashcroftpolls.com/2019/09/my-northern-ireland-survey-finds-the-union-on-a-knife-edge/.
3. 'Irish Unification Becoming Likelier: Time to Start Thinking About What It Might Mean', *Economist*, 13 February 2020.
4. 'No Deal Brexit: Could Open Path to Irish Unity', *New York Times*, 15 February 2019.
5. 'Why the Idea of a United Ireland is Back in Play', *Financial Times*, 30 November 2018.
6. Capital Economics, *A Primer on Irish Unification*, 17 February 2020, www.capitaleconomics.com/publications/european-economics/european-economics-update/a-primer-on-irish-reunification/.
7. 'Do the Irish Want Unification?', *Financial Times*, 14 November 2019, www.ft.com/content/86cc29f6-05a5-11ea-9afa-d9e2401fa7ca.
8. J. Fitzgerald and E. Morgenroth, 'The Northern Ireland Economy: Problems and Prospects', Trinity Economics Papers, No. 0619, Trinity College Dublin, Department of Economics, revised August 2019.

9. British Office of National Statistics, *Country and Regional Public Sector Finances*, Revenue Tables, 2018–2019.

10. S. McGuinness and A. Bergin, 'The Political Economy of a Northern Ireland Border Poll', IZA Institute of Labour Economics, July 2019, table 1.

11. S. McGuinness and M. Sheehan, 'Regional Convergence in the UK, 1970–1995', *Applied Economic Letters*, No. 5 (1968), pp. 653–8.

12. M. Bourke, 'The Economic Case for Irish Unity', p. 4, https://issuu.com/sinn feinireland/docs/economic_case_for_irish_unity.

13. M. McDowell, 'What Exactly Do We Mean by Irish Unity', paper presented to the John F Kennedy School, New Ross, 7 September 2019.

14. Ibid.

15. Ibid.

16. R. Humphries, *Countdown to Unity: Debating Irish Unification*, Dublin: Irish Academic Press, 2008, p. 6.

17. Ibid.

18. R. Humphries, 'What Brexit Means for a 20 year old Agreement', *Irish Examiner*, 9 August 2018.

19. R. Humphries, *Countdown to Unity*, p. 205.

20. J. McGarry and B. O'Leary, *Explaining Northern Ireland*, Oxford: Blackwell, 1995, p. 62.

21. B. O'Leary, *A Treatise on Northern Ireland, Volume 3, Consociation and Confederation*, Oxford: OUP, p. 312.

22. Ibid., p. 316.

23. Ibid., p. 312.

24. Ibid., p. 314.

25. Ibid, p. 316.

26. 'Poll: NHS Could Be Crucial in Border Poll with Support for United Ireland and Union Running Neck-and-Neck', *Belfast Telegraph*, 25 October 2020.

27. O'Leary, *A Treatise on Northern Ireland*, Volume 3, p. 346.

28. Ibid., p. 313.

29. 'When is "an Independent Study" on Irish Unification Not Independent?', *Slugger O Toole*, 21 November 2015.

30. KLC Consulting, *Modelling Irish Unity*, Vancouver: KLC, 2015, p. x.

31. Ibid., p.3.

32. Ibid., p. 1.

33. KLC Consulting, *The Costs of Non-Unification: Brexit and the Unification of Ireland*, Vancouver: KLC, 2018, p. 3.

34. Sinn Féin, *United Ireland – Better for Jobs, Enterprise and Research*, Dublin: Sinn Féin, no date, p. 8.

35. Ibid., p. 9.

36. Sinn Féin, *Towards a United Ireland*, Dublin: Sinn Féin, 2016, p. 9.

37. Ibid.

38. Ibid.

39. Ibid., p. 8.
40. Ibid.
41. 'Goldman Sachs with €200 million of Irish Assets Pays No Tax', *Irish Times*, 17 August 2016.
42. 'Revealed: Starbucks Paid Only €45 Tax in Ireland Last Year', *The Sun*, 4 September 2016.
43. P. Krugman, 'Leprechaun Economics and Neo-Lafferism', *New York Times*, 8 November 2017.
44. The relevant information can be found in the following reports: www.revenue.ie/en/corporate/documents/research/ct-analysis-2019.pdf p.1 and CSO Stat Bank @ https://statbank.cso.ie/px/pxeirestat/Database/eirestat/National%20Income%20and%20Expenditure%20Annual%20Results%202018/National%20Income%20and%20Expenditure%20Annual%20Results%202018_statbank.asp?SP=National%20Income%20and%20Expenditure%20Annual%20Results%202018&Planguage=0.
45. 'Funding and Commissioning', *The Wheel*, 24 August 2018, www.wheel.ie/policy-and-research/issues/funding-and-commissioning.
46. 'Political Stability Helps Drive Irish Recovery', *Financial Times*, 27 January 2012.
47. 'Harland and Wolff Occupation: Historic Struggles Saves Jobs', *Socialist Party*, 2 October 2019, https://socialistparty.ie/2019/10/harland-wolff-occupation-historic-struggle-saves-jobs/.
48. 'Lebanon's Thawra', Middle East Research and Information Project, Winter 2019, https://merip.org/2019/12/lebanons-thawra/.

Index

Thanks to our Patreon Subscribers:

Abdul Alkalimat
Andrew Perry

Who have shown their generosity and comradeship in difficult times.

Check out the other perks you get by subscribing to our Patreon – visit patreon.com/plutopress. Subscriptions start from £3 a month.

The Pluto Press Newsletter

Hello friend of Pluto!

Want to stay on top of the best radical books
we publish?

Then sign up to be the first to hear about our
new books, as well as special events,
podcasts and videos.

You'll also get 50% off your first order with us
when you sign up.

Come and join us!

Go to bit.ly/PlutoNewsletter